Oxford Children's
Colour
Dictionary

**Includes writing tips from best-selling authors
Charlie Higson, Andy Stanton, Jeremy Strong
and Jacqueline Wilson**

Compiled by Sheila Dignen,
Morven Dooner, Kate Mohideen

OXFORD
UNIVERSITY PRESS

OXFORD
UNIVERSITY PRESS

Great Clarendon Street, Oxford OX2 6DP.
United Kingdom

Oxford University Press is a department of the University of Oxford.
It furthers the University's objective of excellence in research, scholarship,
and education by publishing worldwide. Oxford is a registered trade mark of
Oxford University Press in the UK and in certain other countries

First published 2000
Second edition 2006
This edition 2014
This new edition is based on the Oxford Junior Illustrated Dictionary 2011.

British Library Cataloguing in Publication Data
Data available
ISBN: 9780192737540

10 9 8 7 6 5 4 3 2

Paper used in the production of this book is a natural,
recyclable product made from wood grown in sustainable forests.
The manufacturing process conforms to the environmental
regulations of the country of origin.

Printed in Malaysia by Vivar Printing Sdn. Bhd.

Acknowledgements:
Top Ten Writing Tips text pp. 184-5 and photo © Charlie Higson 2014
Top Ten Writing Tips text pp. 186-7 and photo © Andy Stanton 2014
Top Ten Writing Tips text pp. 188-9 © Jeremy Strong 2014
Jeremy Strong photo © Justin Stoddart 2014
Top Ten Writing Tips text and photo pp. 190-1 © Jacqueline Wilson 2014

TEACHERS
For inspirational support plus
free resources and eBooks
www.oxfordprimary.co.uk

PARENTS
Help your child's reading
with essential tips, phonics
support and free eBooks
www.oxfordowl.co.uk

Contents

Introduction

Is homework too much like hard work? Does grammar make you groan? Is spelling a struggle? This new edition of the **Oxford Children's Colour Dictionary** is here to help.

Writing scary, spooky, funny, and gory stories can be fun and easy. Putting together a report for school can be straightforward. Just follow the grammar, punctuation and spelling tips at the beginning of this dictionary to get your writing in good shape. Look up words in the dictionary to check your spellings and meanings. If you need inspiration, check out the secrets of top authors Charlie Higson, Andy Stanton, Jeremy Strong, and Jacqueline Wilson at the back of the book.

Make quick work of homework by using the tools in this dictionary!

How to use a **dictionary**

catch words
the first and last words on the page

alphabet
all the letters are listed and the letter for the page is highlighted

headword
the word you look up, in alphabetical order

tip
tip to help with spelling

definition
what the word means and if a word has more than one meaning, the definitions are numbered

example
examples that show how headwords are used in a sentence

word class
what type of word the word is, for example noun, verb, adjective or adverb

---

glow / government

weather. Gloves have separate parts for your thumb and each finger.

glow *verb* glows, glowing, glowed to shine with a warm, gentle light

glue *noun* glues a sticky substance that you use for sticking things together

gnarled *adjective* Something that is gnarled is bent and twisted because it is very old. *We sat on a gnarled old tree trunk.*

❗ gn- in this word sounds like n-

gnome *noun* gnomes a small, ugly fairy in stories

go *verb* goes, going, went, gone 1 When you go somewhere, you move or travel so that you are there. 2 If a machine is going, it is working. 3 to become *Clay goes hard when you bake it.*

goal *noun* goals 1 the net where you must kick or throw the ball to score a point in a game such as football or netball 2 something that you want to achieve

goat *noun* goats an animal with horns that is kept on farms for its milk

god *noun* gods 1 a person or thing that people worship 2 or God the being or spirit that is worshipped in Christianity, Islam and Judaism, and is believed to have created the universe

goggles *noun* special thick glasses that you wear to protect your eyes, for example when you are swimming

go-kart *noun* go-karts a type of small car that people use for racing

gold *noun* a shiny, yellow metal that is very valuable

golf *noun* Golf is a game that you play by hitting small, white balls with sticks called **golf clubs**. You have to hit the balls into holes in the ground.

good *adjective* better, best 1 nice, pleasant, or enjoyable 2 kind and honest 3 When you are good, you behave well and do not do anything naughty. 4 If you are good at something, you can do it well.

goodbye *interjection* the word you say to someone when you are leaving them

goods *noun* things that people buy and sell

goose *noun* geese a large bird that is kept on farms for its meat and eggs

gorilla *noun* gorillas A gorilla is an African animal like a very large monkey with long arms and no tail. A gorilla is a type of ape.

government *noun* governments the group of people who are in charge of a country

a
b
c
d
e
f
g
h
i
j
k
l
m
n
o
p
q
r
s
t
u
v
w
x
y
z
71

Top Ten Grammar Tips

We use words to communicate and we use grammar to organize words. We organize words into sentences. The words in a sentence need to work together to make the meaning clear.

1 Every word in a sentence has a job to do. Words do different jobs depending on their **word class** or part of speech. The word classes are **noun, verb, adjective, adverb, preposition, conjunction** and **determiner.**

2 A **sentence** tells you something, asks you something, tells you to do something, or exclaims about something.

3 All sentences start with a **capital letter**, and end with a **full stop**, a **question mark** or an **exclamation mark**.

4 All sentences have a **verb**. Often, the verb names an action, such as **run**, **play**, **laugh** or **carry**, but there are also verbs which don't name actions, such as **am/is/are**, **have/has**, **think** and **like**.

5 In a sentence, the person or thing that does the action of the verb needs to agree with the verb. Read your sentences and check they make sense.

The bird eats the seed. ✓
The bird eat the seed. ✗

6 When you are writing, think about when something happens. Is it in the **past** or the **present**? Check that the verbs are in the same tense in each sentence.

I **went** to the house and **knocks** on the door. ✗
I **went** to the house and **knocked** on the door. ✓

7 Use **direct speech** to show what people say. Put inverted commas ' ' or " " around their words.

'**That was brilliant!' Sarah shouted.** ✓
That was brilliant! Sarah shouted. ✗

8 **Adjectives** give more information about a noun. You can use more than one for each noun. Think about the best words to describe your nouns!

9 **Paragraphs** will make your writing easy to read and understand. Paragraphs contain sentences which are about the same idea or thought. A new paragraph may move onto another idea or part of the story.

10 Think about what you are writing and choose your words carefully. If you are writing to a friend, you can use **informal** language. If you are writing a story or schoolwork, then use more **formal** words.

Top Ten Punctuation Tips

Punctuation marks make meaning clear. Here are some tips to help you use punctuation marks so that your sentences are easy to understand.

1. Begin a sentence with a **capital letter**.

2. End a sentence with a **full stop**. It shows that the sentence is finished.

3. If your sentence asks a question, use a **question mark** at the end.

4. If you are writing something urgent, surprising, or if it shows anger, use an **exclamation mark** at the end of the sentence.

5. If you are writing a list of things, use a **comma** to separate each one.

6. A **comma** is also useful when you want to show where a pause in a sentence should be when you read it. A **dash** can show an even longer pause.

full stop   comma   semi colon   colon   question mark

7 A **comma** might mean the difference between life and death! In this sentence we will eat Granny up:
Let's eat Granny!
Put a comma in the right place and we invite Granny to eat with us:
Let's eat, Granny!

8 A **colon** can be useful for writing about facts. You can use it to introduce a list or examples. Remember, you don't need a capital letter after a colon unless the word is a proper noun.

9 A **hyphen** is small but makes a big difference.
A man eating tiger is very different to **a man-eating tiger**. Can you see how it makes a difference?

10 **Apostrophes** are useful to show two things – that letters are missed out (**does + not = doesn't**), *and* that something belongs to someone or something (**the dog's tail**). They don't make plurals though!

exclamation mark   hyphen   ellipses   brackets   dash

Top Ten Spelling Tips

Spelling can be tricky! Here are some tips to help you with your spelling.

1 Try to break difficult words into smaller sections such as **choc-o-late**, **def-in-ite-ly** or **ex-per-i-ment**.

2 Make up a mnemonic for difficult words such as **because** – **b**ig **e**lephants **c**an **a**lways **u**nderstand **s**mall **e**lephants.

3 Sometimes little rhymes help.

i before e except after c when the sound is /ee/

e before i is always the way when the sound is /ay/

4 Most verbs add '-ed' to make a past tense, but some don't. Try using a dictionary to check past tenses for words like **rise**, **strike**, **teach** and **think**. (They are **rose**, **struck**, **taught** and **thought**.)

5 Some words sound the same, but are spelled differently. Try to learn which one to use and make sure to read your sentence to check you chose the right one.

here hear	**they're their there**
to, too two	**pore pour poor**

6 The letter group 'ph' always makes an /f/ sound.

photograph	**phrase**

7 Some words are spelled the same but have different meanings and might sound different.

rose   **My favourite flower is a rose.**
           I rose from the sofa slowly and carefully.

tear   **There is a tear in my eye!**
           There is a tear in my page.

8 Some words have silent letters in them. When you find a word like this, try to remember it for the next time you want to use it.

island   talk   would   write   where   scissors

9 It is easy to confuse **it's** and **its**. If you can say 'it is' or 'it has' instead of 'its' in your sentence, then you need an apostrophe.

It is raining. = It's raining. ✓
It has stopped raining. = It's stopped raining. ✓
The dog wagged it is tail. ✗

10 Apostrophes are also used to show that letters have been missed out of a word.

does + not = doesn't

Top words you need to spell*

afraid
air
are
around
astronaut
bare
bear
because
believe
boat
bread
bright
brown
carrot
catch
chief
clue
coach
coin
complete
couldn't
crawl
creep
cried
dare
dear
didn't
dinosaur
don't
down
draw
dream
drew
dying
each
elephant
enjoy
fair

fairies
fairy
families
family
fetch
field
flew
friend
garden
goal
goes
grew
hair
happy
have
head
hear
here
high
hole
horse
house
hurt
hutch
I
I'm
its
it's
I've
join
jumper
kitchen
lie
light
made
meat
meet
morning

mouth
near
new
night
of
off
once
one
opened
our
pair
pear
pie
point
practising
pull
put
quicker
quickest
rabbit
read
really
rescue
ride
right
road
rude
said
saw
school
sea
see
share
shirt
shore
show
sketch
soil

sound
summer
surprise
their
there
they
thief
think
threw
tie
to
toe
too
tried
undo
unfair
until
use
very
wait
way
wear
week
well
wheel
when
where
which
while
with
wore
yawn
year
you
your
zoo

*based on the national curriculum and Oxford Children's Corpus research

Aa

a, an *determiner* One of something. You use **a** when you are talking about something that starts with a consonant, for example *a tree, a bus, a dog*, and you use **an** when you are talking about something that starts with a vowel, for example *an orange, an apple, an umbrella*.

abbreviation *noun* abbreviations a short way of writing a word *Dr is an abbreviation for doctor.*

ability *noun* abilities If you have the ability to do something, you can do it.

able *adjective* If you are able to do something, you can do it.

about *preposition* **1** on the subject of *I like reading books about animals.* **2** more or less, but not exactly *There are about twenty-five children in my class.*

above *adverb & preposition* **1** higher than *Planes often fly above the clouds.* **2** more than *The film is only for children above the age of 12.*

abroad *adverb* When you go abroad, you go to another country.

absolutely *adverb* completely

absorb *verb* absorbs, absorbing, absorbed *(in science)* To absorb liquid means to soak it up.

accept *verb* accepts, accepting, accepted to take something after someone has offered it to you

accident *noun* accidents **1** When there is an accident, something bad happens and someone gets hurt. **2** If something that you did was an accident, you did not do it deliberately. **accidentally** *adverb* not deliberately

account *noun* accounts **1** If you give an account of something that happened, you describe what happened. **2** If you have a bank account, you keep money in a bank and can take it out when you need it.

accurate *adjective* exactly right or correct *He gave the police an accurate description of the thief.*

ache *verb* aches, aching, ached (rhymes with *bake*) If a part of your body aches, it hurts.

achieve *verb* achieves, achieving, achieved to manage to do something after trying very hard

acid *noun* acids *(in science)* An acid is a chemical. There are many different kinds of acid. Lemons contain a type of acid which makes them taste sour. Some acids are very strong and can burn your clothes and skin.

acrobat *noun* acrobats someone who entertains people by doing exciting jumping and balancing tricks

across *preposition* **1** from one side to the other *We walked across the road.* **2** on the other side of something *The park is across the river.*

act verb acts, acting, acted **1** to do something **2** to take part in a play

action noun actions **1** When there is a lot of action, a lot of exciting things are happening. **2** An action is something that you do.

active adjective If you are active, you are busy doing things.

activity noun activities **1** When there is a lot of activity, people are busy doing things all around you. **2** something enjoyable that you do for fun

actor noun actors a person who acts in a play or film

actress noun actresses a woman who acts in a play or film

actually adverb really I thought it was a wolf, but actually it was a dog.

add verb adds, adding, added **1** (in mathematics) When you add numbers together, you count them together to make a bigger number. **2** to put something with other things or mix it in with other things I added some more sugar to the mixture.

address noun addresses **1** Your address is where you live. **2** Someone's email address is the set of letters or numbers that you use to send them an email.

admire verb admires, admiring, admired **1** to like someone and think that they are very good Which famous person do you admire the most? **2** to look at something and think that it is nice

admit verb admits, admitting, admitted If you admit that you did something wrong, you tell people that you did it.

adore verb adores, adoring, adored to like something a lot I adore ice cream!

adult noun adults someone who is grown up

adventure noun adventures something exciting that happens to you

advert noun adverts An advert or **advertisement** is a picture or short film that shows you something and tries to persuade you to buy it.

advertise verb advertises, advertising, advertised to tell people about something so that they will want to buy it

advice noun If you give someone advice, you tell them what they should do.

advise verb advises, advising, advised If you advise someone to do something, you tell them they should do it.

aeroplane noun aeroplanes a large machine that can travel through the air and carry passengers or goods

affect verb affects, affecting, affected to make something different in some way Will the rain affect our plans?

affection noun the feeling you have when you like someone

afford verb affords, affording, afforded If you can afford something, you have enough money to pay for it.

afraid adjective frightened

after preposition **1** later than We got home after lunch. **2** following someone, or trying to catch them The dog ran after me.

afternoon noun afternoons the time from the middle of the day until the evening

again adverb once more Try again!

against preposition **1** next to something and touching it He leant against the wall. **2** on the opposite side to someone in a game or battle *We've got a match against Luton on Saturday.*

age *noun* Your age is how old you are.

ago *adverb* in the past *I first started dancing three years ago.*

agree *verb* agrees, agreeing, agreed If you agree with someone, you have the same ideas as them and you think that they are right.

ahead *adverb* in front of someone else *I went on ahead to open the gate.*

aim *verb* aims, aiming, aimed **1** If you aim at something, you point a gun or other weapon at it. *Aim at the centre of the target.* **2** When you aim something, you try to throw it or kick it in a particular direction. *He aimed the ball into the far corner of the net.*

air *noun* the gas all around us, which we breathe

airport *noun* airports a place where planes take off and land and passengers can get on and off

alarm *noun* alarms a loud sound that warns people of danger

album *noun* albums **1** a book to put things like photographs or stamps in **2** a CD with several pieces of music on it

alien *noun* aliens In stories, an alien is a person or creature from another planet.

alike *adjective* Things that are alike are similar in some way. *Although Sarah and I are not sisters, everyone says we look alike.*

alive *adjective* living

all *determiner & pronoun* **1** everyone or everything *Are you all listening?* **2** the whole of something *Have you eaten all the cake?*

Allah *noun* the Muslim name for God

allergic *adjective* If you are allergic to something, it makes you ill, for example it makes you sneeze or gives you a rash.

allergy *noun* allergies An allergy is something that makes you ill when you eat or touch it. It often makes you sneeze or gives you a rash. *I have an allergy to peanuts.*

alligator *noun* alligators An alligator is an animal that looks like a crocodile. Alligators are reptiles and live in parts of North and South America and China.

alliteration *noun* the use of words that begin with the same sound to create a special effect in writing, for example *five fat fishes*

allow *verb* allows, allowing, allowed If you allow someone to do something, you let them do it and do not try to stop them. *We're not allowed to play football in the playground.*

all right *adjective* **1** If you are all right, you are safe and well, and not hurt. **2** If something is all right, it is quite good but not very good.

almost *adverb* very nearly *We're almost home.*

alone *adjective* If you are alone, there is no one with you.

along *adverb & preposition* from one end to the other *He ran along the top of the wall.*

alphabet *noun* alphabets all the letters that we use in writing, arranged in a particular order

already *adverb* before now *When we got to the station, the train had already left.*

also *adverb* as well *I love football and also tennis.*

although *conjunction* even though *We kept on running, although we were tired.*

altogether *adverb* including all the people or things

always *adverb* at all times, or every time *Joshua is always late!*

amaze *verb* amazes, amazing, amazed to make you feel very surprised amazed *adjective* surprised

ambition *noun* ambitions something that you want to do very much

ambulance *noun* ambulances a van in which people who are ill or injured are taken to hospital

among *preposition* **1** in the middle of *Somewhere among all these books was the one I was looking for.* **2** between *Share the sweets among you.*

amount *noun* amounts a quantity of something

amphibian *noun* amphibians an animal that lives some of its life in water, and some on land

amuse *verb* amuses, amusing, amused **1** If something amuses you, you find it funny and it makes you laugh. **2** To amuse yourself means to find things to do. *We played games to amuse ourselves.*

ancient *adjective* Something that is ancient is very old.

and *conjunction* a word that you use to join two words or phrases together

angel *noun* angels a messenger sent by God

anger *noun* a strong feeling that you get when you are not pleased

angle *noun* angles the corner where two lines meet

angry *adjective* angrier, angriest annoyed or cross angrily *adverb* If you say something angrily, you are annoyed or cross.

animal *noun* animals An animal is anything that lives and can move about. Birds, fish, snakes, wasps, and elephants are all animals.

ankle *noun* ankles the thin part of your leg where it is joined to your foot

anniversary *noun* anniversaries a day when you remember something special that happened on the same day in the past

announce *verb* announces, announcing, announced to tell everyone about something *Tomorrow we will announce the winner of the competition.*

annoy *verb* annoys, annoying, annoyed to make someone angry **annoying** *adjective* If something is annoying, it makes you angry.

annual *noun* annuals a book with cartoons, stories, and jokes that comes out once a year
annual *adjective* An annual event happens once every year.

another *determiner & pronoun* one more *Can I have another biscuit, please? Would you like another?*

answer *noun* answers something you say or write to someone who has asked you a question
answer *verb* answers, answering, answered to say something to someone after they have asked you a question *I can answer the question.*

ant *noun* ants Ants are tiny insects that live in large groups.

antelope *noun* antelopes a wild animal that looks like a deer and lives in Africa and parts of Asia

anticlockwise *adverb* If something moves anticlockwise, it moves round in a circle in the opposite direction to the hands of a clock.

antique *noun* antiques something that is very old and worth money

antiseptic *noun* antiseptics a chemical that kills germs

anxious *adjective* worried

any *determiner & pronoun* **1** some *Have you got any orange juice?* **2** no special one *Take any book you want.*

anybody, anyone *pronoun* any person *I didn't see anybody at the park.*

anything *pronoun* any thing *I can't see anything in the dark.*

anywhere *adverb* in any place *I can't find my book anywhere.*

apart *adverb* If you keep things apart, you keep them away from each other.

ape *noun* apes An ape is an animal like a large monkey with long arms and no tail. Gorillas and chimpanzees are types of ape.

apex *noun* apexes the highest point of something

apologize *verb* apologizes, apologizing, apologized to say that you are sorry

apology *noun* apologies You say or write an apology when you are sorry for something you have done.

a b c d e f g h i j k l m n o p q r s t u v w x y z

17

A
B
C
D
E
F
G
H
I
J
K
L
M
N
O
P
Q
R
S
T
U
V
W
X
Y
Z

apparatus *noun* the special equipment that you use to do something

appear *verb* appears, appearing, appeared **1** When something appears, it comes into view and you can see it. **2** to seem *This appears to be the wrong key.*

appearance *noun* **1** Your appearance is what you look like. **2** when something appears *The audience cheered after the appearance of the band on the stage.*

appetite *noun* appetites If you have an appetite, you feel hungry. *I'm not hungry. I've lost my appetite.*

applaud *verb* applauds, applauding, applauded to clap to show that you are pleased

apple *noun* apples a round, crisp, juicy fruit

appreciate *verb* appreciates, appreciating, appreciated to feel glad because you have something *You don't seem to appreciate all your toys.*

approach *verb* approaches, approaching, approached to get nearer to something or someone

approve *verb* approves, approving, approved If you approve of something, you think that it is good or suitable.

approximate *adjective* An approximate amount is almost correct, but not exact. *The approximate time of arrival is two o'clock.*

April *noun* the fourth month of the year

apron *noun* aprons something that you wear over your clothes to keep them clean when you are cooking or painting

aquarium *noun* aquariums a large glass tank for keeping fish and other sea animals in

arch *noun* arches a curved part of a bridge or building

architect *noun* architects a person who draws plans for new buildings

area *noun* areas **1** a piece of land *There's a play area behind the library.* **2** When you measure the area of something, you measure how big it is.

argue *verb* argues, arguing, argued When people argue, they talk in an angry way to each other because they do not agree with each other.

arm *noun* arms **1** Your arms are the long parts of your body that are joined to your shoulders. Your hands are on the ends of your arms. **2** Arms are weapons.

armour *noun* metal clothes that soldiers and knights wore in battles long ago

army *noun* armies a large group of people who are trained to fight on land in a war

around *adverb & preposition* all round *We spent the afternoon wandering around town.*

arrange *verb* arranges, arranging, arranged **1** to put things somewhere neatly so that they look nice or are in the right position *She arranged the books into two neat piles.* **2** to make plans so that something will happen *We arranged to meet at two o'clock.*

arrest *verb* arrests, arresting, arrested When the police arrest someone, they take them prisoner.

arrive *verb* arrives, arriving, arrived to get somewhere at the end of a journey

arrow *noun* arrows a stick with a pointed end, which you shoot from a bow

art *noun* drawing and painting

article *noun* articles **1** a thing or an object **2** a piece of writing in a newspaper or magazine

artificial *adjective* not natural, but made by people or machines *The artificial flowers looked just like real ones.*

artist *noun* artists someone who draws or paints pictures

as *conjunction* **1** when *I fell over as I was coming downstairs.* **2** because *As it's cold, I think you should put a coat on.*

ashamed *adjective* If you feel ashamed, you feel sorry and guilty because you have done something bad.

ask *verb* asks, asking, asked **1** If you ask someone a question, you say it to them so that they will tell you the answer. **2** If you ask for something, you say that you want it.

asleep *adjective* sleeping

assembly *noun* assemblies the time when the whole school meets together

assistant *noun* assistants **1** someone whose job is to help an important person **2** someone who serves customers in a shop

asthma *noun* Someone who has asthma sometimes finds it difficult to breathe.

astonish *verb* astonishes, astonishing, astonished to surprise someone a lot

astronaut *noun* astronauts someone who travels in space

at *preposition* **1** in a place *Tom is at home.* **2** when it is a particular time *I'll meet you at two o'clock.*

athlete *noun* athletes someone who does athletics

athletics *noun* sports in which people run, jump, and throw things

atlas *noun* atlases a book of maps

a
b
c
d
e
f
g
h
i
j
k
l
m
n
o
p
q
r
s
t
u
v
w
x
y
z

atmosphere *noun* the air around the earth

atom *noun* atoms *(in science)* one of the very tiny parts that everything is made up of

attach *verb* attaches, attaching, attached to join or fasten things together

attachment *noun* attachments a file that you send to someone with an email

attack *verb* attacks, attacking, attacked to fight somone and try to hurt them

attempt *verb* attempts, attempting, attempted to try to do something

attend *verb* attends, attending, attended If you attend school, you go to school. If you attend an event, you go to watch it.

attention *noun* When you pay attention, you listen carefully to what someone is saying, or watch what they are doing.

attic *noun* attics a room inside the roof of a house

attract *verb* attracts, attracting, attracted **1** If something attracts you, you feel interested in it. *A noise attracted my attention.* **2** to make something come nearer *A magnet will attract some types of metal.*

attractive *adjective* An attractive thing is pleasant to look at. An attractive person is beautiful or handsome.

audience *noun* audiences all the people who have come to a place to see or hear something

August *noun* the eighth month of the year

aunt, aunty *noun* aunts, aunties the sister of your mother or father, or your uncle's wife

author *noun* authors someone who writes books or stories

autograph *noun* autographs When a famous person gives you their autograph, they write their name down for you to keep.

automatic *adjective* Something that is automatic works on its own, without a person controlling it.

autumn *noun* the time of the year when leaves fall off the trees and it gets colder

available *adjective* If something is available, it is there for you to use or buy. *Do you have tennis rackets available for hire?*

avalanche *noun* avalanches a large amount of snow or rock that slides suddenly down a mountain

avenue *noun* avenues a wide road in a town or city

average *adjective* ordinary or usual *What's the average height in your class?*

avoid *verb* avoids, avoiding, avoided to keep away from someone or something

awake *adjective* not sleeping

award *noun* awards a prize

aware *adjective* If you are aware of something, you know about it.

away *adverb* **1** not here *Ali is away today.* **2** to another place *Put your books away now.*

awful *adjective* horrible or very bad

awkward *adjective* **1** difficult to do or difficult to use *The bags were big and* *awkward to carry.* **2** If you feel awkward, you feel embarrassed.

axe *noun* **axes** a sharp tool for chopping wood

Bb

baby *noun* **babies** a very young child

back *noun* **backs** **1** the part of your body that is between your neck and your bottom **2** the long part of an animal's body between its head and its tail **3** the part of something that is opposite the front *We sat in the back of the car.*

back *adverb* If you go back to a place, you go there again. *He ran back home.*

background *noun* everything that you can see behind the main thing in a picture

backwards *adverb* **1** towards the place that is behind you *She fell over backwards.* **2** in the opposite way to usual *Can you count backwards?*

bad *adjective* **worse, worst** **1** Something that is bad is nasty or horrible. *We couldn't go out because of the bad weather.* **2** A bad person does things that are against the law.

badge *noun* **badges** a small thing that you pin or sew onto your clothes

badger *noun* **badgers** A badger is an animal that digs holes in the ground. It has a white face with black stripes on it.

badly *adverb* **1** If you do something badly, you do not do it very well. **2** If you are badly hurt or upset, you are hurt or upset a lot.

badminton *noun* a game in which people use a racket to hit a very light cone called a shuttlecock over a net

bag *noun* **bags** something that you use for carrying things in

Baisakhi *noun* a Sikh festival which takes place in April

bake *verb* **bakes, baking, baked** to cook food in an oven

baker *noun* **bakers** someone whose job is to make or sell bread and cakes

balance *noun* **balances** If you have good balance, you can hold your body steady and not fall over.

balance *verb* **balances, balancing, balanced** **1** to hold your body steady and not fall over *Can you balance on a tightrope?* **2** to put something somewhere carefully so that it does not fall *He balanced a coin on the end of his finger.*

balcony *noun* **balconies** **1** a small platform outside an upstairs window of a building, where people can stand or sit **2** the seats upstairs in a cinema or theatre

bald *adjective* Someone who is bald has no hair on their head.

ball *noun* **balls** **1** a round object that you hit, kick, or throw in games **2** a big party where people wear very smart clothes and dance with each other

ballet *noun* ballets a type of dancing in which dancers dance on the very tips of their toes

balloon *noun* balloons **1** a small, colourful rubber bag that you can fill with air and use for playing with or to decorate a room for a party **2** A hot air balloon is a very big bag that is filled with hot air or gas so that it floats in the sky.

banana *noun* bananas a long, yellow fruit that grows in hot countries

band *noun* bands **1** a group of people who do something together **2** a group of people who play music together **3** a thin strip of material *We had to wear name bands round our wrists.*

bandage *noun* bandages a strip of material that you wrap round part of your body if you have hurt it

bang *noun* bangs a sudden very loud noise

bang *verb* bangs, banging, banged **1** to hit something hard *He banged on the window.* **2** to make a sudden loud noise *The door banged shut.*

bank *noun* banks **1** A bank is a place where people can keep their money safely. Banks also lend money to people. **2** the ground near the edge of a river or lake *We walked along the bank of the river.*

banner *noun* banners a long, thin flag with words written on it

bar *noun* bars **1** a long piece of wood or metal **2** a block of chocolate or soap **3** a place that serves food and drinks at a counter

barbecue *noun* barbecues **1** a party where people sit outside and cook food over a fire **2** a metal frame that you put food on to cook it over a fire outside

barber *noun* barbers a hairdresser for men and boys

bare *adjective* barer, barest **1** If a part of your body is bare, it has nothing covering it. **2** If something is bare, it has nothing on it or in it.

bargain *noun* bargains something that you buy very cheaply, for much less than its usual price

bark *noun* the hard covering round the trunk and branches of a tree

bark *verb* barks, barking, barked When a dog barks, it makes a loud, rough sound.

bar mitzvah *noun* bar mitzvahs a celebration for a Jewish boy when he reaches the age of 13

barn *noun* barns a large building on a farm, where a farmer keeps animals, hay, or grain

barrel *noun* barrels a round, wooden container that beer, wine, or water is kept in

base *noun* bases the part at the bottom of an object, which it stands on

basic *adjective* simple but very important *You need to learn the basic skills first.*

basin *noun* basins a large bowl

basket *noun* baskets A basket is a container that you carry things in. A basket is made of thin strips of straw, plastic, or metal that are twisted or woven together.

basketball *noun* a game in which two teams try to score points by bouncing a ball and throwing it in a high net

bat *noun* bats **1** a small animal with wings that flies and hunts for food at night **2** a piece of wood that you use for hitting a ball in a game

bat *verb* bats, batting, batted When you bat in a game, you try to hit the ball with a bat.

bath *noun* baths (rhymes with *path*) a large container which you can fill with water to sit in and wash yourself

bathroom *noun* bathrooms a room with a bath, washbasin, and toilet

battery *noun* batteries A battery is an object that contains a store of electricity. You put batteries inside torches and radios to make them work.

battle *noun* battles a big fight between two groups of people

bawl *verb* bawls, bawling, bawled to shout or cry very loudly

bay *noun* bays a place on the coast where the land bends inwards and sea fills the space

be *verb* am, are, is; was, were; been, being **1** If you are something, you exist and you are doing something. *I am alive. The dog is in the park. Dad is in the kitchen. I was sitting in the classroom.* **2** You use **be** when something is going to happen. *Football practice is tomorrow. Mum is going to pick me up. We are going to the shops.* **3** You use **be** when you are talking about feeling something. *I am very happy. The teacher was angry that I had forgotten my homework. I have been sad.*

beach *noun* beaches an area of sand or pebbles by the edge of the sea

bead *noun* beads A bead is a small piece of wood, glass, or plastic with a hole through the middle. You thread beads on a string to make a necklace.

beak *noun* beaks A bird's beak is its mouth, which is hard and pointed.

beam *noun* beams A beam of light is a ray of light that shines onto something.

bean *noun* beans Beans are the seeds of some plants which you can eat. Sometimes you eat just the seeds, and sometimes you eat the seeds and the pod that they grow in.

bear *noun* bears a large wild animal with thick fur and sharp teeth and claws

bear *verb* bears, bearing, bore, borne If you cannot bear something, you hate it. *I cannot bear to see animals in pain.*

beard *noun* beards hair growing on a man's chin

beat *verb* beats, beating, beaten **1** to hit someone hard a lot of times **2** If you beat someone, you win a game against them. **3** When you beat a mixture, you stir it hard. *Dad beat some eggs to make an omelette.*

beat *noun* beats the regular rhythm in a piece of music

beautiful *adjective* **1** Something that is beautiful is very nice to look at, hear, or smell. **2** Someone who is beautiful has a lovely face.

because *conjunction* for the reason that *My dad was angry because I was late.*

> Remember **b**ig **e**lephants **c**an **a**lways **u**nderstand **s**mall **e**lephants.

become *verb* becomes, becoming, became, become to start to be *She became quite upset when we told her about the kitten.*

bed *noun* beds a piece of furniture that you sleep on

bedroom *noun* bedrooms a room where you sleep

bee *noun* bees A bee is an insect that can fly and sting you. Bees use a sweet liquid called nectar from flowers to make honey.

beef *noun* meat from a cow

beetle *noun* beetles an insect with hard, shiny wings

before *adverb, conjunction & preposition* **1** earlier than *We usually have maths before lunch.* **2** already *Have you been here before?* **3** in front of *The girl vanished before my eyes.*

beg *verb* begs, begging, begged If you beg someone to do something, you ask them very strongly to do it.

begin *verb* begins, beginning, began, begun to start

behave *verb* behaves, behaving, behaved **1** The way you behave is the way you speak and do things. **2** If you behave yourself, you are polite and do not do anything that is rude or naughty.

behind *adverb & preposition* at the back of *I hid behind the wall.*

belief *noun* beliefs something that you believe is true

believe *verb* believes, believing, believed to feel sure that something is true *I don't believe you—I think you're lying!*

> Remember **i** before **e** except after **c** when the sound is **/ee/**.

bell *noun* bells a metal object that rings when something hits it

bellow *verb* bellows, bellowing, bellowed to shout very loudly

belong *verb* belongs, belonging, belonged **1** If something belongs to you, it is yours. **2** If something belongs in a place, it goes there.

below *preposition* **1** underneath *Can you swim below the surface of the water?* **2** less than *The temperature was below freezing last night.*

belt *noun* **belts** a band of leather or other material that you wear round your waist

bench *noun* **benches** a long wooden or stone seat for more than one person

bend *verb* **bends, bending, bent** **1** to make something curved and not straight **2** When you bend down, you lean forward so that your head is nearer to the ground.
bend *noun* **bends** a part of a road or river that curves round

beneath *preposition* underneath

berry *noun* **berries** a small, round fruit with seeds in it

beside *preposition* at the side of *Dan was standing beside me.*

best *adjective* better than any other *Who's the best swimmer in your class?*

better *adjective* **1** If one thing is better than another, it is more interesting, more useful, or more exciting. **2** If you are better than someone else, you are able to do something more quickly or more successfully. **3** When you are better, you are well again after an illness.

between *preposition* **1** in the middle of two people or things *I sat between Mum and Dad.* **2** among *Share the money between you.*

beware *verb* If you tell someone to beware, you are warning them to be careful.

Bible *noun* **Bibles** the holy book of the Christian religion

bicycle *noun* **bicycles** something with two wheels, which you sit on and ride along by pushing pedals round with your feet

big *adjective* **bigger, biggest** large and not small

bike *noun* **bikes** a bicycle

bill *noun* **bills** a piece of paper that tells you how much money you owe someone

bin *noun* **bins** a container for putting rubbish in

biology *noun* the study of animals and plants

bird *noun* **birds** any animal with feathers, wings, and a beak

birth *noun* **births** when a baby leaves its mother's body and is born

birthday *noun* **birthdays** the day each year when you remember and celebrate the day you were born

biscuit *noun* **biscuits** a kind of small, crisp cake

a b c d e f g h i j k l m n o p q r s t u v w x y z

A
B
C
D
E
F
G
H
I
J
K
L
M
N
O
P
Q
R
S
T
U
V
W
X
Y
Z

bit *noun* bits a small amount of something

bite *verb* bites, biting, bit, bitten to use your teeth to cut something

bite *noun* bites a mouthful cut off by biting

black *adjective* **1** Something that is black is the colour of the sky on a very dark night. **2** Someone who is black has a skin that is naturally dark in colour.

blackbird *noun* blackbirds A blackbird is a type of bird. The male is black with an orange beak, but the female is brown.

blackboard *noun* blackboards a smooth, dark board that you can write on with chalk

blame *verb* blames, blaming, blamed When you blame someone, you say that it is their fault that something bad has happened. *Everyone blamed me for the broken window, but it wasn't my fault!*

blank *adjective* A blank piece of paper has nothing written or drawn on it.

blanket *noun* blankets a thick, warm cover that you put on a bed

blaze *noun* blazes a large, strong fire

blaze *verb* blazes, blazing, blazed to burn brightly

blazer *noun* blazers a type of jacket, especially one that children wear to school as part of their school uniform

bleed *verb* bleeds, bleeding, bled If a part of your body is bleeding, blood is coming out of it.

blind *adjective* Someone who is blind cannot see.

blind *noun* blinds a piece of material that you pull down to cover a window

blink *verb* blinks, blinking, blinked to close your eyes and then open them again quickly

block *noun* blocks **1** a thick piece of stone or wood **2** a tall building with lots of flats or offices inside *We live in a block of flats near the city centre.*

block *verb* blocks, blocking, blocked If something is blocking a road or pipe, it is in the way and nothing can get past it.

blog *noun* blogs a website on which someone writes regularly about their own life or opinions blogger *noun* someone who regularly writes a blog

blond, blonde *adjective* Someone who is blond has fair or light-coloured hair.

blood *noun* the red liquid that is pumped round inside your body

blossom *noun* blossoms the flowers on a tree

blouse *noun* blouses a shirt that a woman or girl wears

blow *noun* blows If you receive a blow, someone hits you hard.

blow *verb* blows, blowing, blew, blown **1** to make air come out of your mouth **2** When the wind blows, it moves along.

blue *adjective* Something that is blue is the colour of the sky on a fine day.

blunt *adjective* blunter, bluntest not sharp *This knife is too blunt to cut anything.*

blush *verb* blushes, blushing, blushed When you blush, your face goes red because you feel shy or guilty.

board *noun* **boards** a flat piece of wood

board *verb* **boards, boarding, boarded** to get onto an aeroplane, bus, ship, or train

boast *verb* **boasts, boasting, boasted** to talk about how clever you are or how well you can do things

boat *noun* **boats** a vehicle that floats on water and can carry people and goods over water

body *noun* **bodies** 1 Your body is every part of you that you can see and touch. 2 A body is a dead person.

boil *verb* **boils, boiling, boiled** 1 When water boils, it bubbles and gives off steam because it is very hot. 2 When you boil something, you cook it in boiling water.

bold *adjective* **bolder, boldest** brave and not afraid

bolt *noun* **bolts** 1 a piece of metal that you slide across to lock a door 2 A bolt is a thick metal pin that looks like a screw with a blunt end. You screw a bolt into a nut to fasten something.

bolt *verb* **bolts, bolting, bolted** When you bolt a door or window, you lock it with a bolt.

bomb *noun* **bombs** a weapon that explodes and hurts people or damages things

bone *noun* **bones** Your bones are the hard white parts inside your body. Your skeleton is made of bones.

bonfire *noun* **bonfires** a large fire that you make outside, especially to burn rubbish

bonnet *noun* **bonnets** the part of a car that covers the engine

book *noun* **books** A book is a set of pages that are joined together inside a cover. You can read a book.

book *verb* **books, booking, booked** to arrange for something to be reserved for you

boot *noun* **boots** 1 a type of shoe that also covers your ankle and part of your leg 2 the part of a car that you carry luggage in

bore *verb* **bores, boring, bored** If something bores you, you find it dull and not interesting.

born *adjective* When a baby is born, it comes out of its mother's body and starts to live.

borrow *verb* **borrows, borrowing, borrowed** to take something and use it for a while and then give it back

both *determiner* & *pronoun* the two of them *Hold it in both hands.*

bother *verb* **bothers, bothering, bothered** 1 to worry you or annoy you 2 If you do not bother to do something, you do not do it because it would take too much effort. *Joe never bothers to answer his text messages.*

bottle *noun* **bottles** a tall glass or plastic container that you keep liquids in

bottom *noun* **bottoms** the lowest part of something *The others waited for us at the bottom of the hill.*

bounce *verb* **bounces, bouncing, bounced** When something bounces, it

A
B
C
D
E
F
G
H
I
J
K
L
M
N
O
P
Q
R
S
T
U
V
W
X
Y
Z

springs back into the air when it hits something hard

bound *verb* bounds, bounding, bounded *adjective* If something is bound to happen, it will definitely happen. *We've got the best team, so we're bound to win.*

bow *noun* bows (rhymes with *go*) **1** a knot with large loops *She tied the ribbon into a bow.* **2** a weapon that you use for shooting arrows

bow *verb* bows, bowing, bowed (rhymes with *cow*) to bend forwards to show respect to someone or to thank people for clapping

bowl *verb* bowls, bowling, bowled When you bowl in a game of cricket, you throw the ball for someone else to hit.

box *noun* boxes a container with straight sides, made of cardboard or plastic

box *verb* boxes, boxing, boxed When people box, they fight by hitting each other with their fists.

boy *noun* boys a male child

bracelet *noun* bracelets a piece of jewellery that you wear round your wrist

Braille *noun* Braille is a way of writing that uses a pattern of raised dots on paper. Blind people can read Braille by touching the dots with their fingers.

brain *noun* brains the part inside your head that controls your body and allows you to think and remember things

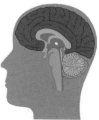

brainy *adjective* brainier, brainiest Someone who is brainy is very clever.

brake *noun* brakes the part of a car or bicycle that makes it slow down and stop

branch *noun* branches a part that grows out from the trunk of a tree

brave *adjective* braver, bravest willing to do dangerous things

bread *noun* a food that is made from flour and water, and baked in the oven

break *verb* breaks, breaking, broke, broken **1** to smash something into several pieces **2** to damage something so that it no longer works **3** If you break a law or a promise, you do something that goes against it. **4** If something breaks down, it stops working. *Our bus broke down on the motorway.*

break *noun* breaks a short rest

breakfast *noun* breakfasts the first meal of the day, which you eat in the morning

breast *noun* breasts **1** A woman's breasts are the parts on the front of her body that can produce milk to feed a baby. **2** The breast on a chicken or other bird is its chest.

breath *noun* breaths the air that you take into your body and then blow out again

breathe *verb* breathes, breathing, breathed to take air into your lungs through your nose or mouth and then blow it out again

breed *noun* breeds a particular type of animal *Poodles are my favourite breed of dog.*

breeze *noun* breezes a gentle wind

brick *noun* bricks A brick is a small block made from baked clay. People use bricks for building houses.

bride *noun* brides a woman who is getting married

bridegroom *noun* bridegrooms a man who is getting married

bridesmaid *noun* bridesmaids a girl or woman who walks behind the bride at her wedding

bridge *noun* bridges something that is built over a river, railway, or road so that people can go across it

brief *adjective* briefer, briefest short and not lasting very long

briefcase *noun* briefcases a small case that you carry books and papers in

bright *adjective* brighter, brightest 1 A bright light shines with a lot of light 2 A bright colour is strong and not dull. 3 A bright day is sunny. 4 Someone who is bright is clever and learns things quickly. **brightly** *adverb* If something shines brightly, it has a lot of light. **brightness** *noun* when something is bright

brilliant *adjective* 1 Someone who is brilliant is very clever, or very good at something. 2 Something that is brilliant is very good.

bring *verb* brings, bringing, brought 1 If you bring something with you, you carry it with you. 2 If you bring someone with you, they come with you.

broad *adjective* broader, broadest wide

broadcast *verb* broadcasts, broadcasting, broadcast to send something out as a television or radio programme

brooch *noun* brooches a piece of jewellery that you pin to your clothes

broom *noun* brooms a brush with a long handle that you use for sweeping floors

brother *noun* brothers a boy who has the same parents as you

brown *adjective* 1 Something that is brown is the colour of soil. 2 Brown bread is made with the whole wheat grain, not just the white part.

bruise *noun* bruises a dark mark on your skin that you get when you have been hit

brush *noun* brushes A brush is an object with short, stiff hairs on the end of a handle. You use a brush for cleaning things, and you also use a brush for painting.
brush *verb* brushes, brushing, brushed to clean something using a brush

a
b
c
d
e
f
g
h
i
j
k
l
m
n
o
p
q
r
s
t
u
v
w
x
y
z

bubble *noun* bubbles Bubbles are small balls of air or gas inside a liquid, for example like the ones you find in fizzy drinks.

bubble *verb* bubbles, bubbling, bubbled When a liquid bubbles, it makes bubbles.

bucket *noun* buckets a container with a handle that you use for carrying water

buckle *noun* buckles the part of a belt that you use to fasten the two ends together

bud *noun* buds a small lump on a plant that will later open into a flower or leaf

Buddha or also **the Buddha** *noun* the person on whose teachings the **Buddhist** religion is based

Buddhist *noun* Buddhists someone who follows the Buddhist religion and the teachings of the Buddha

bug *noun* bugs **1** an insect **2** a germ that gets into your body and makes you ill

build *verb* builds, building, built to make something by joining or fixing different parts together

builder *noun* builders someone who builds houses and other buildings

building *noun* buildings a structure like a house, school, shop, or church

bulb *noun* bulbs the part of an electric lamp that gives out light

bull *noun* bulls a male cow, elephant, or whale

bulldozer *noun* bulldozers a heavy machine that moves earth and makes land flat

bullet *noun* bullets a small piece of metal that is fired from a gun

bully *verb* bullies, bullying, bullied to hurt someone or be unkind to them

bully *noun* bullies someone who hurts other people or is unkind to them

bump *verb* bumps, bumping, bumped to knock or hit something

bump *noun* bumps **1** the noise that something makes when it falls to the ground **2** a small lump on your skin that you get when you have knocked it

bumper *noun* bumpers A bumper is a bar along the front or back of a car. The bumper protects the car if it hits something.

bun *noun* buns **1** a small, round cake **2** a round piece of bread

bunch *noun* bunches a group of things that are tied together *What a lovely bunch of flowers!*

bundle *noun* bundles a group of things that are tied together *She was carrying a bundle of old clothes.*

bungalow *noun* bungalows a house without any upstairs rooms

A B C D E F G H I J K L M N O P Q R S T U V W X Y Z

bunk *noun* bunks a bed that has another bed above or below it *Can I sleep in the top bunk?*

burger *noun* burgers a piece of minced meat that has been made into a round, flat cake and cooked

burglar *noun* burglars someone who goes into a building and steals things

burn *verb* burns, burning, burned, burnt
1 When something burns, it catches fire. **2** If you burn something, you damage it or destroy it using fire or heat. **3** If you burn yourself, you hurt your skin with fire or heat.

burrow *noun* burrows a hole in the ground that an animal lives in

burst *verb* bursts, bursting, burst to suddenly break open

bury *verb* buries, burying, buried (rhymes with *merry*) **1** to put something in a hole in the ground and cover it over **2** When a dead person is buried, their body is put into the ground.

bus *noun* buses a vehicle that a lot of people can travel in

bush *noun* bushes a plant that looks like a small tree

business *noun* businesses **1** When people do business, they buy and sell things. **2** a shop or company that makes or sells things

busy *adjective* busier, busiest **1** If you are busy, you have a lot of things to do. **2** A busy place has a lot of people and traffic in it.

but *conjunction* however

butcher *noun* butchers someone who cuts up meat and sells it in a shop

butter *noun* a yellow food that is made from milk

butterfly *noun* butterflies an insect with large colourful wings

button *noun* buttons **1** a small round thing that you use to fasten clothes by pushing it through a small hole in the clothes **2** a part of a machine that you press to switch it on or off

buy *verb* buys, buying, bought to get something by giving someone money for it

buzz *verb* buzzes, buzzing, buzzed to make a sound like a bee

by *preposition* **1** near *You can leave your shoes by the front door.* **2** travelling in *We're going by train.*

a
b
c
d
e
f
g
h
i
j
k
l
m
n
o
p
q
r
s
t
u
v
w
x
y
z

Cc

cab *noun* **cabs** **1** a taxi **2** the part at the front of a lorry, bus, or train where the driver sits

cabbage *noun* **cabbages** a round, green vegetable with a lot of leaves that are wrapped tightly round each other

cabin *noun* **cabins** **1** a room for passengers in a ship or an aeroplane **2** a small hut

cable *noun* **cables** **1** strong, thick wire or rope **2** A cable is a bundle of wires that are held together in a plastic covering. They carry electricity or television signals.

cafe *noun* **cafes** a place where you can buy a drink or food and sit down to eat or drink it

cage *noun* **cages** a box or small room with bars across it for keeping animals or birds in

cake *noun* **cakes** a sweet food that you make with flour, fat, eggs, and sugar and bake in the oven

calculate *verb* **calculates, calculating, calculated** When you calculate an amount, you do a sum and work out how many or how much it is.

calculator *noun* **calculators** a machine that you use to do sums

calendar *noun* **calendars** A calendar is a list of all the days, weeks, and months in a year. You can write on a calendar things that you are going to do each day.

calf *noun* **calves** **1** a young cow, elephant, or whale **2** the back part of your leg between your knee and your ankle

call *verb* **calls, calling, called** **1** When you call to someone, you speak loudly so that they can hear you. *'Look out!' he called.* **2** to tell someone to come to you *Mum called us in for tea.* **3** When you call someone a name, you give them that name. *We decided to call the puppy Patch.* **4** to telephone someone

calm *adjective* **calmer, calmest** **1** If the sea or the weather is calm, it is still and not stormy. **2** If you are calm, you are quiet and not noisy or excited.

camel *noun* **camels** a big animal with one or two humps on its back

camera *noun* **cameras** a machine that you use for taking photographs

camouflage *verb* **camouflages, camouflaging, camouflaged** If something is camouflaged, it is hidden because it looks very like the things around it.

camp *noun* **camps** a place where people stay for a short time in tents or small huts

camp *verb* **camps, camping, camped** to sleep in a tent

can *noun* **cans** a tin with food or drink in

can *verb* **could** If you can do something, you are able to do it. *Can you swim?*

canal *noun* **canals** a river that people have made for boats to travel on

cancel *verb* **cancels, cancelling, cancelled** When you cancel something that was arranged, you say that it will not happen.

candle *noun* **candles** A candle is a stick of wax with string through the centre. You light the string and it burns slowly to give you light.

cannot *verb* can not

canoe *noun* canoes a light, narrow boat that you sit in and paddle along

can't *verb* can not

canvas *noun* a type of strong cloth that is used for making tents and sails

cap *noun* caps **1** a soft hat with a stiff part that sticks out at the front, over your eyes **2** a lid for a bottle or other container

capital *noun* capitals a country's most important city

captain *noun* captains **1** the person in charge of a ship or aeroplane **2** the person in charge of a team, who tells the others what to do

caption *noun* captions words that are printed next to a picture and tell you what the picture is about

capture *verb* captures, capturing, captured to catch someone *My grandfather was captured by enemy soldiers during the war.*

car *noun* cars something that you can drive along in on roads

caravan *noun* caravans a small house on wheels that can be pulled from place to place

card *noun* cards **1** thick, stiff paper **2** A card is a piece of card with a picture and a message on it. You send cards to people at special times like their birthday or Christmas. **3** Cards are small pieces of card with numbers or pictures on them, that you use to play games.

cardboard *noun* very thick, strong paper

cardigan *noun* cardigans a knitted jumper that has buttons down the front

care *noun* **1** If you take care when you are doing something, you do it carefully. **2** If you take care of someone, you look after them.

care *verb* cares, caring, cared **1** If you care about something, it is important to you. *I don't care where I sit.* **2** If you care for someone, you look after them.

careful *adjective* If you are careful, you make sure that you do things safely and well so that you do not have an accident. **carefully** *adverb* If you do something carefully, you make sure that you do it safely and well so that you do not have an accident.

careless *adjective* If you are careless, you are not careful and so you make mistakes or have an accident.

caretaker *noun* caretakers someone whose job is to look after a building

carnival *noun* carnivals a large party that takes place in the streets

carpenter *noun* carpenters someone whose job is to make things out of wood

carpet *noun* carpets a thick, soft material that is put on a floor to cover it

carriage *noun* carriages **1** The carriages on a train are the parts where people sit. **2** something that is pulled by horses for people to travel in

carrot *noun* **carrots** a long, thin, orange vegetable

carry *verb* **carries, carrying, carried 1** to hold something in your hands or arms and take it somewhere **2** If you carry on doing something, you keep doing it.

cart *noun* **carts** a wooden vehicle that you can put things in to take them somewhere

carton *noun* **cartons** a small plastic or cardboard box in which food or drink is sold

cartoon *noun* **cartoons 1** a funny drawing that makes people laugh **2** a film that has drawings instead of real people

cartwheel *noun* **cartwheels** When you do a cartwheel, you put your hands on the ground and swing your legs into the air in a circle.

carve *verb* **carves, carving, carved 1** to make something by cutting wood or stone into the right shape **2** to cut slices from meat

case *noun* **cases 1** a box for keeping things in **2** a suitcase

cash *noun* money

cast *verb* **casts, casting, cast** To cast a spell on someone means to say a spell that will affect them.

castle *noun* **castles** a large, strong building with thick, stone walls

cat *noun* **cats** A cat is a furry animal that people often keep as a pet. Lions, tigers, and leopards are large wild cats.

catalogue *noun* **catalogues** a list of all the things that you can buy from a place, sometimes with pictures of the things

catch *verb* **catches, catching, caught 1** If you catch something that is moving through the air, you get hold of it. **2** To catch someone means to find them and take them prisoner. **3** If you catch an illness, you get it. **4** When you catch a bus or train, you get on it.

caterpillar *noun* **caterpillars** a small animal that looks like a worm and will turn into a butterfly or moth

cathedral *noun* **cathedrals** a big, important church

cattle *noun* cows and bulls

cause *verb* **causes, causing, caused** To cause something to happen means to make it happen

cautious *adjective* very careful not to do anything that might be dangerous

cave *noun* caves a big hole in the rock under the ground or inside a mountain

CD *noun* CDs A CD is a round, flat disc on which music or computer information can be stored. CD is short for **compact disc**.

ceiling *noun* ceilings the part of a room above your head

celebrate *verb* celebrates, celebrating, celebrated to do something special because it is an important day *Hindus and Sikhs celebrate Diwali in October or November.* celebration *noun* when you do something special on an important day

celebrity *noun* celebrities a famous person

cell *noun* cells 1 a small room in which a prisoner is kept in a prison 2 *(in science)* Cells are the tiny parts that all living things are made of.

cellar *noun* cellars a room underneath a building

Celsius *adjective* We can measure temperature in degrees Celsius. Water boils at 100 degrees Celsius.

cemetery *noun* cemeteries a place where dead people are buried

centigrade *adjective* We can measure temperature in degrees centigrade. Water boils at 100 degrees centigrade.

centimetre *noun* centimetres We can measure length in centimetres. There are 100 centimetres in one metre.

centre *noun* centres 1 the part in the middle of something 2 a place where you go to do certain things *Have you been to the new sports centre yet?*

century *noun* centuries a hundred years

cereal *noun* cereals 1 Cereals are plants such as wheat and corn that are grown by farmers for their seeds. 2 A breakfast cereal is a food that you eat at breakfast. Cereals are often made from wheat, oats, or rice, and you eat them with milk.

ceremony *noun* ceremonies A ceremony is an event at which something important is announced to people. There is usually a ceremony when people get married, or when someone has died.

certain *adjective* sure that something is true

certificate *noun* certificates a piece of paper that says you have achieved something

chain *noun* chains a metal rope that is made of a line of metal rings fastened together

chair *noun* chairs a seat for one person to sit on

chalk *noun* chalks a white or coloured stick that you use for writing on a blackboard

champion *noun* champions the person who has won a game or competition and shown that they are the best

chance *noun* chances 1 a time when it is possible for you to do something 2 When something happens by chance, it just happens, with no one planning or organizing it.

change *verb* changes, changing, changed **1** to make something different *If you don't like your first design, you can always change it.* **2** to become different *Caterpillars change into butterflies or moths.* **3** to get rid of something, and get a different one instead

change *noun* changes **1** Change is the money you get back when you give too much money to pay for something. **2** When there is a change, something becomes different.

channel *noun* channels **1** a narrow area of sea **2** a television station

chaos *noun* When there is chaos, everything is very confused and no one knows what is happening.

chapter *noun* chapters one part of a book

character *noun* characters **1** a person in a story **2** Your character is the sort of person you are.

charge *noun* charges the amount of money that you have to pay for something

charge *verb* charges, charging, charged **1** If you charge money for something, you ask for money. **2** If you charge at someone, you rush at them suddenly. in charge If you are in charge of something, you have the job of organizing it or looking after it.

charity *noun* charities an organization that raises money and uses it to help people who are poor or need help

charm *noun* charms **1** If someone has charm, they are pleasant and polite and so people like them. **2** a small ornament that you wear to bring good luck

chart *noun* charts **1** a big map **2** a sheet of paper that has rows of numbers or dates on it the charts a list of the pop songs that are most popular each week

chase *verb* chases, chasing, chased to run after somone and try to catch them

chat *verb* chats, chatting, chatted to talk in a friendly way to someone

chatter *verb* chatters, chattering, chattered **1** to talk a lot about things that are not very important **2** When your teeth chatter, they bang together because you are cold.

cheap *adjective* cheaper, cheapest not costing very much money cheaply *adverb* If something is sold cheaply then it does not cost very much money.

cheat *verb* cheats, cheating, cheated to break the rules in a game or test so that you can do well

cheat *noun* cheats someone who cheats in a game or test

check *verb* checks, checking, checked to look at something carefully to make sure that it is right

cheek *noun* cheeks **1** Your cheeks are the sides of your face. **2** Cheek is talking or behaving in a rude way towards someone.

cheeky *adjective* cheekier, cheekiest If you are cheeky, you are rude to someone and do not show that you respect them.

cheer *verb* cheers, cheering, cheered to shout to show that you are pleased

cheerful *adjective* happy

cheese *noun* cheeses a type of food that is made from milk and has a strong, salty taste

A B C D E F G H I J K L M N O P Q R S T U V W X Y Z

chemist *noun* chemists someone who makes or sells medicines

chemistry *noun* the subject in which you study the substances that things are made of and how these substances behave, for example when they are mixed together

cherry *noun* cherries a small round red fruit with a stone in the middle

chess *noun* a game in which two people move special pieces across a black and white board

chest *noun* chests 1 a big, strong box 2 the front part of your body between your neck and your waist

chew *verb* chews, chewing, chewed to keep biting on food in your mouth before you swallow it

chick *noun* chicks a baby bird

chicken *noun* chickens a bird that is kept on farms for its meat and eggs

chickenpox *noun* an illness that gives you red itchy spots on your body

chief *noun* chiefs a leader who is in charge of other people

child *noun* children 1 a young boy or girl 2 someone's son or daughter

childhood *noun* childhoods the time when you are a child

childish *adjective* Someone who is childish behaves in a silly way, like a young child

chilly *adjective* chillier, chilliest If you are chilly, you are slightly cold. If the weather is chilly, it is quite cold.

chime *verb* chimes, chiming, chimed When a clock or bell chimes, it makes a ringing sound.

chimney *noun* chimneys a tall pipe that takes smoke away from a fire inside a building

chimpanzee *noun* chimpanzees A chimpanzee is an African ape. Chimpanzees look like large monkeys and have long arms and no tail.

chin *noun* chins the part at the bottom of your face, under your mouth

chip *noun* chips 1 Chips are small pieces of fried potato. 2 A computer chip is the small electronic part inside it that makes it work.

chocolate *noun* chocolates a sweet food that is made from cocoa and sugar

choice *noun* choices 1 When you make a choice, you choose something. 2 If there is a choice, there are several different things to choose from.

choir *noun* choirs a group of people who sing together

choke *verb* chokes, choking, choked When you choke, you cannot breathe properly.

choose *verb* chooses, choosing, chose, chosen When you choose something, you decide that it is the one you want.

chop *verb* chops, chopping, chopped to cut something with a knife or axe

chop *noun* chops a thick slice of pork or lamb with a bone still attached to it

chorus *noun* choruses the part of a song or poem that you repeat after each verse

ch- in this word sounds like **k-**

Christian *noun* Christians someone who follows the Christian religion and believes in Jesus Christ

a b c d e f g h i j k l m n o p q r s t u v w x y z

Christmas *noun* Christmases 25 December, when Christians celebrate the birth of Jesus Christ

chrysalis *noun* chrysalises the hard cover that a caterpillar makes round itself before it changes into a butterfly or moth

chuckle *verb* chuckles, chuckling, chuckled to laugh quietly to yourself

church *noun* churches a building where Christians pray and worship

cinema *noun* cinemas a place where people go to watch films

circle *noun* circles a round shape like a ring or a wheel

circumference *noun* circumferences how much a circle measures round its edge

circus *noun* circuses a show in which clowns, acrobats, and sometimes animals perform in a large tent

city *noun* cities a big town

claim *verb* claims, claiming, claimed **1** When you claim something, you say that you want it because it is yours. **2** If you claim that something is true, you say that it is true.

class *noun* classes a group of children who learn things together

classroom *noun* classrooms a room where children have lessons

claw *noun* claws An animal's claws are its sharp nails.

clay *noun* Clay is a type of sticky mud that becomes very hard when it dries out. Clay is used for making pots and pottery.

clean *adjective* cleaner, cleanest Something that is clean has no dirt on it.

clean *verb* cleans, cleaning, cleaned to take the dirt off something so that it is clean

clear *adjective* clearer, clearest **1** If water or glass is clear, it is not dirty and you can see through it. **2** If a picture or sound is clear, you can see it or hear it easily. **3** If something is clear, you can understand it. **4** If a place is clear, there is nothing blocking it or getting in the way.

clear *verb* clears, clearing, cleared To clear a place means to get rid of things that are in the way. *I helped clear the table.*
clearly *adverb* If you can see something clearly there is nothing blocking it or getting in the way.

clever *adjective* cleverer, cleverest Someone who is clever learns things quickly and easily.

click *verb* clicks, clicking, clicked **1** When something clicks, it makes a short sound like the sound a light switch makes. **2** *(in ICT)* When you click on something on a computer, you move the cursor so that it is on that thing and then you press the button on the mouse.

cliff *noun* **cliffs** a steep hill made of rock next to the sea

climate *noun* **climates** the sort of weather that a place has

climb *verb* **climbs, climbing, climbed** 1 to go upwards *She climbed the stairs slowly.* 2 to use your hands and feet to move over things *They climbed over the rocks.*

clinic *noun* **clinics** a place where you can go to see a doctor or nurse

cloak *noun* **cloaks** a piece of clothing that you wrap around your shoulders and fasten round your neck

cloakroom *noun* **cloakrooms** the room where you can hang your coat

clock *noun* **clocks** a machine that shows you the time

clockwise *adverb* If something moves clockwise, it moves round in a circle in the same direction as the hands of a clock.

close *adjective* **closer, closest** (rhymes with *dose*) 1 If you are close to something, you are near it. 2 If you take a close look at something, or keep a close watch on something, you do it very carefully.

close *verb* **closes, closing, closed** (rhymes with *doze*) 1 to shut something 2 When a shop closes, it is no longer open and people cannot go there.

closed *adjective* not open

cloth *noun* material for making things like clothes and curtains

clothes, clothing *noun* the things that you wear to cover your body

cloud *noun* **clouds** Clouds are the large grey or white things that sometimes float high in the sky. **cloudy** *adjective* If a sky is cloudy there are lots of clouds.

clown *noun* **clowns** someone in a circus who wears funny clothes and make-up and does silly things to make people laugh

club *noun* **clubs** 1 a group of people who get together because they are interested in doing the same thing 2 a thick stick that is used as a weapon

a
b
c
d
e
f
g
h
i
j
k
l
m
n
o
p
q
r
s
t
u
v
w
x
y
z

clue *noun* **clues** something that helps you to find the answer to a puzzle

clumsy *adjective* **clumsier, clumsiest** If you are clumsy, you are not careful and so are likely to knock things over or drop things.

clutch *verb* **clutches, clutching, clutched** to hold on to something very tightly

coach *noun* **coaches** 1 a bus that takes people on long journeys 2 someone who trains people in a sport

coal *noun* Coal is a type of hard, black rock that people burn on fires. Coal is found under the ground.

coast *noun* **coasts** the land that is right next to the sea

coat *noun* **coats** 1 a piece of clothing with sleeves that you wear on top of other clothes to keep warm 2 An animal's coat is the hair or fur that covers its body.

cobweb *noun* **cobwebs** a thin, sticky net that a spider spins to catch insects

cocoa *noun* Cocoa is a brown powder that tastes of chocolate. It is used for making hot chocolate drinks and also for making chocolate cakes and biscuits.

coconut *noun* **coconuts** A coconut is a big, round, hard nut that grows on palm trees. It is brown and hairy on the outside and it has sweet, white flesh inside that you can eat.

cocoon *noun* **cocoons** a covering that some insects spin from silky threads to protect themselves while they are changing into their adult form

cod *noun* **cod** a sea fish that you can eat

code *noun* **codes** a set of signs or letters that you use for sending messages secretly

coffee *noun* **coffees** a hot drink that is made by adding hot water to roasted coffee beans that have been ground into a powder

coin *noun* **coins** a piece of metal money

cold *adjective* **colder, coldest** 1 not hot 2 not friendly

cold *noun* **colds** an illness that makes you sneeze and gives you a runny nose

collage *noun* **collages** a picture that you make by gluing small pieces of paper and material

collapse *verb* **collapses, collapsing, collapsed** 1 If something collapses, it falls down. 2 If someone collapses, they fall over because they are ill.

collar *noun* **collars** 1 the part of a piece of clothing that goes round your neck 2 a thin band of leather or material that goes round an animal's neck

collect *verb* **collects, collecting, collected** 1 If you collect things, you get them and keep them together. 2 When you collect someone, you go to a place and get them. **collection** *noun* a set of things that someone has collected

college *noun* **colleges** a place where you can go to study after you have left school

colour *noun* **colours** Red, green, blue, and yellow are different colours.

column *noun* **columns** **1** a thick stone post that supports or decorates a building **2** a line of numbers or words one below the other

comb *noun* **combs** (rhymes with *home*) A comb is a strip of plastic or metal with a row of thin teeth along it. You use a comb to make your hair neat and tidy.

combine *verb* **combines, combining, combined** to join or mix things together

come *verb* **comes, coming, came, come** **1** To come to a place means to move towards it. *Do you want to come to my house after school?* **2** to arrive in a place *Has the letter come yet?*

comedy *noun* **comedies** a play, film, or TV programme that is funny and makes you laugh

comet *noun* **comets** an object that moves around the sun and looks like a bright star with a tail

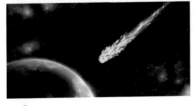

comfort *verb* **comforts, comforting, comforted** to be kind to someone and try to make them feel better when they are hurt or upset

comfortable *adjective* **1** If something is comfortable, it is pleasant to use or to wear and does not hurt you at all. *The bed was large and very comfortable.* **2** If you are comfortable, you are relaxed and are not in any pain.

comic *adjective* Something that is comic is funny.

comic *noun* **comics** a magazine for children that has stories told in pictures

command *verb* **commands, commanding, commanded** to tell someone to do something

common *adjective* **commoner, commonest** normal and ordinary

common sense *noun* If you have common sense, you are usually sensible and make the right decisions about what to do and how to behave.

communicate *verb* **communicates, communicating, communicated** When people communicate, they talk or write to each other.

compact disc *noun* **compact discs** a CD

company *noun* **companies** **1** a group of people who make and sell things, or do things together **2** If you have company, you are not alone.

compare *verb* **compares, comparing, compared** When you compare things, you try to see how they are the same and how they are different.

compass *noun* compasses **1** an instrument with a needle that always points north **2** A compass is an instrument that you use for drawing circles. It is also called a **pair of compasses**.

competition *noun* competitions a game or race that people take part in and try to win

complain *verb* complains, complaining, complained to say that you are not happy about something or do not like something

complete *adjective* **1** Something that is complete has all its parts and has nothing missing. **2** finished **3** in every way *Winning the game was a complete surprise.* **completely** *adverb* totally

complicated *adjective* difficult to understand or do

computer *noun* computers A computer is a machine which can store information and do calculations. You can also play games on computers.

concentrate *verb* concentrates, concentrating, concentrated to think hard about the thing you are doing

concern *verb* concerns, concerning, concerned If something concerns you, it is important to you and you should be interested in it. If something does not concern you, it is nothing to do with you.

concerned *adjective* If you are concerned about something, you are worried about it.

concert *noun* concerts a show in which people play music for other people to listen to

concrete *noun* a mixture of cement and sand used for making buildings and paths

condition *noun* conditions **1** The condition something is in is how new or clean it is, and how well it works. If it is in good condition, it looks new and works properly. If it is in bad condition, it is old or dirty, or does not work properly. **2** something you must do before you can do or have something else *You can go to the fair on condition that you're home by eight o'clock.*

cone *noun* cones **1** a shape that is round at one end and goes in to a point at the other end **2** a hard, brown fruit that grows on pine trees and fir trees

confess *verb* confesses, confessing, confessed to admit that you have done something wrong

confident *adjective* not nervous or afraid

confuse *verb* confuses, confusing, confused **1** If something confuses you, you cannot understand it. **2** If you confuse things, you get them muddled up in your mind.

congratulate *verb* congratulates, congratulating, congratulated to tell someone that you are pleased that something special has happened to them

connect *verb* connects, connecting, connected to join things together *You need to connect the printer to your computer.*

conquer *verb* conquers, conquering, conquered to beat people in a battle or war

conscious *adjective* awake and able to understand what is happening around you

conservation *noun* taking good care of the world's air, water, plants, and animals

consider *verb* considers, considering, considered to think about something carefully

consonant *noun* consonants Consonants are all the letters of the alphabet except a, e, i, o, and u, which are vowels.

constant *adjective* Something that is constant goes on all the time.

construct *verb* constructs, constructing, constructed to build something

contain *verb* contains, containing, contained to have something inside

container *noun* containers A container is anything that you can put other things into. Buckets, cups, bags, boxes, and jars are all containers.

contents *noun* The contents of something are the things that are inside it.

contest *noun* contests a competition

continent *noun* continents A continent is one of the seven very large areas of land in the world. Asia, Europe, and Africa are all continents.

continue *verb* continues, continuing, continued If you continue doing something, you go on doing it.

continuous *adjective* Something that is continuous goes on happening and never stops.

contradict *verb* contradicts, contradicting, contradicted If you contradict someone, you say that what they have said is wrong.

control *noun* controls The controls are the switches and buttons that you use to make a machine work.

control *verb* controls, controlling, controlled to make something do what you want it to do

conversation *noun* conversations When people have a conversation, they talk to each other.

convince *verb* convinces, convincing, convinced to make someone believe something

cook *verb* cooks, cooking, cooked to prepare food and heat it so that it is ready to eat

cook *noun* cooks someone whose job is to cook

cooker *noun* A cooker is a machine on which you cook food.

cookie *noun* a kind of small, crisp cake

cool *adjective* cooler, coolest slightly cold

cope *verb* copes, coping, coped If you can cope with something, you can manage to do it.

copper *noun* a shiny brown metal

copy *verb* copies, copying, copied **1** to write something down or draw it in the same way as it has already been written or drawn **2** (*in ICT*) When you copy something from one file to another file on a computer, you move it to the second file but do not delete it from the first file. **3** to do exactly the same as someone

copy *noun* copies something that is made to look exactly like something else

coral *noun* a type of rock that is made in the sea from the bodies of tiny creatures

cord *noun* **cords** a thin rope

core *noun* **cores** the hard part in the middle of an apple or pear

cork *noun* **corks** something that is pushed into the top of a bottle of wine to close it

corn *noun* the seeds of plants such as wheat, which we use as food

corner *noun* **corners** **1** the place where two edges meet **2** the place where two streets meet

correct *adjective* right and without any mistakes

correct *verb* **corrects, correcting, corrected** to find the mistakes in something and put them right **correction** *noun* When you make a correction, you change a mistake and put it right. **correctly** *adverb* When you do something correctly, you do it right.

corridor *noun* **corridors** a passage in a building with rooms leading off it

cost *verb* **costs, costing, cost** The amount that something costs is the amount you have to pay to buy it.

costume *noun* **costumes** clothes that you wear for acting in a play

cosy *adjective* **cosier, cosiest** A cosy place is warm and comfortable.

cot *noun* **cots** a bed with sides for a baby

cottage *noun* **cottages** a small house in the country

cotton *noun* **1** thread that you use for sewing **2** a type of cloth that is used for making clothes

cough *verb* **coughs, coughing, coughed** (rhymes with *off*) to make a rough sound in your throat and push air out through your mouth

council *noun* **councils** a group of people who are chosen to discuss things and make decisions for everyone

count *verb* **counts, counting, counted** **1** When you count things, you use numbers to say how many there are **2** When you count, you say numbers in order. *Can you count to 1000?*

counter *noun* **counters** **1** the table where you pay for things in a shop **2** a small, round piece of plastic that you use for playing some games

country *noun* **countries** **1** A country is a land with its own people and laws. England, Australia, and China are all countries. **2** The country is land that is not in a town.

couple *noun* **couples** **1** two people who are married or going out with each other **2** A couple of things means two of them.

coupon *noun* **coupons** a special piece of paper which you can use to pay for something

courage *noun* the feeling you have when you are not afraid, and you dare to do something difficult or dangerous **courageous** *adjective* If someone is courageous or if they do something courageous, they do not feel afraid of something that is dangerous or difficult.

course *noun* **courses** **1** a set of lessons **2** a piece of ground where people play golf or run races

court *noun* **courts** **1** a piece of ground that is marked out so that people can play a game such as netball or tennis **2** a building where people decide whether someone is guilty of committing a crime **3** The court of a king or queen is the place where they live and rule the country.

cousin *noun* **cousins** a child of your aunt or uncle

cover *verb* **covers, covering, covered** When you cover something, you put something else over it.

cover *noun* **covers** a piece of material which goes over or round something

cow *noun* **cows** a large animal that is kept on farms for its milk and meat

coward *noun* **cowards** someone who is afraid when they ought to be brave

cowboy *noun* **cowboys** a man who looks after the cattle on large farms in America

crab *noun* **crabs** A crab is an animal with a hard shell on its back, which lives in the sea. Crabs have ten legs and large, powerful claws for catching food.

crack *noun* **cracks** **1** a thin line on something where it has nearly broken **2** a sudden loud noise *We heard a crack of thunder.*

crack *verb* **cracks, cracking, cracked** **1** to break something so that it has lines on it but does not break into pieces **2** to make a sharp noise like the noise a dry twig makes when you break it

cradle *noun* **cradles** a bed with sides for a young baby

crane *noun* **cranes** a large machine for lifting heavy things

crash *noun* **crashes** **1** an accident in which a car, lorry, train, or plane hits something **2** the noise of something falling or crashing

crash *verb* **crashes, crashing, crashed** **1** to bump into something else and make a loud noise **2** *(in ICT)* If a computer crashes, it stops working suddenly.

crate *noun* **crates** a large box

crawl *verb* **crawls, crawling, crawled** **1** to move along on your hands and knees **2** When a car or train crawls along, it moves very slowly.

crayon *noun* **crayons** a coloured pencil

crazy *adjective* **crazier, craziest** Someone who is crazy does very silly or strange things. Something that is crazy is very silly or strange.

creak *verb* **creaks, creaking, creaked** to make a rough, squeaking noise

cream *noun* Cream is a thick white liquid that is taken from milk. You eat cream with fruit and other sweet foods.

create *verb* **creates, creating, created** to make something new

A
B
C
D
E
F
G
H
I
J
K
L
M
N
O
P
Q
R
S
T
U
V
W
X
Y
Z

creature *noun* creatures any animal

creep *verb* creeps, creeping, crept **1** to move along with your body very close to the ground **2** to walk very quietly and secretly

creep *noun* creeps **1** a nasty person **2** If something gives you the creeps, it frightens you.

crescent *noun* crescents a curved shape, like the shape of a new moon

crew *noun* crews a group of people who work together on a boat or aeroplane

cricket *noun* **1** a game in which two teams hit a ball with a bat and try to score runs by running between two wickets **2** an insect that makes a loud high chirping sound

crime *noun* crimes something bad that a person does, which is against the law

criminal *noun* criminals someone who has done something bad that is against the law

crisp **1** Food that is crisp is dry and breaks easily. **2** Fruit that is crisp is firm and fresh.

crisp *noun* crisps Crisps are thin, crisp slices of fried potato that you eat as a snack.

criticize *verb* criticizes, criticizing, criticized to say that someone has done something wrong

crocodile *noun* crocodiles A crocodile is a large animal that lives in rivers in some hot countries. Crocodiles are reptiles, and have short legs, a long body, and sharp teeth.

crooked *adjective* not straight

crop *noun* crops a type of plant which farmers grow as food

cross *adjective* crosser, crossest angry

cross *noun* crosses a mark like **x** or **+**

cross *verb* crosses, crossing, crossed **1** When you cross a road or a river, you go across it. **2** When you cross your arms or legs, you put one over the other. **3** When you cross out writing, you draw a line through it.

crossing *noun* crossings a place where you can cross the road safely

crow *noun* crows a big, black bird

crowd *noun* crowds a large number of people

crown *noun* crowns a special hat made of silver or gold which a king or queen wears

cruel *adjective* crueller, cruellest If you are cruel to someone, you hurt them or are very unkind to them.

crumb *noun* crumbs Crumbs are very small pieces of bread or cake.

crumble *verb* crumbles, crumbling, crumbled to break into a lot of small pieces

crumple *verb* crumples, crumpling, crumpled to make something very creased *My clothes were all crumpled in the bottom of my bag.*

crunch *verb* crunches, crunching, crunched to eat food by breaking it noisily with your teeth

crush *verb* crushes, crushing, crushed to squash something by pressing it hard

crust *noun* **crusts** the hard part around the outside of bread

cry *verb* **cries, crying, cried** **1** When you cry, tears come out of your eyes. **2** When you cry, you shout something.

crystal *noun* **crystals** Crystal is a type of mineral that is found in rock. It is hard and clear like glass.

cub *noun* **cubs** a young bear, lion, tiger, fox, or wolf

cube *noun* **cubes** A cube is a square shape like the shape of a dice. Cubes have six square sides that are all the same size.

cuckoo *noun* **cuckoos** a bird that lays its eggs in other birds' nests

cucumber *noun* **cucumbers** a long, green vegetable that you eat raw in salads

cuddle *verb* **cuddles, cuddling, cuddled** to put your arms round someone to show that you love them

cunning *adjective* clever and very good at getting what you want

cup *noun* **cups** **1** a container with a handle, which you use for drinking from **2** a silver cup that is given as a prize to the winner of a competition

cupboard *noun* **cupboards** a piece of furniture with doors on the front, which you use for keeping things in

cure *verb* **cures, curing, cured** to make someone better after they have been ill

curious *adjective* **1** If you are curious about something, you want to know more about it. **2** Something that is curious is strange or unusual.

curl *noun* **curls** a piece of hair that is curved, not straight

currant *noun* **currants** a small dried grape

current *noun* **currents** A current of water, air, or electricity is an amount of it that is moving in one direction.

curry *noun* **curries** meat or vegetables in a spicy sauce

cursor *noun* **cursors** the mark which shows your position on a computer screen

curtain *noun* **curtains** a piece of cloth that you can pull in front of a window to cover it

curve *noun* **curves** a line that is bent smoothly like the letter C **curved** *adjective* When something is curved, it is bent smoothly like the letter C.

cushion *noun* **cushions** a soft object that you put on a chair to sit on or lean against

custom *noun* **customs** If something is a custom, you do it because people have done it in that way for a long time.

customer *noun* **customers** someone who buys something in a shop

cut *verb* **cuts, cutting, cut** **1** If you cut yourself, you break a part of your skin on something sharp. *He fell over and cut his knee.* **2** to use a knife or scissors to break something into pieces **3** *(in ICT)* to delete something on a computer

a b c d e f g h i j k l m n o p q r s t u v w x y z

cut *noun* **cuts** If you have a cut on your skin, your skin has been broken by something sharp.

cutlery *noun* knives, forks, and spoons

cyber- *prefix* Words that begin with **cyber** have something to do with the Internet. *I checked my emails at the cybercafe.*

cycle *verb* **cycles, cycling, cycled** to ride a bicycle

cylinder *noun* **cylinders** a shape that looks like a tube with flat, round ends

cymbals *noun* two round pieces of metal that you bang together when you are playing music

Dd

dad, daddy *noun* **dads, daddies** your father

daffodil *noun* **daffodils** a yellow flower that grows in the spring

daily *adverb* every day

dairy *noun* **dairies** a place where people make cheese, butter, and yoghurt from milk

daisy *noun* **daisies** a small flower with white petals and a yellow centre

damage *verb* **damages, damaging, damaged** to break something or spoil it

damp *adjective* **damper, dampest** slightly wet

dance *verb* **dances, dancing, danced** to move about in time to music

dance *noun* **dances** 1 When you do a dance, you move about in time to music. 2 A dance is a party where people dance.

danger *noun* **dangers** When there is danger, there is the chance that something horrible might happen and someone might get hurt.

dangerous *adjective* Something that is dangerous might kill or hurt you.

dare *verb* **dares, daring, dared** 1 If you dare to do something, you are brave enough to do it. 2 If you dare someone to do something, you tell them to do it to show how brave they are.

dark *adjective* **darker, darkest** 1 If a place is dark, there is no light in it. 2 nearly black in colour

data *noun* information about something

database *noun* **databases** a store of information that is kept on a computer

date *noun* **dates** **1** If you say what the date is, you say what day of the month and what year it is. **2** If you have a date with someone, you have arranged to go out with them. **3** a sweet, brown fruit that grows on a palm tree

daughter *noun* **daughters** someone's female child

dawn *noun* the time of day when the sun rises and it becomes light

day *noun* **days** **1** a period of twenty-four hours **2** the part of the day when it is light

dazzle *verb* **dazzles, dazzling, dazzled** If a bright light dazzles you, you cannot see anything because it is shining in your eyes.

dead *adjective* not alive

deaf *adjective* **deafer, deafest** Someone who is deaf cannot hear.

deal *verb* **deals, dealing, dealt** **1** When you deal out cards, you give them to each person at the beginning of a game. **2** When you deal with something, you do the work that needs to be done on it.

dear *adjective* **dearer, dearest** **1** If someone is dear to you, you love them a lot. **2** Something you write before someone's name at the start of a letter.

death *noun* **deaths** the time when someone dies

deceive *verb* **deceives, deceiving, deceived** to make someone believe something that is not true

> Remember **i** before **e** except after **c** when the sound is **/ee/**.

December *noun* the twelfth and last month of the year

decide *verb* **decides, deciding, decided** to choose to do something

decimal *noun* **decimals** *(in mathematics)* a number that has tenths shown as numbers after a dot, for example *2.5*

decision *noun* **decisions** When you make a decision, you decide what you are going to do.

deck *noun* **decks** a floor in a ship or bus

decorate *verb* **decorates, decorating, decorated** **1** to make something look nice or pretty **2** to put paint or wallpaper on the walls of a room

decrease *verb* **decreases, decreasing, decreased** to become less

deep *adjective* **deeper, deepest** Something that is deep goes down a long way from the top. *Be careful, the water's quite deep.* **deeply** *adverb* If you breathe deeply, you take a lot of air into your lungs.

deer *noun* **deer** A deer is an animal that eats grass and can run fast. Male deer have long horns called **antlers**.

defeat *verb* **defeats, defeating, defeated** to beat someone in a game or battle

defend *verb* **defends, defending, defended** to keep a place safe and stop people from attacking it

definite *adjective* Something that is definite is certain. **definitely** *adverb* You say that you will definitely do something if you are certain that you will.

definition *noun* **definitions** a sentence that explains what a word means

degree *noun* **degrees** We can measure how hot or cold something is in degrees. You can write the number of degrees using

a b c **d** e f g h i j k l m n o p q r s t u v w x y z

the sign °. *The temperature could be over 30°C today.*

delay *verb* **delays, delaying, delayed 1** If you are delayed, something makes you late. *The train was delayed by heavy snow.* **2** to put off doing something until later *We'll delay giving the prizes until everyone is here.*

delete *verb* **deletes, deleting, deleted** When you delete something that you have written, you rub it out or remove it.

deliberate *adjective* If something is deliberate, someone has done it on purpose. **deliberately** *adverb* on purpose

delicate *adjective* Something that is delicate will break easily.

delicious *adjective* Something that is delicious tastes very nice.

delight *verb* **delights, delighting, delighted** to make you feel very happy

deliver *verb* **delivers, delivering, delivered** to take something to someone's house

demand *verb* **demands, demanding, demanded** to ask for something very strongly

demonstrate *verb* **demonstrates, demonstrating, demonstrated** to show someone how to do something

demonstration *noun* **demonstrations 1** If you give someone a demonstration of something, you show them how to do it. **2** When there is a demonstration, a lot of people march through the streets to show that they are angry about something.

den *noun* **dens 1** a place where a wild animal lives **2** a secret place where you can hide

dentist *noun* **dentists** someone whose job is to check and look after people's teeth

deny *verb* **denies, denying, denied** to say that something is not true

depart *verb* **departs, departing, departed** to leave a place

depend *verb* **depends, depending, depended** If you depend on someone, you need them to help you. *The young lions depend on their mother for food.*

depth *noun* **depths** how deep something is

descend *verb* **descends, descending, descended** to go down

describe *verb* **describes, describing, described** to talk about something and say what it is like **description** *noun* When you give a description of something, you say what it is like.

desert *noun* **deserts** dry land where very few plants can grow

deserted *adjective* A place that is deserted is empty, with no one in it.

deserve *verb* deserves, deserving, deserved If you deserve a punishment or reward, you should get it.

design *verb* designs, designing, designed to plan something and draw a picture of it

desk *noun* desks a table where you can read, write, and keep books

dessert *noun* desserts sweet food that you eat at the end of a meal

destroy *verb* destroys, destroying, destroyed to break something or spoil it so badly that you cannot use it again

detail *noun* details one small part of something, or one small piece of information about it

detective *noun* detectives someone who looks at clues and tries to find out who committed a crime

determined *adjective* If you are determined to do something, you have made up your mind that you want to do it.

develop *verb* develops, developing, developed to change and grow *Seeds develop into plants.*

dew *noun* tiny drops of water that form on the ground during the night

diagonal *adjective* A diagonal line goes from one corner of something to the opposite corner.

diagram *noun* diagrams a picture that shows what something is like or explains how it works

dial *verb* dials, dialling, dialled to call a number on a telephone *He dialled 999 and asked for an ambulance.*

diameter *noun* diameters the distance across the centre of a circle

diamond *noun* diamonds **1** a very hard jewel that looks like clear glass **2** a shape that looks like a square standing on one of its corners

diary *noun* diaries a book where you write down the things that you do each day

dice *noun* dice A dice is a small cube with each side marked with a different number of dots. You use dice in some games.

dictionary *noun* dictionaries a book that explains what words mean and shows you how to spell them

die *verb* dies, dying, died to stop living

a
b
c
d
e
f
g
h
i
j
k
l
m
n
o
p
q
r
s
t
u
v
w
x
y
z

diet *noun* **diets** **1** Your diet is the kind of food that you eat. **2** If you go on a diet, you eat less food because you want to become thinner.

difference *noun* **differences** A difference between things is a way in which they are different.

different *adjective* not the same

difficult *adjective* not easy

dig *verb* **digs, digging, dug** to move soil away and make a hole in the ground

digit *noun* **digits** (in mathematics) one of the numbers between 0 and 9

digital *adjective* **1** A digital watch or clock shows the time with numbers, rather than with hands. **2** A digital camera or television uses a special kind of electronic signal to make pictures.

dinghy *noun* **dinghies** a small sailing boat

dining room *noun* **dining rooms** a room where people have their meals

dinner *noun* **dinners** the main meal of the day

dinosaur *noun* **dinosaurs** an animal like a huge lizard that lived millions of years ago

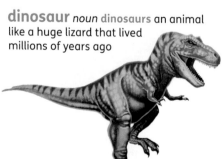

dip *verb* **dips, dipping, dipped** to put something into liquid and leave it there for only a short time

direct *adjective* If you go somewhere in a direct way, you go straight there, without going anywhere else first. *We got on the direct train to London.*

direct *verb* **directs, directing, directed** **1** If you direct someone to a place, you explain to them how to get there. **2** The person who directs a play or film organizes it and tells everyone what they should do.

direction *noun* **directions** The direction you are going in is the way you are going.

dirt *noun* dust or mud

dirty *adjective* **dirtier, dirtiest** Something that is dirty has mud or dirt on it.

disabled *adjective* Someone who is disabled finds it hard to do some things because a part of their body does not work properly.

disagree *verb* **disagrees, disagreeing, disagreed** If you disagree with someone, you think that they are wrong.

disappear *verb* **disappears, disappearing, disappeared** When something disappears, it goes away and you cannot see it any more.

disappoint *verb* **disappoints, disappointing, disappointed** If something disappoints you, you feel sad because it is not as good as you thought it would be.

disapprove *verb* **disapproves, disapproving, disapproved** If you disapprove of something, you do not like it and do not think that it is right.

disaster *noun* **disasters** something very bad that happens

disc or **disk** *noun* discs or disks **1** any round, flat object **2** A disc is a round, flat piece of plastic that has music or computer information on it. This is also called a **compact disc**.

disco *noun* discos a party where you dance to pop music

discover *verb* discovers, discovering, discovered to find something, or find out about it

discuss *verb* discusses, discussing, discussed to talk about something

disease *noun* diseases an illness

disguise *noun* disguises special clothes that you wear so that you will look different and people will not recognize you

dish *noun* dishes **1** a container in which food is served **2** food that has been prepared and cooked in a particular way

dishonest *adjective* Someone who is dishonest is not honest and does not tell the truth.

dislike *verb* dislikes, disliking, disliked If you dislike something, you do not like it.

display *noun* displays a show or exhibition

dissolve *verb* dissolves, dissolving, dissolved When something dissolves in water, it mixes with the water so that you cannot see it.

distance *noun* distances the amount of space between two places

district *noun* districts part of a town, city, or country

disturb *verb* disturbs, disturbing, disturbed to interrupt someone and stop them from doing something

dive *verb* dives, diving, dived to jump into water head first

diver *noun* divers someone who dives into water and swims around under the water, wearing special breathing equipment

divide *verb* divides, dividing, divided **1** to share things out *Divide the sweets equally between you.* **2** to split something into smaller parts *The cake was divided into eight pieces.* **3** *(in mathematics)* When you divide numbers, you find out how many times one number goes into another. *Six divided by two is three, $6 \div 2 = 3$.*

divorce *verb* divorces, divorcing, divorced When two people divorce, they end their marriage.

Diwali *noun* Diwali is an important Hindu festival at which lamps are lit. It is held in October or November.

dizzy *adjective* dizzier, dizziest If you feel dizzy, you feel as if everything is spinning round you.

do *verb* does, doing, did, done When you do something, you carry out that action. *She did a little dance in the middle of the room.*

doctor *noun* doctors someone whose job is to give people medicines and treatment when they are ill

document *noun* documents **1** an important piece of paper with official information on it **2** *(in ICT)* a piece of work that you write and store on a computer

a b c **d** e f g h i j k l m n o p q r s t u v w x y z

dog *noun* **dogs** A dog is an animal people often keep as a pet. Dogs can bark, and you can train them to obey you.

doll *noun* **dolls** a toy in the shape of a baby or person

dollar *noun* **dollars** A dollar is a unit of money. Dollars are used in the United States of America, Australia, and some other countries.

dolphin *noun* **dolphins** A dolphin is a large animal that swims like a fish and lives in the sea. Dolphins are mammals, and breathe air.

donkey *noun* **donkeys** an animal that looks like a small horse with long ears

don't *verb* do not *Don't be silly!*

door *noun* **doors** something that you can open and go through to get into a place

dot *noun* **dots** a small spot that looks like a full stop

double *adjective* Something that is double the size of something else is twice as big.

double *verb* **doubles, doubling, doubled** to make an amount twice as big

doubt *noun* **doubts** (rhymes with *out*) If you have doubts about something, you are not sure about it.

doubt *verb* **doubts, doubting, doubted** (rhymes with *out*) If you doubt something, you do not believe it. *I doubt that we'll hear from him again.*

down *adverb* & *preposition* towards a lower place *It fell down. Run down the hill.*

download *verb* **downloads, downloading, downloaded** (*in ICT*) to copy information from the Internet onto your computer

doze *verb* **dozes, dozing, dozed** If you are dozing, you are nearly asleep. If you doze off, you fall asleep.

dozen *noun* **dozens** a set of 12 *I bought a dozen eggs.*

drag *verb* **drags, dragging, dragged** to pull something heavy along the ground

dragon *noun* **dragons** a large monster with wings in a story

drain *noun* **drains** a pipe that carries water away under the ground

drama *noun* acting in a play or story

dramatic *adjective* very exciting

draw *verb* **draws, drawing, drew, drawn** **1** to make a picture with a pen, pencil, or crayon **2** When you draw curtains, you open them or close them. **3** When two people draw in a game, they have the same score at the end of the game. *We drew 1–1.*

drawer *noun* **drawers** a part of a piece of furniture that you can pull out and use for keeping things in

drawing *noun* **drawings** a picture that someone has drawn

dreadful *adjective* very bad

dream *noun* **dreams** **1** things that you seem to see when you are asleep **2** something that you would like very much *My dream is to become a pop singer.*

dream *verb* **dreams, dreaming, dreamed, dreamt** **1** to seem to see things in your head when you are asleep **2** to think about something because you would like to do it *He had always dreamt of being an Olympic champion.*

dress *noun* dresses A dress is a piece of clothing that a woman or girl wears. It has a skirt, and also covers the top half of her body.

dress *verb* dresses, dressing, dressed When you dress, you put on clothes. You can also say that you **get dressed**.

drill *noun* drills a tool that you use for making holes

drink *verb* drinks, drinking, drank, drunk to swallow liquid

drink *noun* drinks a liquid that you take into your mouth and swallow

drip *verb* drips, dripping, dripped When water drips, it falls in small drops.

drive *verb* drives, driving, drove, driven to control a car, bus, train, or lorry

drizzle *noun* very light rain

drop *noun* drops a very small amount of liquid

drop *verb* drops, dropping, dropped If you drop something, you do not hold it tightly enough and it falls out of your hands.

drought *noun* droughts (rhymes with *out*) a time when there is very little rain and the ground becomes very dry

drown *verb* drowns, drowning, drowned to die because you are under water and cannot breathe

drug *noun* drugs **1** a medicine that can help you feel better if you are ill or in pain **2** A drug is a substance that some people take for pleasure because it changes the way they feel or behave. This type of drug is against the law and dangerous.

drum *noun* drums a hollow musical instrument that you bang with a stick or with your hands

dry *adjective* drier, driest not wet or damp

duck *noun* ducks a bird that lives near water and swims on the water

due *adjective* The time that something is due is the time you expect it to arrive.

dull *adjective* duller, dullest **1** not very bright **2** boring and not interesting

dungeon *noun* dungeons a prison underneath a castle

during *preposition* while something else is going on

dust *noun* dry dirt that is like powder

dustbin *noun* dustbins a large container that you use for putting rubbish in

duty *noun* duties If it is your duty to do something, you have to do it.

duvet *noun* duvets a thick, warm cover for a bed

DVD *noun* DVDs A DVD is a round, flat disc on which music, pictures, or film can be stored. DVD is short for **digital versatile disc**.

dye *verb* dyes, dyeing, dyed to change the colour of something by putting it in a special coloured liquid

dyslexic *adjective* Someone who is dyslexic finds it difficult to learn to read

a
b
c
d
e
f
g
h
i
j
k
l
m
n
o
p
q
r
s
t
u
v
w
x
y
z

and write because their brain muddles up letters and words.

Ee

each *determiner* every *She gave each child a present.*

eager *adjective* very keen to do something

eagle *noun* **eagles** An eagle is a large bird that hunts and eats small animals. Eagles live in mountain areas.

ear *noun* **ears** Your ears are the parts of your body that you use for hearing.

early *adjective* **earlier, earliest 1** If you are early, you arrive before people are expecting you. *We were ten minutes early.* **2** When it is early in the day, it is in the morning, not the afternoon or evening.

earn *verb* **earns, earning, earned** to get money by working for it

earphone *noun* **earphones** Earphones are small speakers that you wear in your ears so that you can listen to music from a music player.

earring *noun* **earrings** Earrings are jewellery that you wear in your ears.

earth *noun* **1** the planet that we all live on **2** the soil in which plants grow

earthquake *noun* **earthquakes** When there is an earthquake, the ground

suddenly shakes. Strong earthquakes can destroy buildings.

east *noun* East is the direction where the sun rises in the morning.

Easter *noun* the day when Christians celebrate Jesus Christ coming back from the dead

easy *adjective* **easier, easiest** If something is easy, you can do it or understand it without any trouble. **easily** *adverb* without any trouble

eat *verb* **eats, eating, ate, eaten** to put food in your mouth and swallow it

e-book *noun* **e-books** An e-book is a book which is published as an electronic file or on the Internet. You can read an e-book on a small computer called an **e-book reader**.

eclipse *noun* **eclipses** When there is an eclipse of the sun, the moon moves in front of it and hides it for a short time. When there is an eclipse of the moon, the moon passes behind the earth and is hidden from the sun for a short time.

edge *noun* **edges** the part along the end or side of something

educate *verb* **educates, educating, educated** to teach someone things they need to know like reading and writing

effect *noun* effects If something has an effect, it makes something else happen. *Some chemicals have a harmful effect on the environment.*

effort *noun* If you put effort into something, you work hard to do it.

egg *noun* eggs An egg is an oval object with a thin shell. Eggs are laid by birds, snakes, and insects. We can cook and eat hens' eggs.

Eid *noun* a Muslim festival that marks the end of Ramadan

eight *noun* eights the number 8

eighteen *noun* the number 18

eighty *noun* the number 80

elastic *noun* a strip of material that can stretch and then go back to its usual size

elbow *noun* elbows the joint in the middle of your arm, where your arm can bend

elect *verb* elects, electing, elected to choose someone by voting for them

electricity *noun* the power or energy that is used to give light and heat and to work machines electric, electrical *adjective* worked by electricity

electronic *adjective* An electronic machine uses electrical signals to control the way it works. Televisions, computers, and automatic washing machines have electronic systems inside them.

elephant *noun* elephants a very big, grey animal with tusks and a very long nose called a trunk

eleven *noun* the number 11

else *adverb* different *Let's do something else today.*

email *noun* emails a message that you send from your computer to someone else's computer

embarrass *verb* embarrasses, embarrassing, embarrassed to make someone feel shy, nervous, or ashamed

emerald *noun* emeralds a green jewel or precious stone

emergency *noun* emergencies When there is an emergency, something very dangerous suddenly happens and people must act quickly so that no one gets hurt.

emotion *noun* emotions Your emotions are your feelings.

empty *adjective* Something that is empty has nothing in it.

enchanted *adjective* under a magic spell

encourage *verb* encourages, encouraging, encouraged to tell someone to do something and make them feel brave enough to do it *Everyone encouraged me to try again.*

encyclopedia *noun* encyclopedias a book that gives you information about a lot of different things

end *noun* ends the place or time where something stops

end *verb* ends, ending, ended to stop

enemy *noun* enemies **1** someone who wants to hurt you **2** the people fighting against you

energetic *adjective* If you are energetic, you have a lot of energy and run round a lot.

energy *noun* **1** If you have energy, you feel strong and fit. **2** Energy is the power that comes from coal, electricity, and gas. Energy makes machines work and gives us heat and light.

engine *noun* engines a machine that can make things move

engineer *noun* engineers someone who makes machines, or plans the building of roads and bridges

enjoy *verb* enjoys, enjoying, enjoyed If you enjoy something, you like doing it or watching it. **enjoyable** *adjective* If something is enjoyable, you like doing it or watching it.

enormous *adjective* very big

enough *adjective* as much as you need of something *I haven't got enough money to buy an ice cream.*

enter *verb* enters, entering, entered **1** to go into a place **2** to take part in a race or competition

entertain *verb* entertains, entertaining, entertained to do things that people enjoy watching, or things that make them laugh

enthusiastic *adjective* very keen on something and wanting to do it

entrance *noun* entrances the way into a place

envelope *noun* envelopes a paper cover that you put a letter in before you send it

environment *noun* environments the world we live in, especially the plants, animals, and things around us

envy *noun* the feeling you have when you would like to have something that someone else has

episode *noun* episodes one programme in a radio or TV serial

equal *adjective* If two things are equal, they are the same size or worth the same amount **equally** *adverb* in the same way or in the same amount *We shared the money equally between us.*

equipment *noun* the things that you need for doing something

error *noun* errors a mistake

erupt *verb* erupts, erupting, erupted When a volcano erupts, hot, liquid rock comes up out of it.

escape *verb* escapes, escaping, escaped to get away from a place and become free

especially *adverb* more than anything else *I love fruit, especially apples.*

estimate *verb* estimates, estimating, estimated to guess how much an amount will be

EU *noun* EU is an abbreviation of **European Union**, which is an organization of countries that work together.

euro *noun* euros A euro is a unit of money. Euros are used in Germany, France and some other countries.

evaporate *verb* evaporates, evaporating, evaporated When water evaporates, it changes into a gas and so disappears.

even *adjective* 1 smooth and level *You need an even surface to work on.* 2 equal 3 (in mathematics) An even number is a number that you can divide by two. 4, 6, and 8 are even numbers.

evening *noun* evenings the time at the end of the day before people go to bed

event *noun* events something important that happens

eventually *adverb* in the end *We got home eventually.*

ever *adverb* at any time *Have you ever been to America?* **for ever** always

every *determiner* each *I go swimming every week.*

There is **er** in the middle of this word.

everybody, **everyone** *pronoun* every person

everything *pronoun* all things

everywhere *adverb* in all places

evidence *noun* anything that proves that something is true, or that something happened

evil *adjective* wicked

exact *adjective* completely right or accurate *Show me the exact spot where you were standing.* **exactly** *adverb* You use **exactly** before an amount or a number of something to say that it is completely right or accurate. *I had exactly 24 pence in my pocket.*

exaggerate *verb* exaggerates, exaggerating, exaggerated to say that something is bigger or better than it really is

exam, **examination** *noun* exams, examinations an important test

examine *verb* examines, examining, examined to look at something very carefully

example *noun* examples 1 one thing that shows what all the others are like 2 Someone who sets an example behaves well and shows other people how they should behave.

excellent *adjective* very good

except *preposition* apart from *Everyone got a prize except me.*

exchange *verb* exchanges, exchanging, exchanged to give something to someone and get something else in return

excite *verb* excites, exciting, excited to make someone feel happy, interested, and keen to do something **excitement** *noun* Excitement is when you feel happy and keen to do something. **exciting** *adjective* Something is exciting when you are happy and keen to do it.

The /s/ sound is spelled with a **c** in this word.

exclaim *verb* exclaims, exclaiming, exclaimed to shout something suddenly because you are surprised or excited

A B C D E F G H I J K L M N O P Q R S T U V W X Y Z

excuse *noun* **excuses** (rhymes with *goose*) a reason you give to try to explain why you have done wrong so that you will not get into trouble

excuse *verb* **excuses, excusing, excused** (rhymes with *choose*) to forgive someone *I'm sorry for interrupting you. Please excuse me.*

exercise *noun* **exercises 1** When you do exercise, you run around or move your body to make your body healthy and strong. **2** a piece of work that you do to make yourself better at something

exhausted *adjective* very tired

exhibition *noun* **exhibitions** a collection of things that are put on show so that people can come to see them

exist *verb* **exists, existing, existed** Things that exist are real, not imaginary.

exit *noun* **exits** the way out of a place

expect *verb* **expects, expecting, expected** to think that something will happen

expensive *adjective* Something that is expensive costs a lot of money.

experience *noun* **experiences 1** If you have experience of something, you have done it before and so know what it is like. **2** something very good or bad that happens to you

experiment *noun* **experiments** a test that you do to find out whether an idea works

expert *noun* **experts** someone who does something very well or knows a lot about something

explain *verb* **explains, explaining, explained** to talk about something so that other people understand it

explode *verb* **explodes, exploding, exploded** to burst or blow up with a loud bang

explore *verb* **explores, exploring, explored** to look around a place carefully to find out what it is like

explosion *noun* **explosions** a loud bang that is made when something bursts or blows up

express *verb* **expresses, expressing, expressed** to talk about your ideas or feelings or show them to other people

expression *noun* **expressions 1** the look on your face **2** a word or phrase

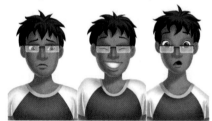

extinct *adjective* Animals that are extinct no longer exist because they are all dead.

extra *adjective* more than you would usually have or do *Bring some extra clothes in case it gets cold.*

extraordinary *adjective* very unusual

extreme *adjective* very great

eye *noun* **eyes** Your eyes are the parts of your body that you use for seeing.

eyesight *noun* your ability to see

Ff

face *noun* **faces** the front part of your head, which has your eyes, nose, and mouth on it

face *verb* **faces, facing, faced** The direction that you are facing is the direction in which you are looking.

fact *noun* **facts** something that we know is true

factory *noun* **factories** a large building where people make things with machines

fade *verb* **fades, fading, faded** **1** to become less bright **2** to become less loud

fail *verb* **fails, failing, failed** If you fail a test, you do not pass it.

failure *noun* **failures** **1** someone who has failed a test, or has not managed to do something very well **2** something that does not work well or is not successful

faint *adjective* **fainter, faintest** **1** A faint sound is not very loud and you cannot hear it very well. **2** A faint colour, mark, or light is not very bright or clear. **3** If you feel faint, you feel dizzy.

faint *verb* **faints, fainting, fainted** If you faint, you feel dizzy and become unconscious for a short time.

fair *adjective* **fairer, fairest** **1** Something that is fair treats everyone in the same way so that everyone is equal. **2** Fair hair is light in colour.

fair *noun* **fairs** a place with a lot of rides and stalls, where you can go to enjoy yourself by going on the rides and trying to win things at the stalls

fairy *noun* **fairies** a small, magical person in a story

fairy tale *noun* **fairy tales** a story for young children in which magic things happen

faithful *adjective* If you are faithful to someone, you always help them and support them.

fake *noun* **fakes** something that has been made to look like a valuable thing, but is not real

fall *verb* **falls, falling, fell, fallen** **1** to drop down towards the ground **2** When you fall asleep, you start sleeping.

false *adjective* not true or real

familiar *adjective* If something is familiar to you, you recognize it or know about it.

family *noun* **families** **1** all the people who are related to you, for example your parents, brothers and sisters, aunts and uncles **2** a group of animals or plants that are closely related

famous *adjective* very well known

fan *noun* **fans** **1** a machine that blows air about to cool a place **2** something that you hold in your hand and wave in front of your face to cool your face **3** someone who supports a famous person or a sports team *Are you a football fan?*

fantastic *adjective* wonderful

fantasy *noun* **fantasies** something that is magical and cannot happen in real life *I like reading fantasy stories.*

far *adverb* **farther, further, farthest, furthest** Something that is far away is a long way away.

fare *noun* **fares** the amount of money that you have to pay to travel on a train, bus, boat, or aeroplane

farm *noun* **farms** a piece of land where someone grows crops and keeps animals for food **farmer** *noun* someone who has a farm

fashion *noun* **fashions** A fashion is a style of clothes that is popular for a short time. Clothes that are **in fashion** are popular now. Clothes that are **out of fashion** are not popular.

fashionable *adjective* in fashion and popular now

fast *adjective* **faster, fastest**
1 Something that is fast moves quickly.
2 If a clock or watch is fast, it shows a time that is later than the right time. *My watch is ten minutes fast.*

fasten *verb* **fastens, fastening, fastened 1** to close something or do it up **2** to tie or join two things together

fat *noun* **1** the white, greasy part of meat **2** a substance such as butter, margarine, or oil used in cooking
fat *adjective* **fatter, fattest** Someone who is fat has a big, round body.

father *noun* **fathers** your male parent

fault *noun* **faults** If something bad is your fault, you made it happen.

favour *noun* **favours** If you do someone a favour, you do something for them.

favourite *adjective* Your favourite thing is the one that you like the most.

> There is an **ou** in the middle of this word.

fear *noun* **fears** the feeling you get when you are frightened because you think something bad is going to happen
fear *verb* **fears, fearing, feared** to be afraid of something

feast *noun* **feasts** a special big meal for a lot of people

feather *noun* **feathers** the light, soft things that a bird has all over its body

February *noun* the second month of the year

feed *verb* **feeds, feeding, fed** to give food to a person or an animal

feel *verb* **feels, feeling, felt 1** to touch something to find out what it is like **2** to have an emotion such as anger, fear, or happiness

feeling *noun* **feelings** something that you feel inside yourself, like anger or love

female *adjective* A female animal or person can become a mother.

fence *noun* **fences** A fence is a kind of wall made from wood or wire. Fences are put round gardens and fields.

ferocious *adjective* fierce and dangerous

ferry *noun* **ferries** a boat that takes people across a river or short stretch of water

festival *noun* **festivals** a special time when people celebrate something

fetch *verb* fetches, fetching, fetched to go and get something

fete *noun* fetes an event outside with games and competitions, and a lot of stalls selling different things

fever *noun* fevers If you have a fever, you have a high temperature and your body feels very hot.

few *determiner & pronoun* A few means a small number.

fewer *adjective* not as many *We scored fewer goals than the other team, so we lost the match.*

fibre *noun* a substance in some foods which we need to help our body digest things properly

fiction *noun* books and stories that are made up and are not true

field *noun* fields a piece of ground with crops or grass growing on it

fierce *adjective* fiercer, fiercest A fierce animal is dangerous because it might bite you or attack you.

fifteen *noun* the number 15

fifty *noun* the number 50

fight *verb* fights, fighting, fought When people fight, they hit each other or attack each other.

figure *noun* figures a number, such as 1, 2, or 3

file *noun* files **1** a book or box that you keep pieces of paper in **2** *(in ICT)* an amount of information that is stored together on a computer

fill *verb* fills, filling, filled **1** When you fill something, you put so much in it that it is full. **2** If food fills you up, it makes you feel full.

film *noun* films **1** a roll of plastic you put in some cameras for taking photographs **2** a moving picture that you watch on a screen at the cinema or on television

filthy *adjective* filthier, filthiest very dirty

fin *noun* fins The fins on a fish are the parts on its sides that it uses to help it swim.

final *adjective* The final thing is the one that comes last.

find *verb* finds, finding, found to see something *I found 50 pence on the ground.*

fine *adjective* finer, finest **1** If the weather is fine, it is sunny. **2** If you feel fine, you feel well and happy.

fine *noun* fines an amount of money that you have to pay because you have done something wrong

finger *noun* fingers Your fingers are the parts of your body on the ends of your hands.

finish *verb* finishes, finishing, finished **1** to come to the end of something **2** to end

fire *noun* fires **1** When there is a fire, something is burning. **2** a machine that gives out heat

A B C D E **F** G H I J K L M N O P Q R S T U V W X Y Z

fire *verb* fires, firing, fired to make a gun shoot

fire engine *noun* fire engines a large truck that carries firefighters and the equipment that they need to put out fires

firefighter *noun* firefighters a person whose job is to put out fires

firework *noun* fireworks something that explodes with coloured lights and loud bangs

first *adjective* The first thing is the one that comes before all the others.

first aid *noun* help that you give to a person who is hurt, before a doctor comes

fish *noun* fishes, fish A fish is an animal that swims and lives in water. Fish have fins to help them swim and scales on their bodies.
fish *verb* fishes, fishing, fished to try to catch fish

fisherman *noun* fishermen a person who catches fish

fist *noun* fists When you make a fist, you close your hand tightly.

fit *adjective* fitter, fittest If you are fit, your body is healthy and strong. *Swimming helps to keep you fit.*
fit *verb* fits, fitting, fitted **1** If something fits you, it is the right size for you to wear.

2 If something fits into a place, it is the right size to go there.

five *noun* fives the number 5

fix *verb* fixes, fixing, fixed **1** to join one thing firmly onto another *My dad fixed the lamp onto my bike for me.* **2** to mend something

fizzy *adjective* fizzier, fizziest A fizzy drink has a lot of tiny bubbles of gas in it.

flag *noun* flags a piece of cloth with a special design on, which is fixed to a pole

flame *noun* flames Flames are the orange, pointed parts that come up out of a fire.

flap *verb* flaps, flapping, flapped When something flaps, it moves up and down or from side to side. *The huge bird flapped its wings and flew off.*

flash *noun* flashes a sudden bright light
flash *verb* flashes, flashing, flashed to shine brightly and then stop shining again

flask *noun* flasks a container that keeps hot drinks hot and cold drinks cold

flat *adjective* flatter, flattest **1** smooth and level, with no bumps **2** A flat battery has no more power in it. **3** A flat tyre or ball does not have enough air in it.
flat *noun* flats a set of rooms that you can live in inside a large building

flavour *noun* flavours the taste that something has when you eat it or drink it

fleece *noun* fleeces a type of warm coat or jacket made of thick material

flesh *noun* the soft part of your body between your bones and your skin

flight *noun* flights **1** a journey in an aeroplane **2** A flight of stairs is a set of stairs.

flipper *noun* flippers The flippers on a seal or a penguin are the parts on the sides of its body that it uses for swimming.

float *verb* floats, floating, floated When something floats, it does not sink but stays on the surface of water.

flock *noun* flocks A flock of sheep or birds is a large group of them.

flood *noun* floods When there is a flood, a lot of water spreads over the land.

flood *verb* floods, flooding, flooded When a river floods, it becomes too full and spills out over the land.

floor *noun* floors **1** the part of a building that you walk on **2** one of the levels in a tall building

flour *noun* Flour is a powder that is made from crushed wheat. You use flour for making bread, pastry, and cakes.

flow *verb* flows, flowing, flowed When water flows, it moves along like a river.

flow chart *noun* flow charts a diagram that shows the different stages of how something happens

flower *noun* flowers the brightly coloured part of a plant

flu *noun* Flu is an illness that gives you a bad cold and makes you ache all over and feel very hot. Flu is short for **influenza**.

flute *noun* flutes a musical instrument which you hold sideways across your mouth and play by blowing across a hole in it

flutter *verb* flutters, fluttering, fluttered to flap gently

fly *noun* flies a small insect with wings

fly *verb* flies, flying, flew, flown to move along through the air

foal *noun* foals a young horse

foam *noun* a thick mass of small bubbles on the top of a liquid

focus *verb* focuses, focusing, focused When you focus a camera or telescope, you move the controls so that you get a clear picture.

fog *noun* thick cloud just above the ground, which makes it difficult to see

fold *verb* folds, folding, folded to bend one part of something over another part

folder *noun* folders **1** a thin cardboard case that you keep pieces of paper in **2** a place where you keep several files together on a computer

follow *verb* follows, following, followed **1** to go after someone **2** to go along a road or path

fond *adjective* fonder, fondest If you are fond of something, you like it a lot. If you are fond of someone, you like them a lot.

a
b
c
d
e
f
g
h
i
j
k
l
m
n
o
p
q
r
s
t
u
v
w
x
y
z

food *noun* **foods** anything that you eat to help you grow and be healthy

food chain *noun* **food chains** *(in science)* A food chain is a set of plants and animals that are linked because each one eats the one below it on the chain. For example, grass is eaten by a rabbit, then a rabbit is eaten by a fox.

foot *noun* **feet** **1** Your feet are the parts of your body that you stand on. **2** We can measure length in feet. One foot is about 30 centimetres.

football *noun* **1** a game in which two teams try to score goals by kicking a ball into a net **2** a ball that you use for playing football

for *preposition* **1** If something is for a person, you are going to give it to that person. *I've bought a present for you.* **2** If you say what something is for, you are saying how you use it. *You need a sharp knife for cutting bread.*

forbid *verb* **forbids, forbidding, forbade, forbidden** To forbid someone to do something means to tell them that they must not do it. If something is forbidden, you are not allowed to do it.

force *noun* **forces** **1** If you use force to do something, you use your strength. **2** *(in science)* A force is something that pushes or pulls an object.

force *verb* **forces, forcing, forced** If you force someone to do something, you make them do it.

forehead *noun* **foreheads** the part of your head that is above your eyes

foreign *adjective* Things that are foreign come from other countries or are to do with other countries. *My brother speaks four foreign languages.*

forest *noun* **forests** an area of land where a lot of trees grow close together

forget *verb* **forgets, forgetting, forgot, forgotten** If you forget something, you do not remember it. *I forgot to do my homework.*

forgive *verb* **forgives, forgiving, forgave, forgiven** to stop being angry with someone

fork *noun* **forks** A fork is a tool with three sharp points called prongs. You use a fork for eating food, and you use a large fork for digging in the ground.

form *noun* **forms** **1** a piece of paper that has writing on it and spaces where you must fill in your name and other information **2** a class in a school **3** a type *A bicycle is a form of transport.*

form *verb* **forms, forming, formed** When something forms, it is made.

formal *adjective* Formal language is language that you write down, not language you use when you are talking to friends.

fortnight *noun* **fortnights** two weeks

fortress *noun* **fortresses** a large building or a group of buildings that is made strong against attack

fortunate *adjective* lucky

fortune *noun* fortunes a very large amount of money

forty *noun* the number 40

forwards, **forward** 1 towards the place that is in front of you *The train moved slowly forwards.* 2 If you are looking forward to something, you are excited because it is going to happen.

fossil *noun* fossils part of a dead plant or animal that has been in the ground for millions of years and has gradually turned to stone

fountain *noun* fountains a jet of water that shoots up into the air

four *noun* fours the number 4

fourteen *noun* the number 14

fox *noun* foxes a wild animal that looks like a dog and has red fur and a long, furry tail

fraction *noun* fractions *(in mathematics)* A fraction is a number that is not a whole number. ⅓, ½, and ¾ are fractions.

fracture *noun* fractures a place where a bone is cracked or broken

fragile *adjective* Something that is fragile will break easily if you drop it.

frame *noun* frames 1 the part round the outside of a picture or a pair of glasses 2 the part that supports an object

freckle *noun* freckles Freckles are the small brown spots that some people have on their skin, especially when they have been in the sun.

free *adjective* freer, freest 1 If you are free, you can go where you want and do what you want to do. 2 If something is free, you do not have to pay for it.

free *verb* frees, freeing, freed to let someone go after they have been locked up

freeze *verb* freezes, freezing, froze, frozen 1 to become very cold and hard and change into ice *The lake froze over last winter.* 2 If you are freezing or frozen, you are very cold.

freezer *noun* freezers a large, very cold container in which you can store frozen food for a long time

frequent *adjective* Something that is frequent happens quite often.

fresh *adjective* fresher, freshest 1 clean and new 2 Fresh food has been made or picked only a short time ago. 3 Fresh air is clean and cool. 4 Fresh water is not salty.

friction *noun* *(in science)* the force which is produced when one thing rubs against another

Friday *noun* Fridays the day after Thursday

fridge *noun* fridges A fridge is a large cool container that you keep food in so

67

that it does not go bad. Fridge is short for **refrigerator**.

friend *noun* friends a person you like and know well friendly *adjective* If you are friendly, you like people and are nice to them. friendship *noun* being friends with someone

fright *noun* frights a sudden feeling of fear frightening *adjective* If something is frightening, it makes you suddenly feel fear.

frighten *verb* frightens, frightening, frightened to make someone feel scared

fringe *noun* freckles short hair that hangs down your forehead

frog *noun* frogs A frog is a small animal with a smooth, wet skin and long back legs. Frogs live near water and can jump by using their strong back legs.

from *preposition* **1** When you go away from a place, you leave that place. *We flew from London to Paris.* **2** If a present is from a person, that person gave it to you.

front *noun* fronts the part of something that faces forwards *We sat at the front of the bus.*

frost *noun* frosts ice that looks like powder and covers the ground when the weather is cold

frown *verb* frowns, frowning, frowned When you frown, you have lines on your forehead because you are angry or worried.

frozen *adjective* Something that is frozen has turned to ice.

fruit *noun* fruits, fruit A fruit is the part of a plant which contains seeds. A lot of fruits taste sweet and are good to eat.

Apples, oranges, and bananas are all types of fruit.

fry *verb* fries, frying, fried to cook food in hot fat

fuel *noun* fuels anything that people burn to give heat or power

full *adjective* fuller, fullest If something is full, it has as much inside it as it can hold. *The room was full of people.*

fun *noun* When you have fun, you enjoy yourself.

funeral *noun* funerals the ceremony that takes place when a dead person is buried or burned

funny *adjective* funnier, funniest **1** Something that is funny makes you laugh or smile. **2** Something that is funny is strange or surprising.

fur *noun* furs the soft hair that covers some animals

furious *adjective* very angry furiously *adverb* If you do or say something furiously, you do it or say it because you are very angry.

furniture *noun* things such as beds and tables that you need inside a house

fuss *verb* fusses, fussing, fussed If you fuss about something, you worry about it too much.

future *noun* the time that will come

fuzzy *adjective* fuzzier, fuzziest A picture or sound that is fuzzy is not very clear.

Gg

galaxy *noun* galaxies A galaxy is a large group of stars and planets. The Milky Way is a galaxy.

gale *noun* gales a very strong wind

gallery *noun* galleries a building or large room where there are paintings on the walls for people to look at

gallon *noun* gallons We can measure liquids in gallons. A gallon is about 4½ litres.

gallop *verb* gallops, galloping, galloped When a horse gallops, it runs as fast as it can.

game *noun* games something that you play for fun

gang *noun* gangs a group of people who spend time together and do things together

gap *noun* gaps a hole, or an empty space between two things

garage *noun* garages 1 a building in which people keep a car, motorbike, or bus 2 a place that sells petrol and mends cars

garden *noun* gardens a piece of ground where people grow flowers, fruit, or vegetables

garlic *noun* a plant like an onion with a very strong smell and taste

gas *noun* gases A gas is any substance that is like air, and is not a solid or a liquid. We can burn some types of gas to give heat to cook with or heat our homes.

gasp *verb* gasps, gasping, gasped to breathe in quickly and noisily because you are surprised, or because you have been running

gate *noun* gates a door in a wall or fence

gather *verb* gathers, gathering, gathered 1 When people gather, they come together. 2 to collect things and bring them together

gaze *verb* gazes, gazing, gazed to look at something for a long time

general *adjective* 1 Something that is general includes most people. *There was general agreement that something had to be done.* 2 Something that is general does not go into details. *We had a general discussion about what life was like in Roman times.*

generally *adverb* usually *It is generally very cold here in the winter.*

generous *adjective* kind and always ready to give or share the things that you have

gentle *adjective* gentler, gentlest If you are gentle, you touch something in a kind, careful way and are not rough. **gently** *adverb* If you do or say something gently, you do it or say it in a careful way, and are not rough.

a b c d e f **g** h i j k l m n o p q r s t u v w x y z

gentleman *noun* gentlemen a polite name for a man

geography *noun* the subject in which you learn about the earth, with its mountains, rivers, countries, and the people who live in them

germ *noun* germs A germ is a tiny living thing that is too small to see. Germs sometimes make you ill if they get inside your body.

get *verb* gets, getting, got **1** When you get something, you receive it, buy it, or earn it, and it becomes yours. *What did you get for your birthday?* **2** to become *Are you getting tired yet?*

ghost *noun* ghosts the shape of a dead person that some people think they can see

> There is a silent **h** in this word.

giant *noun* giants a very big person, especially in stories

gift *noun* gifts a present

gigantic *adjective* very big

giggle *verb* giggles, giggling, giggled to laugh in a silly way

ginger *noun* a spice with a strong, hot taste

ginger *adjective* Ginger hair is a reddish-orange colour.

giraffe *noun* giraffes A giraffe is a very tall African animal with a very long neck. Giraffes are the tallest animals in the world.

girl *noun* girls a female child

give *verb* gives, giving, gave, given to let someone have something

glad *adjective* happy about something

glance *verb* glances, glancing, glanced to look at something quickly

glare *verb* glares, glaring, glared to look at someone angrily

glass *noun* glasses **1** the hard, clear substance that windows are made of **2** a cup made of glass, which you drink out of

glasses *noun* two round pieces of glass in a frame, which some people wear over their eyes to help them to see better

gleam *verb* gleams, gleaming, gleamed to shine

glide *verb* glides, gliding, glided to move along very smoothly

glider *noun* gliders a type of aeroplane without an engine

glitter *verb* glitters, glittering, glittered to shine and sparkle brightly

globe *noun* globes a ball with the map of the whole world on it

gloomy *adjective* gloomier, gloomiest **1** A gloomy place is dark. **2** If you feel gloomy, you feel sad.

glossy *adjective* glossier, glossiest smooth and shiny

glove *noun* gloves A glove is something that you wear on your hands in cold weather. Gloves have separate parts for your thumb and each finger.

glow *verb* glows, glowing, glowed to shine with a warm, gentle light

glue *noun* glues a sticky substance that you use for sticking things together

gnarled *adjective* Something that is gnarled is bent and twisted because it is very old. *We sat on a gnarled old tree trunk.*

gn- in this word sounds like n-

gnome *noun* gnomes a small, ugly fairy in stories

go *verb* goes, going, went, gone **1** When you go somewhere, you move or travel so that you are there. **2** If a machine is going, it is working. **3** to become *Clay goes hard when you bake it.*

goal *noun* goals **1** the net where you must kick or throw the ball to score a point in a game such as football or netball **2** something that you want to achieve

goat *noun* goats an animal with horns that is kept on farms for its milk

god *noun* gods **1** a person or thing that people worship **2** or **God** the being or spirit that is worshipped in Christianity, Islam and Judaism, and is believed to have created the universe

goggles *noun* special thick glasses that you wear to protect your eyes, for example when you are swimming

go-kart *noun* go-karts a type of small car that people use for racing

gold *noun* a shiny, yellow metal that is very valuable

golf *noun* Golf is a game that you play by hitting small, white balls with sticks called **golf clubs**. You have to hit the balls into holes in the ground.

good *adjective* better, best **1** nice, pleasant, or enjoyable **2** kind and honest **3** When you are good, you behave well and do not do anything naughty. **4** If you are good at something, you can do it well.

goodbye *interjection* the word you say to someone when you are leaving them

goods *noun* things that people buy and sell

goose *noun* geese a large bird that is kept on farms for its meat and eggs

gorilla *noun* gorillas A gorilla is an African animal like a very large monkey with long arms and no tail. A gorilla is a type of ape.

government *noun* governments the group of people who are in charge of a country

grab *verb* grabs, grabbing, grabbed to take hold of something quickly or roughly

graceful *adjective* Someone who is graceful moves in a smooth, gentle way.

gradual *adjective* happening slowly, bit by bit, not all at once **gradually** *adverb* If something happens gradually, it happens slowly. *I was gradually beginning to feel better.*

graffiti *noun* writing and pictures that people have scribbled or scratched onto walls

grain *noun* grains **1** Grain is the seeds of plants like corn and wheat. **2** A grain of salt or sand is one tiny bit of it.

gram *noun* grams We can measure weight in grams. There are 1000 grams in one kilogram.

grammar *noun* all the rules of a language, which tell us how to put the words together correctly

grand *adjective* grander, grandest very big and important

grandchild *noun* grandchildren Someone's grandchild is a child of their son or daughter. A grandchild can also be called a **granddaughter**, or a **grandson**.

grandparent *noun* grandparents Your grandparents are the parents of your father or mother. You can also call your grandparents your **grandmother** and **grandfather**. A grandmother is often called **grandma** or **granny**. A grandfather is often called **grandpa** or **grandad**.

grape *noun* grapes a small, soft green or purple fruit that grows in bunches

grapefruit *noun* grapefruits a large, sour-tasting fruit that has thick yellow skin

graph *noun* graphs a diagram that shows information about something

grasp *verb* grasps, grasping, grasped to get hold of something and hold it tightly

grass *noun* grasses a green plant that covers the ground and is used for lawns and parks

grasshopper *noun* grasshoppers an insect that has long back legs and can jump a long way

grate *verb* grates, grating, grated to cut food into very small pieces by rubbing it against a rough tool

grateful *adjective* If you are grateful for something, you are glad that you have it.

grave *noun* graves a place where a dead person is buried in the ground

gravity *noun* (in science) the force that pulls things towards the earth

graze *verb* grazes, grazing, grazed to hurt a part of your body by scraping it against something and making it bleed

grease *noun* a thick, oily substance

great *adjective* greater, greatest **1** very big and impressive **2** very clever and important **3** very good

greedy *adjective* greedier, greediest Someone who is greedy wants more food or money than they need.

green *adjective* Something that is green is the colour of grass.

greengrocer *noun* greengrocers someone who sells fruit and vegetables in a shop

greenhouse *noun* greenhouses a glass building that people use for growing plants in

greet *verb* greets, greeting, greeted to welcome someone and say hello to them

grey *adjective* (rhymes with *day*) Something that is grey is the colour of the sky on a cloudy day.

grid *noun* grids a pattern of straight lines that cross over each other to make squares

grill *verb* grills, grilling, grilled to cook food on metal bars either under or over heat

grin *verb* grins, grinning, grinned to smile in a cheerful way

grind *verb* grinds, grinding, ground to crush something into tiny bits

grip *verb* grips, gripping, gripped to hold on to something tightly

groan *verb* groans, groaning, groaned to make a low sound because you are in pain or are disappointed about something

grocery *noun* groceries a shop that sells tea, sugar, jam, and other kinds of food

ground *noun* grounds **1** The ground is the earth. **2** A sports ground is a piece of land that people play sport on.

group *noun* groups **1** a number of people, animals, or things that are together or belong together **2** a number of people who play music together

grow *verb* grows, growing, grew, grown **1** to become bigger **2** When you grow plants you put them in the ground and look after them. **3** to become *Everyone was beginning to grow tired.*

growl *verb* growls, growling, growled When an animal growls, it makes a deep, angry sound in its throat.

grown-up *noun* grown-ups a man or woman who is not a child any more

growth *noun* the way in which something grows and gets bigger

grumble *verb* grumbles, grumbling, grumbled to complain about something

grunt *verb* grunts, grunting, grunted to make a rough sound

guarantee *noun* guarantees a promise that something you have bought will be mended or replaced free if it goes wrong

guard *verb* guards, guarding, guarded **1** to watch a place to keep it safe from other people **2** to watch a person to keep them safe or to stop them from escaping

guard *noun* guards someone who protects a place or watches a person to keep them safe or stop them from escaping

guess *verb* guesses, guessing, guessed to say what you think the answer to a question is when you do not really know *Can you guess what I've got in my pocket?*

guest *noun* guests a person who is invited to a party or is invited to stay in someone else's home for a short time

guide *noun* guides **1** a person who shows you around a place **2** a book that gives you information about something

guide *verb* guides, guiding, guided to lead or take someone to a place

guilty *adjective* guiltier, guiltiest **1** If you are guilty, you have done something wrong. *The prisoner was found guilty of murder.* **2** If you feel guilty, you feel bad because you have done something wrong.

guitar *noun* guitars A guitar is a musical instrument with strings across it. You hold a guitar in front of your body and play it by pulling on the strings with your fingers.

gulp *verb* gulps, gulping, gulped to swallow food or drink very quickly

gum *noun* gums **1** Your gums are the hard pink parts of your mouth that are around your teeth. **2** Gum is a sweet that you chew but do not swallow.

gun *noun* guns a weapon that fires bullets from a metal tube

gurdwara *noun* gurdwaras a Sikh temple

guru *noun* gurus a Hindu or Sikh religious leader

gust *noun* gusts A gust of wind is a sudden rush of wind.

gym *noun* gyms A gym is a large room with special equipment for doing exercises. A gym is also called a **gymnasium**.

gymnastics *noun* special exercises that you do to make your body strong and to show how well you can bend, stretch, and twist your body

Hh

habit *noun* habits If something that you do is a habit, you do it without thinking, because you have done it so often before.

habitat *noun* habitats the place where an animal or plant usually lives or grows

hail *noun* small pieces of ice that fall from the sky like rain

hair *noun* hairs Your hair is the long, soft stuff that grows on your head. An animal's hair is the soft stuff that grows all over its body.

hairdresser *noun* hairdressers someone who cuts people's hair

hairy *adjective* hairier, hairiest Something that is hairy is covered with hair. A person who is hairy has a lot of hair on their body.

Hajj *noun* the journey to Mecca that all Muslims try to make at least once in their lives

half *noun* halves One half of something is one of two equal parts that the thing is divided into. It can also be written as ½.

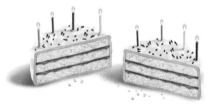

halfway *adverb* in the middle *I'll meet you halfway between my house and your house.*

hall *noun* halls **1** the part of a house that is just inside the front door **2** a very big room **3** a large, important building

Hallowe'en *noun* 31 October, when people dress up, often as ghosts or witches

halve *verb* halves, halving, halved to cut something into two equal parts

ham *noun* meat from a pig's leg that has been salted or smoked

hammer *noun* hammers a heavy tool that you use for hitting nails

hand *noun* hands Your hands are the parts of your body at the ends of your arms.

handbag *noun* handbags a small bag in which women carry money and other things

handkerchief *noun* handkerchiefs a piece of material you use for blowing your nose

handle *noun* handles the part of something that you hold in your hand

handle *verb* handles, handling, handled to pick something up and hold it in your hands

handsome *adjective* A handsome man or boy is attractive to look at.

handwriting *noun* the way in which you write

handy *adjective* handier, handiest useful and easy to use

hang *verb* hangs, hanging, hung When you hang something up, you put it on a hook or nail.

hanger *noun* hangers a piece of wood or metal that you hang clothes on

Hanukkah *noun* the Jewish festival of lights, which lasts for eight days and begins in December

happen *verb* happens, happening, happened **1** to take place **2** If you happen to do something, you do it by chance, without planning to do it.

happy *adjective* happier, happiest When you are happy, you feel pleased and you are enjoying yourself. happiness *noun* Happiness is when you are pleased and are enjoying yourself.

harbour *noun* harbours a place where people can tie up boats and leave them

hard *adjective* harder, hardest **1** not soft **2** difficult

hard *adverb* When you work hard, you work a lot and with a lot of effort.

hard disk *noun* **hard disks** *(in ICT)* the part inside a computer where information is stored

hardly *adverb* If you can hardly do something, you can only just do it.

hare *noun* **hares** A hare is an animal that looks like a big rabbit with very long ears. Hares have strong back legs and can run very fast.

harm *verb* **harms, harming, harmed** To harm something means to damage it or spoil it in some way. To harm someone means to hurt them.

harvest *noun* **harvests** the time when farmers gather in the crops that they have grown

hat *noun* **hats** something that you wear on your head

hatch *verb* **hatches, hatching, hatched** When a baby bird or animal hatches, it comes out of an egg and is born.

hate *verb* **hates, hating, hated** If you hate something, you do not like it at all. If you hate someone, you do not like them at all.

haunted *adjective* A haunted place is one where people believe there are ghosts.

have *verb* **has, having, had** 1 to own something 2 If you have an illness, you are suffering from it. 3 If you have to do something, you must do it.

hay *noun* dry grass that people use to feed animals

he *pronoun* You use **he** when you are talking about a man, boy, or male animal.

head *noun* **heads** 1 the part at the top of your body that contains your brain, eyes, and mouth 2 the person in charge of something

headache *noun* **headaches** If you have a headache, your head hurts.

headlight *noun* **headlights** one of the lights on a car that you use at night so that you can see where you are going

headline *noun* **headlines** the words in large print at the top of a piece of writing in a newspaper

headphones *noun* a set of small speakers that you wear over your ears so that you can listen to music from a music player

headquarters *noun* the place where an organization is based, and where the people in charge of it work

headteacher *noun* **headteachers** A headteacher is the person in charge of all the teachers and children in a school. A headteacher is also called a **headmaster** or **headmistress**.

heal *verb* **heals, healing, healed** When a cut or broken bone heals, it gets better.

health *noun* Your health is how well you are.

healthy *adjective* **healthier, healthiest** 1 When you are healthy, you are not ill. 2 Things that are healthy are good for you and keep you fit and well.

heap *noun* **heaps** an untidy pile of things

hear *verb* **hears, hearing, heard** to notice something through your ears

> This sounds the same as **here**.

hearing *noun* your ability to hear things

heart *noun* **hearts** **1** the part of your body in your chest that pumps blood all round your body **2** a curved shape that looks like the shape of a heart and is used to represent love

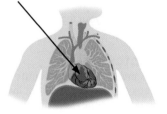

heat *noun* the hot feeling you get from a fire or from the sun
heat *verb* **heats, heating, heated** to make something warm or hot

heaven *noun* Heaven is the place where some people believe that a god lives. Some people believe that people go to heaven when they die.

heavy *adjective* **heavier, heaviest** Something that is heavy weighs a lot and is hard to lift.

hedge *noun* **hedges** a line of bushes that are growing very close together and make a sort of wall round a garden or field

hedgehog *noun* **hedgehogs** a small animal that is covered with spines like sharp needles

heel *noun* **heels** the back part of your foot

height *noun* **heights** (rhymes with *bite*) The height of something is how high it is. The height of a person is how tall they are.

helicopter *noun* **helicopters** a flying machine with a big propeller that spins round on its roof

hello, hallo *interjection* the word you say to someone when you meet them

helmet *noun* **helmets** a strong hat that you wear to protect your head

help *verb* **helps, helping, helped** **1** to do something for someone that makes things easier for them **2** When you help yourself to something, you take it. **helpful** *adjective* If you are helpful, you do something for someone that makes things easier for them.

helping *noun* **helpings** an amount of food that you give to one person

helpless *adjective* not able to look after yourself

hen *noun* **hens** a bird that is kept on farms for the eggs that it lays

heptagon *noun* **heptagons** a shape with seven straight sides

her *determiner* You use **her** when you are talking about something belonging to a woman, girl or female animal.

herb *noun* **herbs** A herb is a plant that people add to food when they are cooking to make it taste nice. Parsley and mint are herbs.

a b c d e f g **h** i j k l m n o p q r s t u v w x y z

herd *noun* **herds** a group of animals that live and feed together

here *adverb* in this place *Please wait here until I get back.*

> This sounds the same as **hear**.

hero *noun* **heroes** **1** a boy or man who has done something very brave **2** the man or boy in a story who is the main character

heroine *noun* **heroines** **1** a girl or woman who has done something very brave **2** the woman or girl in a story who is the main character

hers *pronoun* You use **hers** when you are talking about something that belongs to a woman, girl, or female animal. *The books are hers.*

hesitate *verb* **hesitates**, **hesitating**, **hesitated** to wait for a little while before you do something because you are not sure what you should do

hexagon *noun* **hexagons** a shape with six straight sides

hibernate *verb* **hibernates**, **hibernating**, **hibernated** When animals hibernate, they spend the winter in a special kind of deep sleep. Bats, tortoises, and hedgehogs all hibernate.

hide *verb* **hides**, **hiding**, **hid**, **hidden** **1** to go to a place where people cannot see you **2** to put something in a secret place so that people cannot find it

high *adjective* **higher**, **highest** **1** very tall *There was a high wall around the garden.* **2** Something that is high up is a long way above the ground. **3** A high voice or sound is not deep or low.

hill *noun* **hills** a bit of ground that is higher than the ground around it

him *pronoun* You use **him** when you are talking about a boy, man or male animal.

Hindu *noun* **Hindus** someone who follows the religion of Hinduism, which is an Indian religion with many gods

hinge *noun* **hinges** A hinge is a piece of metal that is fixed to a door and to the wall. A hinge can move so that you can open and shut the door.

hint *verb* **hints**, **hinting**, **hinted** to suggest something without saying exactly what you mean

hip *noun* **hips** Your hips are the parts of your body where your legs join the rest of your body.

hippopotamus *noun* **hippopotamuses** A hippopotamus is a very large, heavy, African animal that lives near water. It is sometimes called a **hippo** for short.

hire *verb* **hires**, **hiring**, **hired** to pay to use something for a short time

his *determiner & pronoun* You use **his** when you are talking about something that belongs to a man, boy or male animal. *That's his lunch. The car is his.*

history *noun* the subject in which you learn about things that happened in the past

hit *verb* **hits**, **hitting**, **hit** To hit something means to bang against it. To hit someone means to knock them or slap them.

hive *noun* **hives** A hive is a special box that bees live in. It is designed so that people can collect the honey that the bees make.

hoarse *adjective* A hoarse voice sounds rough and deep.

hobby *noun* **hobbies** something that you do for fun in your spare time

hockey *noun* a game in which two teams try to score goals by hitting a ball into a net with a special stick

hold *verb* **holds, holding, held** **1** to have something in your hands **2** The amount that something holds is the amount that you can put inside it.

hole *noun* **holes** a gap or an empty space in something

Holi *noun* a Hindu festival that takes place in the spring

holiday *noun* **holidays** a time when you do not have to go to school or work

hollow *adjective* Something that is hollow has an empty space inside it.

holy *adjective* **holier, holiest** Something that is holy is special because it has something to do with a god or religion.

home *noun* **homes** the place where you live

home page *noun* **home pages** the main page on a website, which you can look at by using the Internet

homework *noun* school work that you do at home, in the evenings or at the weekend

honest *adjective* Someone who is honest does not steal or cheat or tell lies.

honey *noun* a sweet, sticky food that is made by bees

hood *noun* **hoods** the part of a coat that you put over your head when it is cold or raining

hoof *noun* **hoofs, hooves** An animal's hooves are the hard parts on its feet.

hook *noun* **hooks** a curved piece of metal that you use for hanging things on or catching things with

hoop *noun* **hoops** a big wooden or plastic ring that you use in games

hoot *verb* **hoots, hooting, hooted** to make a sound like an owl or the horn of a car

hop *verb* **hops, hopping, hopped** **1** to jump on one foot **2** When animals hop, they jump with two feet together.

hope *verb* **hopes, hoping, hoped** If you hope that something will happen, you want it to happen.

hopeful *adjective* If you are hopeful, you think that something you want to happen will happen. **hopefully** *adverb* If you do something hopefully you do it in a hopeful way, or you are hopeful that something will happen.

hopeless *adjective* **1** You say that something is hopeless when you think that it is never going to work. **2** If you are hopeless at something, you are very bad at it.

A
B
C
D
E
F
G
H
I
J
K
L
M
N
O
P
Q
R
S
T
U
V
W
X
Y
Z

horizon *noun* the line in the distance where the sky and the land or sea seem to meet

horizontal *adjective* flat and level

horn *noun* horns **1** The horns on some animals are the hard, pointed parts that grow on their heads. **2** the part on a car that makes a loud noise to warn people when there is danger

horrible *adjective* very nasty or frightening

horror *noun* a feeling of very great fear

horse *noun* horses a big animal that people can ride on or use to pull carts

hospital *noun* hospitals a place where people who are ill or hurt are looked after until they are better

hot *adjective* hotter, hottest **1** very warm **2** Hot food has a strong, spicy taste.

hotel *noun* hotels a building where you can pay to stay the night and to have meals

hour *noun* hours We measure time in hours. There are sixty minutes in one hour, and twenty-four hours in one day.

house *noun* houses a building where people live

hover *verb* hovers, hovering, hovered to stay in one place in the air

hovercraft *noun* hovercraft a type of boat that travels on a cushion of air just above the surface of the water

how *adverb* **1** a word that you use to ask questions *How old are you?* **2** a word you use to explain the way something works or happens *He explained how a camera works.*

however *adverb* **1** no matter how much *You'll never catch him, however fast you run.* **2** in spite of this *We were losing 3–0 at half time. However, we still kept trying.*

howl *verb* howls, howling, howled to make a long, high sound, like the sound of an animal crying or a strong wind blowing

hug *verb* hugs, hugging, hugged to hold someone in your arms to show you love them

huge *adjective* very big

hum *verb* hums, humming, hummed to sing a tune with your lips closed

human *noun* humans A human is a man, woman, or child. A human is also called a **human being**.

humour *noun* If you have a sense of humour, you enjoy laughing at things.

hundred *noun* hundreds the number 100

hungry *adjective* hungrier, hungriest If you are hungry, you feel that you need food. hungrily *adverb* in a way that shows you are hungry *He ate the bread and cheese hungrily.*

hunt *verb* hunts, hunting, hunted **1** to chase and kill animals for food or as a sport **2** When you hunt for something, you look for it in a lot of different places.

hurricane *noun* hurricanes a storm with a very strong wind

hurry *verb* hurries, hurrying, hurried to walk or run quickly, or try to do something quickly

hurt *verb* hurts, hurting, hurt **1** to make someone feel pain **2** If a part of your body hurts, it feels sore.

husband *noun* husbands the man a woman is married to

hut *noun* huts a small building made of wood

hutch *noun* hutches a small box or cage that you keep a pet rabbit in

hymn *noun* hymns (rhymes with *him*) a Christian song that praises God

Ii

I *pronoun* You use **I** when you are talking about yourself.

ice *noun* water that has frozen hard

iceberg *noun* icebergs a very big piece of ice floating in the sea

ice cream *noun* ice creams a very cold, frozen food that is made from milk or cream and flavoured with sugar and fruit or chocolate

ice skate *noun* ice skates a boot with a special blade on the bottom, which you use for skating on ice

icicle *noun* icicles a thin, pointed piece of ice hanging down from a high place

icing *noun* a sweet mixture that you spread over cakes to decorate them

ICT *noun* ICT is the subject in which you study computers. It stands for **information and communication technology**.

icy *adjective* icier, iciest **1** very cold **2** When the road is icy, it is slippery because it is covered with ice.

idea *noun* ideas When you have an idea, you think of something that you could do.

ideal *adjective* perfect

identical *adjective* exactly the same

idol *noun* idols a famous person that a lot of people love

if *conjunction* **1** You use **if** when you are talking about something that might happen. *If you go to the park, can you take your brother?* **2** You use **if** when you are talking about a choice between two things. *Do you know if you want to go to the park or not?* **3** on the condition that *I'll take him to the park if we're allowed sweets.*

ignore *verb* ignores, ignoring, ignored to refuse to speak to someone or take any notice of them

ill *adjective* not very well

illness *noun* illnesses An illness is something that makes people ill. Measles, chickenpox, and colds are illnesses.

illustrate *verb* illustrates, illustrating, illustrated to add pictures to a book or story

imaginary *adjective* Something that is imaginary does not really exist, but is only in your mind or in a story.

imagine *verb* imagines, imagining, imagined to make a picture of something in your mind

Imam *noun* Imams a Muslim religious leader

a
b
c
d
e
f
g
h
i
j
k
l
m
n
o
p
q
r
s
t
u
v
w
x
y
z

imitate *verb* imitates, imitating, imitated to copy the way someone speaks or behaves

imitation *noun* imitations something that has been made to look like something valuable

immediate *adjective* Something that is immediate happens straight away. immediately *adverb* straight away

impatient *adjective* Someone who is impatient gets bored and angry if they have to wait for something.

important *adjective* 1 If something is important, you must think about it carefully and seriously. 2 An important person is special and well known.

impossible *adjective* If something is impossible, no one can do it. *It's impossible to undo this knot.*

improve *verb* improves, improving, improved 1 to make something better 2 to get better

in *preposition* 1 inside *My pencil case is in my bag.* 2 wearing *I was still in my school uniform.*

inch *noun* inches We can measure length in inches. One inch is about 2½ centimetres.

include *verb* includes, including, included If you include something you put it with other things and make it part of the set or group. If you include someone, you let them join a group.

increase *verb* increases, increasing, increased When an amount increases, it gets bigger.

index *noun* indexes a list at the back of a book, which tells you what things are in the book and where to find them

individual *adjective* for just one person *You can have group lessons or individual lessons.*

infant *noun* infants a very young child

influence *verb* influences, influencing, influenced to change the way that someone thinks or behaves

informal *adjective* Informal language is language that you use when you are talking to friends.

information *noun* facts about something *We're collecting information about rainforests.*

ingredient *noun* ingredients Ingredients are the things that you mix together when you are cooking something.

injection *noun* injections When you have an injection, a doctor puts a needle into your arm to put medicine into your body.

injure *verb* injures, injuring, injured to hurt someone

ink *noun* inks the coloured liquid inside a pen, which comes out onto the paper when you write

inn *noun* inns a small hotel

innocent *adjective* If you are innocent, you have not done anything wrong.

insect *noun* insects An insect is a small creature with six legs. Flies, ants,

A B C D E F G H **I** J K L M N O P Q R S T U V W X Y Z

butterflies, and ladybirds are all different types of insect.

insert *verb* inserts, inserting, inserted
1 When you insert something, you put it into a hole or a slot. *He inserted a coin into the slot.* **2** (*in ICT*) When you insert something into a computer document, you add it.

inside *adverb & preposition* in something *Come inside, it's cold. It is inside the box.*

insist *verb* insists, insisting, insisted
If you insist on something, you say very firmly that you want to do it.

inspect *verb* inspects, inspecting, inspected to look at something very carefully to check that it is all right

instant *adjective* **1** Something that is instant happens immediately. **2** Instant food is food that you can make very quickly.

instead *adverb* in place of something else *They gave us water instead of lemonade.*

instrument *noun* instruments
something that you use for playing music

insult *verb* insults, insulting, insulted
to upset someone by saying rude or nasty things to them

intelligent *adjective* clever and able to learn things quickly

intend *verb* intends, intending, intended to plan to do something

intentional *adjective* done on purpose

interactive *adjective* (*in ICT*) An interactive computer program is one in which you can change and control things.

interest *verb* interests, interesting, interested If something interests you, you think it is exciting and you want to see it or learn about it. **interesting** *adjective* If something is interesting, you think it is exciting and want to see it or learn about it.

interfere *verb* interferes, interfering, interfered to get involved with something that has nothing to do with you

international *adjective* involving people from different countries

Internet *noun* a system that allows computers all over the world to get information and send messages to each other

interrupt *verb* interrupts, interrupting, interrupted to disturb somone while they are talking or working, and make them stop

interval *noun* intervals a short break in the middle of a play or concert

interview *verb* interviews, interviewing, interviewed to ask someone questions to find out what they are like, or what they think, or what they know

into *preposition* in *He threw a stone into the water.*

introduce *verb* introduces, introducing, introduced to bring people together and let them meet each other

Salim and Sarah kindly introduced me to the professor.

introduction *noun* introductions a short part at the beginning of a book or piece of music

invent *verb* invents, inventing, invented If you invent something new, you are the first person to make it or think of it.

investigate *verb* investigates, investigating, investigated to try to find out about something

invisible *adjective* If something is invisible, no one can see it.

invite *verb* invites, inviting, invited to ask someone to come to your house or to go somewhere with you

iron *noun* irons **1** a type of strong, heavy metal **2** An iron is an object that you use for making clothes smooth and flat. It has a flat piece of metal with a handle, and you heat it before you use it.

irritate *verb* irritates, irritating, irritated to make someone feel annoyed

Islam *noun* the religion that Muslims follow

island *noun* islands a piece of land with water all round it

it *pronoun* You use **it** when you're talking about something that has already been mentioned.

itch *verb* itches, itching, itched When your skin itches, it is uncomfortable and feels as if you need to scratch it. **itchy** *adjective* If your skin is itchy, it is uncomfortable and feels as if you need to scratch it.

item *noun* items one thing in a list or group of things

its *determiner* You use **its** when you're talking about something that belongs to something that has already been mentioned. *The horse threw back its head.*

it's **1** it is *It's raining.* **2** it has *It's been raining.*

jacket *noun* jackets a short coat

jagged *adjective* Something that is jagged has a sharp, uneven edge. *We climbed over the jagged rocks.*

jail *noun* jails a prison

jam *noun* jams **1** a thick, sweet, sticky food that is made by cooking fruit and sugar together **2** If there is a traffic jam, there are too many cars on the road and they cannot move forward.

jam *verb* jams, jamming, jammed When something jams, it gets stuck and you cannot move it.

January *noun* the first month of the year

jar *noun* jars a glass container that food is kept in

jaw *noun* jaws Your jaws are the bones that hold your teeth in place. You move your lower jaw to open your mouth.

jealous *adjective* If you are jealous of someone, you are unhappy because they have something that you would like, or they can do something better than you can.

jeans *noun* trousers that are made of strong cotton cloth

jelly *noun* jellies a sweet food made from fruit and sugar that shakes when you move it

jellyfish *noun* jellyfish A jellyfish is a sea animal that has a soft, clear body. Some types of jellyfish can sting you.

jerk *verb* jerks, jerking, jerked to move suddenly and roughly

jet *noun* jets 1 A jet of water is a thin stream that comes out of a small hole very quickly. 2 a fast aeroplane

jewel *noun* jewels a beautiful and valuable stone

jewellery *noun* jewels or ornaments that you wear, such as necklaces, bracelets, earrings, and rings

Jewish *adjective* Someone who is Jewish follows the religion of Judaism.

jigsaw puzzle *noun* jigsaw puzzles a set of small pieces of cardboard or wood that fit together to make a picture

job *noun* jobs 1 the work that someone does to earn money 2 something useful that you have to do

jog *verb* jogs, jogging, jogged 1 to run slowly 2 to knock or bump something

join *verb* joins, joining, joined 1 When you join things together, you fasten or tie them together. 2 to become a member of a club or group

joint *noun* joints 1 Your joints are the parts of your arms and legs that you can bend and turn. Your ankles, elbows, and hips are all joints. 2 a large piece of meat

joke *noun* jokes something you say or do to make people laugh

joke *verb* jokes, joking, joked to say things to make people laugh

jolt *verb* jolts, jolting, jolted 1 to move with sudden and rough movements 2 to knock or bump something

journal *noun* journals a diary in which someone writes about what they do each day

journalist *noun* journalists someone who writes about the news in a newspaper

journey *noun* journeys When you go on a journey, you travel somewhere.

joy *noun* a feeling of great happiness

Judaism *noun* the religion that Jewish people follow

judge *verb* judges, judging, judged to say how good or bad something is

jug *noun* jugs a container with a handle that you use for pouring out water and other liquids

juggle *verb* juggles, juggling, juggled to keep throwing several balls or other things into the air and catching them again quickly

juice *noun* juices the liquid that is in fruit and vegetables

July *noun* the seventh month of the year

jump *verb* jumps, jumping, jumped to push yourself up into the air

jumper *noun* jumpers a warm piece of clothing with long sleeves which you wear on the top half of your body

June *noun* the sixth month of the year

jungle *noun* jungles a thick forest in a hot country

junior *adjective* for young children

junk *noun* useless things that people do not want any more

just *adverb* 1 exactly *This game is just what I wanted.* 2 hardly *I only just caught the bus.* 3 recently *She has just left.* 4 only *I'll just brush my hair and then we can go.*

justice *noun* fair treatment for everyone

Kk

kangaroo *noun* kangaroos A kangaroo is an Australian animal that jumps along on its strong back legs. Female kangaroos have pouches in which they carry their babies.

keen *adjective* keener, keenest 1 If you are keen on something, you like it. 2 If you are keen to do something, you want to do it.

keep *verb* keeps, keeping, kept 1 If you keep something, you have it for yourself and do not get rid of it or give it to anyone else. 2 When you keep something in a certain way, you make it stay that way. *I like to keep my hair short in the summer.* 3 If you keep doing something, you go on doing it.

kennel *noun* kennels a little hut for a dog to sleep in

kerb *noun* kerbs the edge of a pavement, where you step down to go onto the road

ketchup *noun* a type of thick, cold tomato sauce

kettle *noun* kettles a container that you boil water in

key *noun* keys 1 a piece of metal that is shaped so that it fits into a lock 2 The keys on a piano or computer keyboard are the parts that you press to make it work.

keyboard *noun* keyboards The keyboard on a piano or computer is the set of keys that you press to make it work.

kick *verb* kicks, kicking, kicked to hit something with your foot

kid *noun* kids 1 a child 2 a young goat

kidnap *verb* kidnaps, kidnapping, kidnapped to take someone away and say that you will only let them go if another person pays you money

kill *verb* kills, killing, killed to make a person or animal die

kilogram *noun* kilograms We can measure weight in kilograms. There are 1000 grams in one kilogram. A kilogram is also called a **kilo**.

kilometre *noun* kilometres We can measure distance in kilometres. There are 1000 metres in one kilometre.

kilt *noun* kilts A kilt is a kind of skirt. In Scotland, men sometimes wear kilts as part of their traditional costume.

kind *noun* kinds a type *A terrier is a kind of dog.*

kind *adjective* kinder, kindest friendly and nice to people *It was very kind of you to help us.*

king *noun* kings a man who rules a country

kingdom *noun* kingdoms a land that is ruled by a king or queen

kiss *verb* kisses, kissing, kissed to touch someone with your lips because you like them or love them

kit *noun* kits **1** the clothes and other things that you need to do a sport **2** a set of parts that you fit together to make something

kitchen *noun* kitchens the room in a house in which people prepare and cook food

kite *noun* kites A kite is a light frame covered in cloth or paper. You hold a kite at the end of a long string and make it fly in the air.

kitten *noun* kittens a young cat

kiwi fruit *noun* kiwi fruits a fruit with a brown, hairy skin and green flesh

knee *noun* knees the part in the middle of your leg, where your leg can bend

kneel *verb* kneels, kneeling, kneeled to go down onto your knees

knife *noun* knives a tool with a long, sharp edge that you use for cutting things

knight *noun* knights a man who wore armour and rode into battle on a horse, in the past

knit *verb* knits, knitting, knitted to make clothes out of wool by twisting the wool over a pair of long needles or using a machine

a b c d e f g h i j **k** l m n o p q r s t u v w x y z

A
B
C
D
E
F
G
H
I
J
K
L
M
N
O
P
Q
R
S
T
U
V
W
X
Y
Z

knob *noun* knobs **1** a round handle on a door or drawer **2** a round button that you turn to make a machine work

knock *verb* knocks, knocking, knocked to bang or hit something

knot *noun* knots the twisted part where pieces of string or cloth have been tied together

know *verb* knows, knowing, knew, known **1** If you know something, you have learned it and have it in your mind. **2** If you know someone, you have met them before and you recognize them.

kn- in this word sounds like **n-**

knowledge *noun* all the things that you know and understand

knuckle *noun* knuckles Your knuckles are the parts where your fingers bend.

koala *noun* koalas a furry Australian animal that lives in trees and looks like a small bear

Koran *noun* the holy book of the religion of Islam

Ll

label *noun* labels a piece of paper or cloth that is put on something to show what it is or tell you something about it

laboratory *noun* laboratories a room in which people do experiments for science

lace *noun* laces **1** Lace is a type of thin, pretty material with a pattern of holes in it. **2** Laces are pieces of string that you use to tie up your shoes.

ladder *noun* ladders A ladder is a tall frame that you can climb up. It has two long poles with short bars between them, which you climb up like steps.

lady *noun* ladies **1** a polite name for a woman **2** a title that is given to some important women

ladybird *noun* ladybirds a red or yellow insect with black spots on its back

lake *noun* lakes a large area of fresh water with land all around it

lamb *noun* lambs a young sheep

lamp *noun* lamps A lamp is a light, especially one that you can hold or move around. The big lights in a street are called **street lamps**.

land *noun* lands **1** Land is the dry part of the earth where there is no water. **2** A land is a country.

land *verb* lands, landing, landed to arrive on land again after being in the air *What time will our plane land?*

lane *noun* lanes **1** a narrow road **2** a strip of road that one line of traffic can drive along

language *noun* languages the words that you use when you speak or write

lantern *noun* lanterns a candle inside a container

lap *noun* laps the flat part of your legs when you are sitting down

laptop *noun* laptops a small computer that you can carry around with you and hold on your knees when you are sitting down

large *adjective* larger, largest big

larva *noun* larvae an animal that looks like a small worm and which will become an insect

last *adjective* The last thing is the one that comes after all the others.

last *verb* lasts, lasting, lasted If something lasts for a certain time, it goes on for that amount of time. *The film lasted two hours.*

late *adjective* later, latest **1** If you are late, you arrive after the time when people are expecting you. *The bus was ten minutes late.* **2** When it is late in the day, it is near the middle or end of the day, not the morning. *Hurry up, it's getting late.*

lately *adverb* not very long ago

laugh *verb* laughs, laughing, laughed to make sounds that show that you are happy or think something is funny

launch *verb* launches, launching, launched to send a rocket or spaceship into space

lava *noun* very hot, liquid rock that comes out of a volcano

law *noun* laws Laws are all the rules that everyone in a country must obey.

lawn *noun* lawns a piece of ground in a garden that is covered with short grass

lawyer *noun* lawyers a person who has studied the law and who talks for people in a court of law

lay *verb* lays, laying, laid **1** to put something somewhere **2** When you lay a table, you put knives and forks on it so that it is ready for a meal. **3** When a bird lays an egg, it produces one.

layer *noun* layers a covering of something on top of something else

lazy *adjective* lazier, laziest Someone who is lazy does not want to work.

lead *verb* leads, leading, led (rhymes with *seed*) **1** to go in front of people and take them somewhere *He led us to the secret cave.* **2** to be in charge of people and tell them what to do **3** If you are leading in a game or competition, you are winning.

lead *noun* leads (rhymes with *seed*) **1** a long strap that you fasten to a dog's collar so that you can keep hold of it and control it **2** If you are in the lead, you are winning in a race or competition.

a
b
c
d
e
f
g
h
i
j
k
l
m
n
o
p
q
r
s
t
u
v
w
x
y
z

lead *noun* (rhymes with *bed*) a type of heavy, grey metal

leaf *noun* **leaves** The leaves on a plant are the green parts that grow at the ends of the stems and branches.

leaflet *noun* **leaflets** a piece of paper that gives you information about something

leak *verb* **leaks, leaking, leaked** If something is leaking, it has a hole or crack in it and liquid can get through.

lean *verb* **leans, leaning, leaned, leant** **1** If you lean forwards or backwards, you bend your body that way. **2** When you lean against something, you rest against it.

leap *verb* **leaps, leaping, leaped, leapt** to jump

learn *verb* **learns, learning, learned, learnt** **1** When you learn about something, you find out about it. **2** When you learn to do something, you find out how to do it.

least *adverb* less than all the others *My mum wanted me to buy the least expensive trainers.*

leather *noun* Leather is a strong material that is made from the skins of animals. Shoes and bags are often made of leather.

leave *verb* **leaves, leaving, left** **1** to go away from a place *I leave home every morning at eight o'clock.* **2** When you leave something in a place, you let it stay there and do not take it away. *I'm sorry, I've left my homework at home.*

ledge *noun* **ledges** a narrow shelf that sticks out from a wall

left *adjective & adverb* The left side of something is the side that is opposite the right side. Most people write with their right hand, not their left hand. *She had a letter in her left hand. Turn left at the traffic lights.*

leg *noun* **legs** **1** Your legs are the parts of your body between your hips and your feet. **2** The legs on a table or chair are the parts that it stands on.

legend *noun* **legends** an old story that has been handed down from the past

lemon *noun* **lemons** a yellow fruit with a very sour taste

lemonade *noun* a fizzy drink made from lemons, sugar, and water

lend *verb* **lends, lending, lent** to let someone use something for a short time

length *noun* how long something is

lens *noun* **lenses** A lens is a curved piece of glass or plastic that makes things look bigger or smaller when you look through it. Glasses and telescopes all have lenses.

less *adjective & adverb* smaller in amount or not as much *Make less noise. It is less important.*

lesson *noun* **lessons** **1** a time when someone is teaching you **2** something that you have to learn

let *verb* lets, letting, let to allow someone to do something *Samir let me use his phone.*

letter *noun* letters **1** one of the signs that we use for writing words, such as *a*, *b*, or *c* **2** a message that you write down and send to someone

lettuce *noun* lettuces a vegetable with green leaves that you eat in salads

level *adjective* **1** flat and smooth **2** If you are level with someone, you are walking or running next to them. **3** If people are level in a game or competition, they have the same number of points.

level *noun* levels If something is at a different level, it is higher or lower.

lever *noun* levers a bar that you pull down to make a machine work

liar *noun* liars someone who tells lies

library *noun* libraries a building or room where a lot of books are kept for people to use or borrow

lick *verb* licks, licking, licked to move your tongue over something

lid *noun* lids a cover on the top of a box or jar

lie *verb* lies, lying, lied to say something that you know is not true

lie *noun* lies something you say that you know is not true

lie *verb* lies, lying, lay, lain **1** When you lie down, you rest with your body spread out on the ground or on a bed. **2** When something lies somewhere, it is there. *Thick snow lay on the ground.*

life *noun* lives Your life is the time when you are alive.

lifeboat *noun* lifeboats a boat that goes out to sea in bad weather to rescue people

lift *verb* lifts, lifting, lifted to pick something up or move it upwards

lift *noun* lifts **1** a machine that takes people up and down inside a building **2** If someone gives you a lift, they take you somewhere in their car.

light *noun* lights **1** brightness that comes from the sun, the stars, fires, and lamps **2** a lamp, bulb, or torch that gives out light

light *adjective* lighter, lightest **1** not heavy **2** A place that is light is not dark, but has plenty of light in it. **3** A light colour is pale and not very bright. *She was wearing a light blue top.*

light *verb* lights, lighting, lit **1** to put light in something so that you can see **2** To light a fire means to make it burn.

lighthouse *noun* lighthouses a tower with a bright light that warns ships about rocks or other dangers

lightning *noun* a bright flash of light that you see in the sky when there is a storm

like *verb* likes, liking, liked to think that something or someone is nice

like *preposition* If one thing is like another, it is similar to it. *This tastes like roast lamb.*

likely *adjective* **likelier**, **likeliest** If something is likely to happen, it will probably happen.

limit *noun* **limits** an amount or a point which people must not go past

limp *verb* **limps**, **limping**, **limped** to walk with uneven steps because you have hurt one of your legs or feet

line *noun* **lines** **1** a long mark like this _____ **2** a row of people or things **3** A railway line is the two metal rails a train moves along. **4** A line of writing is the words that are written next to each other on a page. *I don't know the next line of the poem.*

link *verb* **links**, **linking**, **linked** To link two things means to join them together. *The Channel Tunnel links Britain to France.*

lion *noun* **lions** A lion is a big, light brown wild cat that lives in Africa and India. A female lion is called a **lioness**.

lip *noun* **lips** Your lips are the parts round the edges of your mouth.

liquid *noun* **liquids** any substance that is like water, and is not a solid or a gas

list *noun* **lists** a number of words or names that are written down one after the other

listen *verb* **listens**, **listening**, **listened** to pay attention so that you can hear something

literacy *noun* **1** Literacy is being able to read and write. **2** the subject in which you study reading and writing

literature *noun* stories, plays, and poetry

litre *noun* **litres** We can measure liquids in litres.

litter *noun* rubbish that people have dropped or left lying about

little *adjective* **1** not very big **2** If you have little of something, you do not have very much. *I've got very little money left as I spent so much on sweets at lunch time.*

live *verb* **lives**, **living**, **lived** **1** to be alive **2** If you live somewhere, that is where your home is.

live *adjective* (rhymes with *dive*) **1** A live animal is alive. **2** A live television programme is not recorded, but is shown as it is happening.

lively *adjective* **livelier**, **liveliest** Someone who is lively has a lot of energy and enjoys having fun.

living *noun* When you earn a living, you earn enough money to live.

living room *noun* **living rooms** the room in a house with comfortable chairs, where people sit and talk or watch television

lizard *noun* **lizards** A lizard is an animal with skin like a snake and four legs. Lizards are reptiles and live in warm countries.

load *noun* **loads** an amount of things that someone is carrying *The lorry brought another load of sand.*

load *verb* **loads, loading, loaded** **1** to put things into a car or lorry *Load the suitcases into the car.* **2** to put bullets in a gun **3** to put a program onto a computer so that you can use it

loaf *noun* **loaves** A loaf of bread is a large piece of bread that you cut into slices to eat.

local *adjective* near where you live

lock *noun* **locks** the part on a door, gate, or window that you can open and shut with a key

lock *verb* **locks, locking, locked** to shut something and fasten it with a key

loft *noun* **lofts** a room in the roof of a house, where you can store things

log *noun* **logs** A log is a part of a tree that has been chopped down. You can burn logs on a fire.

log *verb* **logs, logging, logged** (*in ICT*) When you log in to a computer, you switch it on so that you can use it. When you log out, you shut it down and switch it off.

lolly *noun* **lollies** a sweet on the end of a stick

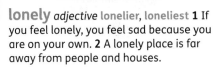

lonely *adjective* **lonelier, loneliest** **1** If you feel lonely, you feel sad because you are on your own. **2** A lonely place is far away from people and houses.

long *adjective* **longer, longest** **1** Something that is long measures a lot from one end to the other **2** Something that is long takes a lot of time.

long *verb* **longs, longing, longed** If you long for something, you want it a lot.

look *verb* **looks, looking, looked** **1** to point your eyes at something so that you can see it *Hey! Look at me!* **2** The way something looks is the way it seems. *That dog doesn't look very friendly.* **3** When you look for something, you try to find it. **4** When you look after someone, you take care of them. **5** When you look forward to something, you feel excited that it is going to happen.

loop *noun* **loops** a ring made in a piece of string or rope

loose *adjective* **looser, loosest** **1** not fixed firmly in place *I've got a loose tooth.* **2** Loose clothes do not fit tightly. **3** If a wild animal is loose, it has escaped and is free.

lord *noun* **lords** a title that is given to some important men

lorry *noun* **lorries** a big truck that is used for carrying heavy things by road

lose *verb* **loses, losing, lost** **1** When you lose something, you do not have it and do not know where it is. **2** When you lose a game, someone else wins.

lost *adjective* If you are lost, you do not know where you are or where you should go. *Don't get lost in the woods!*

lot *noun* **lots** A lot means a large number or a large amount. *I've got lots of friends.*

lottery *noun* **lotteries** a competition in which people buy tickets or choose numbers, and win a prize if their tickets or numbers are picked

loud *adjective* louder, loudest Something that is loud makes a lot of noise.
loudly *adverb* If you do or say something loudly, you do it or say it so that it makes a lot of noise.

lounge *noun* lounges a room with comfortable chairs in it, where people can sit and talk or watch television

love *noun* the strong feeling you have when you like someone very much
love *verb* loves, loving, loved to like someone or something very much

lovely *adjective* lovelier, loveliest beautiful or very nice

low *adjective* lower, lowest 1 not high 2 A low price is a small price. 3 A low voice or sound is deep.

loyal *adjective* If you are loyal to someone, you always help them and support them.

luck *noun* Luck is when something happens by chance, without anyone planning it.

lucky *adjective* luckier, luckiest If you are lucky, you have good luck.

luggage *noun* bags and suitcases that you take with you on a journey

lump *noun* lumps 1 a piece of something 2 a bump on your skin that you get when you have knocked it

lunar *adjective* Lunar means to do with the moon *Have you ever seen a lunar eclipse?*

lunch *noun* lunches a meal that you eat in the middle of the day

lung *noun* lungs Your lungs are the parts inside your chest that you use for breathing.

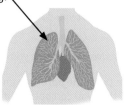

luxury *noun* luxuries something expensive that you like but do not really need

Mm

machine *noun* machines something that has an engine and moving parts, and can do a job or make things

mad *adjective* madder, maddest 1 Someone who is mad is ill in their mind. 2 If you are mad about something, you like it a lot. 3 very angry

magazine *noun* magazines a thin book that is made and sold every week or month with different stories and pictures in it

magic *noun* In stories, magic is the power that some people have to make

impossible and wonderful things happen.
magical *adjective* having the power to make impossible and wonderful things happen

magician *noun* **magicians 1** a person who does magic tricks to entertain people **2** a person in stories who has the power to use magic

magnet *noun* **magnets** a piece of metal that attracts pieces of iron or steel towards it **magnetic** *adjective* If something is magnetic, it attracts pieces of iron or steel towards it.

magnificent *adjective* very good or beautiful

magnify *verb* **magnifies, magnifying, magnified** to make something look bigger

mail *noun* letters, cards, and parcels that are sent through the post and delivered to people's houses

main *adjective* The main thing is the biggest or most important one. *You shouldn't cycle on the main road.*

make *verb* **makes, making, made 1** to create something *Please don't make too much mess.* **2** To make something happen means to cause it to happen. *The horrible smell made me feel sick.* **3** If you make someone do something, you force them to do it. **4** If you make something up, you invent it and it is not true.

male *adjective* A male person or animal can become a father.

mammal *noun* **mammals** A mammal is an animal that gives birth to live babies and feeds its young with its own milk. Cats, dogs, whales, lions, and people are all mammals.

man *noun* **men** a grown-up male person

manage *verb* **manages, managing, managed 1** If you manage to do something difficult, you do it after trying very hard. **2** to be in charge of a shop or business

mango *noun* **mangoes** a fruit with sweet, yellow flesh, which grows in hot countries

manner *noun* The manner in which you do something is the way you do it.

manners *noun* Your manners are the ways in which you behave when you are talking to people or eating your food.

many *determiner & pronoun* a large number *Were there many people on the bus? Many think skiing is expensive.*

map *noun* **maps** a drawing of a town, a country, or the world

marathon *noun* **marathons** a running race which is about forty kilometres long

marble *noun* **marbles** **1** Marbles are small, glass balls that you use to play games with. **2** Marble is a type of smooth stone that is used for building or making statues.

March *noun* the third month of the year

march *verb* **marches, marching, marched** to walk with regular steps like a soldier

margarine *noun* a food that looks and tastes like butter, but is made from vegetable oils

margin *noun* **margins** an empty space on the side of a page, where there is no writing

mark *noun* **marks** **1** a dirty stain or spot on something **2** the number or letter that you get for a piece of work that shows how well you have done

mark *verb* **marks, marking, marked** to give a piece of work a number or letter to show how good it is

market *noun* **markets** a group of stalls where people sell food and other things

marmalade *noun* jam made from oranges or lemons

marry *verb* **marries, marrying, married** to become someone's husband or wife

marsh *noun* **marshes** a piece of very wet, soft ground

marvellous *adjective* wonderful

mask *noun* **masks** something that you wear over your face to hide it or protect it

massive *adjective* very big

mat *noun* **mats** **1** a small carpet **2** something that you put under a hot plate on a table

match *noun* **matches** **1** a small, thin stick that makes a flame when you rub it against something rough **2** a game that two people or teams play against each other

match *verb* **matches, matching, matched** Things that match are the same or go well together.

material *noun* **materials** **1** A material is something that you use to make things with. **2** Material is cloth.

mathematics, maths *noun* the subject in which you learn about numbers, measurement, and shapes, also sometimes called **numeracy**

matter *noun* **matters** **1** something that you need to talk about or deal with **2** When you ask someone what the matter is, you are asking what is wrong.

matter *verb* **matters, mattering, mattered** to be important *It doesn't matter if you are a bit late.*

mattress *noun* **mattresses** the soft part of a bed that you lie on

May *noun* the fifth month of the year

may *verb* **1** If you may do something, you are allowed to do it. *May I have a drink, please?* **2** If something may happen, it is possible that it will happen. *It may rain later.*

maybe *adverb* perhaps

mayor *noun* mayors A mayor is the person in charge of the council of a town or city. A woman who is a mayor can also be called a **mayoress**.

maze *noun* mazes a set of lines or paths that twist and turn so much that it is very easy to lose your way

me *pronoun* You use **me** to talk about yourself.

meadow *noun* meadows a field of grass and flowers

meal *noun* meals the food that you eat at breakfast, lunch, dinner, tea, or supper

mean *verb* means, meaning, meant When you say what a word means, you say what it describes or shows.

mean *adjective* meaner, meanest **1** not liking to share things **2** unkind

meaning *noun* meanings The meaning of a word is what it means.

meanwhile *adverb* during the time something else is happening *Ben went to phone the fire brigade. Meanwhile I made sure there was no one left in the building.*

measles *noun* an illness that gives you red spots all over your body

measure *verb* measures, measuring, measured to find out how big something is or how much there is

measurement *noun* measurements a number that you get when you measure something

meat *noun* the flesh from animals that we can eat

mechanical *adjective* Something that is mechanical has parts that move like a machine. *They used a mechanical digger to dig a deep ditch.*

medal *noun* medals a special piece of metal that is given to someone who has won a competition or done something very brave

medicine *noun* medicines a special liquid or tablet that you take when you are ill to make you better

medium *adjective* not very big and not very small, but in the middle

meet *verb* meets, meeting, met When people meet, they see each other and talk to each other.

meeting *noun* meetings When people have a meeting, they meet to talk about something.

a
b
c
d
e
f
g
h
i
j
k
l
m
n
o
p
q
r
s
t
u
v
w
x
y
z

melt *verb* melts, melting, melted When something melts, it becomes a liquid because it has become warm. *Ice melts as it warms up.*

member *noun* members someone who belongs to a club or group

memory *noun* memories **1** Your memory is your ability to remember things. *Have you got a good memory?* **2** something that you can remember **3** the part in a computer that stores information

mend *verb* mends, mending, mended When you mend something that is broken, you fix it or put it right so that you can use it again.

mental *adjective* happening in your mind

mention *verb* mentions, mentioning, mentioned to talk about something

menu *noun* menus **1** a list of the different kinds of food you can choose for your meal **2** *(in ICT)* a list that appears on a computer screen showing the different things you can ask the computer to do

mercy *noun* If you show mercy to someone, you are kind and do not punish them.

mermaid *noun* mermaids In stories, a mermaid is a sea creature that looks like a woman but has a fish's tail instead of legs.

merry *adjective* merrier, merriest cheerful and laughing

mess *noun* If something is a mess, it is very untidy. messy *adjective* very untidy

message *noun* messages words that you write down or record for someone when you cannot see them or speak to them yourself

metal *noun* metals Metal is a strong material. Gold, silver, iron, and tin are all types of metal.

meteor *noun* meteors A meteor is a piece of rock or metal that flies through space and burns up when it gets near the earth. A piece of rock or metal that falls to earth without burning up is called a **meteorite**.

meter *noun* meters a machine that measures how much of something has been used

method *noun* methods the way in which you do something

metre *noun* metres We can measure length in metres. There are 100 centimetres in a metre.

metric *adjective* The metric system of measurement uses units of 10 and 100. Millimetres, centimetres, and metres are all part of the metric system.

miaow *verb* miaows, miaowing, miaowed When a cat miaows, it makes a long, high sound.

microphone *noun* microphones something that you speak into when you want to record your voice or make it sound louder

microscope *noun* microscopes an instrument that makes tiny things look bigger

microwave *noun* microwaves an oven that cooks food very quickly by passing special radio waves through it

midday *noun* twelve o'clock in the middle of the day

middle *noun* middles **1** the part near the centre of something, not at the edges *There was a huge puddle in the middle of the playground.* **2** the part that is not near the beginning or end of something *The phone rang in the middle of the night.*

midnight *noun* twelve o'clock at night

mild *adjective* milder, mildest Mild weather is quite warm.

mile *noun* miles We can measure distance in miles. One mile is the same as about 1½ kilometres.

military *adjective* Military things are used by soldiers.

milk *noun* Milk is a white liquid that you can drink. All female mammals make milk to feed their babies.

millennium *noun* milleniums, millennia a period of 1000 years

millimetre *noun* millimetres We can measure length in millimetres. There are 1000 millimetres in one metre.

million *noun* millions the number 1,000,000

millionaire *noun* millionaires a very rich person who has more than a million pounds or dollars

mince *noun* meat that has been cut into very small pieces

mind *noun* minds Your mind is your ability to think, and all the thoughts and memories that you have.

mind *verb* minds, minding, minded If you do not mind about something, it does not upset or worry you.

mine *pronoun* You use **mine** when you want to say something belongs to you.

mine *noun* mines a place where people work to dig coal, metal, or stones out of the ground

mineral *noun* minerals Minerals are things such as salt that form naturally in the ground.

mint *noun* mints **1** a green plant that is added to food to give it flavour **2** a sweet that tastes of mint

minus *preposition & adjective (in mathematics)* **1** take away *Six minus two is four, 6−2 = 4.* **2** A minus number is less than 0. *The temperature outside was minus three.*

minute *noun* minutes We measure time in minutes. There are sixty seconds in one minute, and sixty minutes in one hour.

minute *adjective* (sounds like *my-newt*) very small

miracle *noun* miracles something wonderful that has happened, although it did not seem possible

mirror *noun* **mirrors** a piece of glass, in which you can see yourself

mischief *noun* If you get into mischief, you do silly or naughty things.

miserable *adjective* very unhappy

miss *verb* **misses, missing, missed** **1** If you miss something, you do not catch it or hit it. *I tried to hit the ball but I missed it.* **2** If you miss someone, you feel sad because they are not with you.

missile *noun* **missiles** a weapon which is thrown or fired through the air

missing *adjective* lost

mist *noun* When there is mist, there is a lot of cloud just above the ground, which makes it difficult to see.

mistake *noun* **mistakes** If you make a mistake, you do something wrong.

mistake *verb* **mistakes, mistaking, mistook, mistaken** If you mistake someone for another person, you think they are the other person.

mix *verb* **mixes, mixing, mixed** When you mix things together, you put them together and stir them.

mixture *noun* **mixtures** something that is made of different things mixed together

moan *verb* **moans, moaning, moaned** When you moan, you make a low sound because you are in pain. When you moan about something, you complain about it.

mobile *adjective* able to be moved or carried around easily

mobile *noun* **1** a decoration for hanging up so that its parts move in currents of air **2** a mobile phone

mobile phone *noun* **mobile phones** A mobile phone is a telephone that you can carry around with you. It is also called a **mobile**.

model *noun* **models** **1** a small copy of something **2** someone who shows new clothes to people by wearing them and walking around in them

modern *adjective* using new ideas, not old-fashioned ones

mole *noun* **moles** a small, furry animal that digs holes and tunnels under the ground

moment *noun* **moments** a very small amount of time

Monday *noun* **Mondays** the day after Sunday

money *noun* the coins and pieces of paper that we use to buy things

monitor *noun* **monitors** *(in ICT)* a computer screen

monkey *noun* **monkeys** A monkey is an animal with fur and a long tail. Monkeys are good at climbing trees.

monster *noun* **monsters** a large, fierce animal in stories

month *noun* **months** A month is a period of 28, 30, or 31 days. There are twelve months in a year.

mood *noun* moods Your mood is the way you feel, for example whether you are happy or sad.

moon *noun* The moon is the large, round thing that you see shining in the sky at night. The moon travels round the earth in space.

moonlight *noun* light from the moon

mop *noun* mops You use a mop for cleaning floors. It has a bundle of loose strings on the end of a long handle.

more *determiner & adverb* larger in number or amount *I have more tops than skirts. Please write more carefully.*

morning *noun* mornings the time from the beginning of the day until the middle of the day

mosque *noun* mosques a building where Muslims pray and worship

mosquito *noun* mosquitoes a small insect that bites people and animals

moss *noun* mosses a plant that forms soft lumps when it grows on the ground or on old walls

most *determiner & adverb* more than any other *Who got the most points? Which story did you like the most?*

moth *noun* moths an insect like a butterfly, that flies around at night

mother *noun* mothers your female parent

motor *noun* motors an engine that makes something move

motorbike, **motorcycle** *noun* motorbikes, motorcycles a large, heavy bicycle with an engine

motorway *noun* motorways a wide, straight road on which people can drive fast and travel a long way

mountain *noun* mountains a very high hill

mouse *noun* mice **1** a small furry animal with a long tail **2** *(in ICT)* A computer mouse is the part that you move about on your desk to choose things on the screen.

moustache *noun* moustaches hair that grows on a man's top lip

mouth *noun* mouths the part of your face that you can open and use for eating and speaking

move *verb* moves, moving, moved **1** to take something from one place and put it in another place **2** to go from one place to another **movement** *noun* when something goes from one place to another

movie *noun* movies a film that you watch on a screen at the cinema or on television

MP3 player *noun* MP3 players a small music player that plays music you have downloaded onto it from the Internet

much *determiner* a lot of *Hurry up! We haven't got much time!*

mud *noun* wet, sticky soil

a
b
c
d
e
f
g
h
i
j
k
l
m
n
o
p
q
r
s
t
u
v
w
x
y
z

muddle *noun* muddles If something is in a muddle, it is messy or untidy.

muffled *adjective* A muffled sound is not clear, and is hard to hear.

mug *noun* mugs a big cup

multiply *verb* multiplies, multiplying, multiplied *(in mathematics)* When you multiply a number, you make it a number of times bigger. *Multiply five by three.* $5 \times 3 = 15$.

mum, **mummy** *noun* mums, mummies your mother

mumble *verb* mumbles, mumbling, mumbled to speak without saying the words clearly

munch *verb* munches, munching, munched to chew something noisily *We munched our way through a whole packet of biscuits.*

murder *verb* murders, murdering, murdered to kill someone on purpose

murmur *verb* murmurs, murmuring, murmured to speak in a very soft, low voice

muscle *noun* muscles Your muscles are the strong parts of your body that you use to make your body move.

museum *noun* museums a place where things from the past are kept for people to go and see

mushroom *noun* mushrooms a small plant with a stem and a grey, round top that you can eat

music *noun* the nice sound that you make when you sing or play instruments

musical *adjective* A musical instrument is an instrument that you use to play music.

musician *noun* musicians a person who plays or composes music

Muslim *noun* Muslims someone who follows the religion of Islam

must *verb* If you must do something, you have to do it.

my *determiner* You use **my** when you are talking about something that belongs to you.

mystery *noun* mysteries If something is a mystery, it is strange and puzzling and you do not understand it. **mysterious** *adjective* strange and difficult to understand

myth *noun* myths a very old story, often one about gods and goddesses

Nn

nail *noun* **nails** **1** Your nails are the hard parts at the ends of your fingers and toes. **2** A nail is a small thin piece of metal with a sharp point at the end. You bang nails into wood with a hammer to hold pieces of wood together.

nail *verb* **nails, nailing, nailed** When you nail pieces of wood together, you join them together with nails.

name *noun* **names** Your name is what people call you.

name *verb* **names, naming, named** to give someone a name

narrow *adjective* **narrower, narrowest** not very wide

nasty *adjective* **nastier, nastiest** **1** horrible **2** mean or unkind

nation *noun* **nations** a country

natural *adjective* **1** made by nature, not by people or machines **2** normal
naturally *adverb* **1** If someone does something naturally, they do it as if they have been born with the ability to do it. *She's a naturally gifted musician.* **2** You use **naturally** if you are talking about doing something that is normal to you. *Naturally I hurried to investigate the noise.*

nature *noun* **1** everything in the world that was not made by people, for example mountains, animals, and plants **2** Your nature is the type of person that you are.

naughty *adjective* **naughtier, naughtiest** If you are naughty, you behave badly.

navy *noun* **navies** an army that fights at sea, in ships

near *adverb, preposition & adjective* **nearer, nearest** not far away *We live near the school.*

nearly *adverb* almost *It's nearly three o'clock.*

neat *adjective* **neater, neatest** clean and tidy

necessary *adjective* If something is necessary, it has to be done.

> Remember, one **c** and a double **s**.

neck *noun* **necks** the part of your body that joins your head to your shoulders

need *verb* **needs, needing, needed** **1** If you need something, you have to have it. **2** If you need to do something, you have to do it.

need *noun* **needs** **1** Your needs are the things that you need. **2** If someone is in need, they do not have enough money, food, or clothes.

needle *noun* **needles** **1** a thin, pointed piece of metal with a hole at one end that you use for sewing **2** A knitting needle is a long, thin stick that you use for knitting.

negative *adjective* **1** A negative sentence is one that has the word *not* or *no* in it. 'Rebecca is not very happy' is a negative sentence. **2** (in mathematics) A negative number is less than 0.

neighbour *noun* **neighbours** Your neighbours are the people who live near you.

nephew *noun* **nephews** the son of your brother or sister

nerve *noun* **nerves** The nerves in your body are the parts that carry messages to

a
b
c
d
e
f
g
h
i
j
k
l
m
n
o
p
q
r
s
t
u
v
w
x
y
z

and from your brain, so that your body can feel and move.

nervous *adjective* slightly afraid

nest *noun* **nests** a home that a bird or small animal makes for its babies

net *noun* **nets** **1** A net is a piece of material with small holes in it. You use a net for catching fish. **2** *(in ICT)* The net is the Internet.

netball *noun* a game in which two teams of players try to score goals by throwing a ball through a round net on a pole

nettle *noun* **nettles** a plant with leaves that can sting you if you touch them

never *adverb* not ever

new *adjective* **newer, newest** **1** Something that is new has just been made or bought and is not old. **2** different *We're moving to a new house.*

news *noun* The news is all the things that are happening in the world, which you can see on television or read about in newspapers.

newspaper *noun* **newspapers** a set of large printed sheets of paper that contain articles about things that are happening in the world

next *adjective* **1** The next thing is the one that is nearest to you. *My friend lives in the next street.* **2** The next thing is the one that comes after this one. *We're going on holiday next week.*

nice *adjective* **nicer, nicest** **1** pleasant or enjoyable **2** kind

nickname *noun* **nicknames** a friendly name that your family or friends call you

niece *noun* **nieces** the daughter of your brother or sister

night *noun* **nights** the time when it is dark

nightmare *noun* **nightmares** a very frightening dream

nil *noun* nothing, the number 0

nine *noun* **nines** the number 9

nineteen *noun* the number 19

ninety *noun* the number 90

no *interjection* You use **no** when you want to give a negative answer to a question.
no *determiner* **1** You use **no** to mean not any. *I have no balloons left.* **2** You use **no** to mean not. *I've asked that they come to the meeting no earlier than six o'clock.*

nobody *pronoun* no person *There's nobody here.*

nocturnal *adjective* Nocturnal animals move around and feed at night.

nod *verb* **nods, nodding, nodded** to move your head up and down to show that you agree with someone

noise *noun* **noises** a sound that you can hear, especially a loud or strange one **noisy** *adjective* If something is noisy, it makes a loud sound. If someone is noisy they make a lot of loud sound. **noisily** *adverb* with a lot of sound

none *pronoun* not any

non-fiction *noun* books that contain true information

nonsense *noun* something silly that does not mean anything

no one *pronoun* nobody

no one is two separate words

normal *adjective* ordinary and not different or surprising

north *noun* North is one of the directions in which you can face or travel. On a map, north is the direction towards the top of the page.

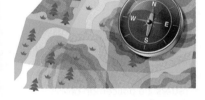

nose *noun* **noses** the part of your face that you use for breathing and smelling

nostril *noun* **nostrils** Your nostrils are the two holes at the end of your nose, which you breathe through.

not *adverb* You use **not** to talk about the opposite or absence of something. *She is not hungry. Granny is not at home.*

note *noun* **notes** **1** a short letter **2** A musical note is one sound in a piece of music. **3** A note is a piece of paper money.

nothing *noun* not anything *There was nothing in the box.*

notice *noun* **notices** **1** a written message that is put up on a wall for people to see **2** If you take no notice of something, you ignore it.
notice *verb* **notices, noticing, noticed** to see something

novel *noun* **novels** a book that tells a long story

November *noun* the eleventh month of the year

now *adverb* at this time *Do you want to go now?*

nowhere *adverb* not anywhere

nudge *verb* **nudges, nudging, nudged** to push someone with your elbow to make them notice something

nuisance *noun* **nuisances** If something is a nuisance, it is annoying.

numb *adjective* If a part of your body is numb, you cannot feel anything with it.

number *noun* **numbers** A number is a word or sign that tells you how many things there are. *1, 2, and 3 are numbers.*

nurse *noun* **nurses** someone who works in a hospital and looks after people who are ill or hurt

nursery *noun* **nurseries** **1** a place where very young children go to play and be looked after **2** a place where people grow plants to sell

nut *noun* **nuts** A nut is a hard fruit that grows on some trees and plants. You can eat some types of nuts.

Oo

oak *noun* oaks a large tree that produces nuts called acorns

oar *noun* oars a pole with a flat part at one end, which you use for rowing a boat

obey *verb* obeys, obeying, obeyed to do what someone tells you to do

object *noun* objects anything that you can see, touch, or hold

obvious *adjective* very easy to see or understand

occasion *noun* occasions an important event

occupy *verb* occupies, occupying, occupied to keep someone busy

occur *verb* occurs, occurring, occurred **1** to happen **2** When something occurs to you, you think of it.

ocean *noun* oceans a big sea

o'clock *adverb* a word you use to say what time it is

octagon *noun* octagons a shape with eight straight sides

October *noun* the tenth month of the year

octopus *noun* octopuses a sea creature with eight tentacles

odd *adjective* odder, oddest **1** strange **2** *(in mathematics)* An odd number cannot be divided by two.

of *preposition* **1** made from *He wore a crown of solid gold.* **2** belonging to *The handle of my bag is broken.*

off *preposition & adverb* **1** down from something or away from something *He fell off the wall.* **2** not switched on *The alarm is off.*

offend *verb* offends, offending, offended to hurt someone's feelings

offer *verb* offers, offering, offered **1** If you offer something to someone, you ask if they would like it. *She offered me a piece of cake.* **2** If you offer to do something, you say that you will do it. *I offered to lay the table.*

office *noun* offices a room with desks, where people work

officer *noun* officers **1** a person in the army, navy, or air force who is in charge of other people and gives them orders **2** a policeman or policewoman

official *adjective* decided or done by a person in charge

often *adverb* many times *We often go swimming on Saturdays.*

oil *noun* Oil is a thick, slippery liquid. You can use some types of oil as fuel, or to make machines work more smoothly. You use other types of oil in cooking.

OK, **okay** *adjective* all right

old *adjective* older, oldest **1** Someone who is old has lived for a long time. **2** Something that is old was made a long time ago.

old-fashioned *adjective* Something that is old-fashioned looks old and not modern.

on *preposition & adverb* **1** on top of *Put your books on your desk.* **2** on the subject of *I've got a new book on dinosaurs.* **3** working *Is the alarm on?*

once *adverb* **1** one time *I only missed school once last term.* **2** at one time *Once dinosaurs roamed the earth.*

one *noun* ones the number 1

onion *noun* onions a round, white vegetable that has a very strong smell and taste

online *adjective (in ICT)* When you work online on a computer, the computer is connected to the Internet.

only *adjective* An only child is a child who has no brothers or sisters.

only *adverb* not more than *It's only four o'clock.*

onto *preposition* on *I stuck a label onto the parcel.*

open *adjective* **1** When a door or window is open, it is not shut. **2** When a shop is open, you can go into it and buy things.

open *verb* opens, opening, opened When you open a door or window, you move it so that it is open.

opening *noun* openings a space or hole in something

operation *noun* operations When you have an operation, doctors mend or take out a part of your body to make you healthy again.

opinion *noun* opinions what you think about something

opponent *noun* opponents the person that you are fighting or playing a game against

opposite *adjective & preposition* **1** facing something *Salim is opposite Sarah.* **2** completely different *North is the opposite direction to south.*

opposite *noun* opposites The opposite of something is the thing that is completely different to it. *Big is the opposite of small.*

optician *noun* opticians someone who tests people's eyes and sells glasses to help them see better

orange *noun* oranges a round, juicy fruit with a thick, orange skin and sweet, juicy flesh

orange *adjective* Something that is orange is the colour that you make when you mix red and yellow together.

orbit *noun* **orbits** When something is in orbit, it is moving round the sun or a planet.

orchard *noun* **orchards** a field where a lot of fruit trees grow

orchestra *noun* **orchestras** a large group of people who play musical instruments together

ch- in this word sounds like **k-**

order *noun* **orders** **1** When you give someone an order, you tell them what they must do. **2** The order that things are in is the way that they are arranged, one after the other.

order *verb* **orders, ordering, ordered** **1** to tell someone that they must do something **2** to ask for something in a shop or restaurant

ordinary *adjective* normal and not different or special

organ *noun* **organs** **1** a musical instrument like a piano with large air pipes where the sound comes out **2** Your organs are the parts inside your body like your heart and brain, that each do a particular job.

organic *adjective* Food that is organic has been grown naturally.

organization *noun* **organizations** a large number of people who work together to do a job

organize *verb* **organizes, organizing, organized** to plan and arrange something

original *adjective* **1** An original part of something was there when it was first made. **2** Something that is original is new and has not been copied from something else.

ornament *noun* **ornaments** something that you put in a place to make it look pretty

orphan *noun* **orphans** a child whose mother and father are dead

other *adjective & pronoun* **1** The other thing is a different thing, not this one. *I can't find my other shoe.* **2** The other person is a different person. *I wonder where the others are.*

otherwise *adverb* or else *Hurry up otherwise we'll be late.*

ought *verb* If you ought to do something, you should do it.

our *determiner* belonging to us

ours *pronoun* You use **ours** when you want to say something belongs to you and at least one other person. *That table is ours.*

ourselves *pronoun* **Ourselves** means we or us and nobody else. *We have asked ourselves the question several times.*

out *adverb* **1** away from *I took the letter out of the envelope.* **2** not at home *We have been out for the day.*

outing *noun* **outings** a trip to a place

outline *noun* **outlines** The outline of something is its shape.

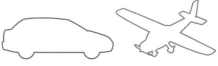

outside *preposition & adverb* not inside

A B C D E F G H I J K L M N O P Q R S T U V W X Y Z

oval *noun* a shape that looks like an egg

oven *noun* ovens the part of a cooker where you can bake or roast food

over *adverb & preposition* **1** across to a place *He walked over to me.* **2** more than *There were over 200 people there.* **3** about *They were fighting over some sweets.*

overcoat *noun* overcoats a thick, warm coat

overdue *adjective* If something is overdue, it is late.

overhead *adverb* above your head *We saw a plane flying overhead.*

overhear *verb* overhears, overhearing, overheard to hear what other people are saying

overtake *verb* overtakes, overtaking, overtook, overtaken to catch someone up and go past them

owe *verb* owes, owing, owed If you owe money to someone, you have to pay it to them.

owl *noun* owls a bird with large eyes that hunts at night for small animals

own *adjective* Something that is your own belongs to you.

own *verb* owns, owning, owned If you own something, it is yours and it belongs to you.

oxygen *noun* the gas in the air that everyone needs to breathe in order to stay alive

ozone *noun* Ozone is a type of oxygen. The **ozone layer** is a layer of ozone high above the earth which protects us from the dangerous rays of the sun.

Pp

pace *noun* paces a step forwards or backwards

pack *noun* packs **1** A pack of things is a number of things that you buy together. **2** A pack of cards is a set of cards that you use for playing games.
pack *verb* packs, packing, packed to put things into a box, bag, or suitcase

package *noun* packages a parcel

packaging *noun* the box or paper that something is wrapped in when you buy it

packet *noun* packets a small box or bag that you buy things in

pad *noun* pads A pad of paper is a set of sheets that are joined together.
pad *verb* pads, padding, padded If something is padded, it is thick and soft because it is filled with thick, soft material.

paddle *verb* paddles, paddling, paddled to walk about in shallow water

padlock *noun* padlocks a lock that you can put on a gate or bicycle

page *noun* pages a piece of paper that is part of a book

pain *noun* pains the feeling that you have in your body when something hurts

a
b
c
d
e
f
g
h
i
j
k
l
m
n
o
p
q
r
s
t
u
v
w
x
y
z

painful *adjective* If something is painful it hurts.

paint *noun* **paints** a coloured liquid that you use for making pictures or putting on walls

paint *verb* **paints, painting, painted** to use paints to make a picture or decorate a wall

painting *noun* **paintings** a picture that has been made using paint

pair *noun* **pairs** two things that belong together

palace *noun* **palaces** a very large house where a king or queen lives

pale *adjective* **paler, palest** **1** If you look pale, your face looks white because you are ill. **2** A pale colour is light and not dark. *She was wearing a pale green jumper.*

palm *noun* **palms** **1** the inside part of your hand **2** A palm tree is a tree that grows in tropical countries.

pan *noun* **pans** a metal pot that you use for cooking

pancake *noun* **pancakes** a flat cake that you make by mixing together flour, milk, and eggs and then frying the mixture in a pan

panda *noun* **pandas** an animal that looks like a large black and white bear

pane *noun* **panes** A pane of glass is a piece of glass in a window.

panic *verb* **panics, panicking, panicked** If you panic, you suddenly feel very frightened and cannot think what to do.

pantomime *noun* **pantomimes** a special play with jokes and songs, which people perform at Christmas

pants *noun* a piece of clothing that you wear over your bottom, underneath your other clothes

paper *noun* **papers** **1** Paper is the thin material that you use to write and draw on. **2** A paper is a newspaper.

parachute *noun* **parachutes** a large piece of cloth that opens over your head and stops you from falling too quickly when you jump out of an aeroplane

parade *noun* **parades** a long line of people marching along, while other people watch them

paragraph *noun* **paragraphs** A paragraph is one section in a long piece of writing. You begin each new paragraph on a new line.

parcel *noun* **parcels** something that is wrapped up in paper

parent *noun* **parents** Your parents are your mother and father.

park *noun* **parks** a large space with grass and trees where people can walk or play **park** *verb* **parks, parking, parked** to leave a car in a place until you need it again

parliament *noun* **parliaments** the people who make the laws of a country

parrot *noun* **parrots** a bird with brightly coloured feathers that lives in tropical forests

part *noun* **parts** One part of something is one bit of it.

particular *adjective* only this one and no other

partly *adverb* not completely

partner *noun* **partners** Your partner is the person you are doing something with, for example when you are working or dancing.

party *noun* **parties** a time when people get together to have fun and celebrate something

pass *verb* **passes, passing, passed** **1** to go past something **2** If you pass something to someone, you pick it up and give it to them. *Please could you pass me the salt?* **3** If you pass a test, you are successful.

passage *noun* **passages** a corridor

passenger *noun* **passengers** a person who is travelling in a bus, train, ship, or aeroplane

Passover *noun* a Jewish religious festival

passport *noun* **passports** A passport is a special book or piece of paper with your name and photograph on it. It shows who you are, and you take it with you when you go to another country.

password *noun* **passwords** a secret word that you use to go into a place or to use a computer

past *noun* the time that has already gone

past *preposition* **1** If you go past something, you go from one side of it to the other side. **2** If it is past a certain time, it is after that time. *We didn't get home until past midnight.*

pasta *noun* Pasta is a type of food made from flour and water. Spaghetti is a type of pasta.

paste *noun* something that is like a very thick, sticky liquid

paste *verb* **pastes, pasting, pasted** *(in ICT)* to add something into a computer document after you have copied it from another document

pastry *noun* a mixture of flour, fat, and water that you roll flat and use for making pies

pat *verb* **pats, patting, patted** to touch something gently with your hand

patch *noun* **patches** a small piece of material that you put over a hole in your clothes

path *noun* **paths** a narrow road that you can walk along but not drive along

patient *noun* **patients** someone who is ill and being looked after by a doctor

patient *adjective* If you are patient, you can wait without getting cross or bored.

pattern *noun* **patterns** a design with lines, shapes, and colours

a
b
c
d
e
f
g
h
i
j
k
l
m
n
o
p
q
r
s
t
u
v
w
x
y
z

pause *noun* **pauses** a short time when you stop what you are doing

pause *verb* **pauses, pausing, paused** to stop what you are doing for a short time

pavement *noun* **pavements** the path that people walk on along the side of a street

paw *noun* **paws** An animal's paws are its feet.

pay *verb* **pays, paying, paid** When you pay for something, you give someone money so that you can have it.

PE *noun* PE is a lesson at school in which you do sports and games. PE is short for **physical education**.

pea *noun* **peas** a small, round, green vegetable

peace *noun* **1** when there is no war **2** when there is no noise

peaceful *adjective* When a place is peaceful, there is no noise.

peach *noun* **peaches** a round, soft, juicy fruit with yellow flesh and a large stone in the middle

peacock *noun* **peacocks** a large bird with long, brightly coloured tail feathers

peak *noun* **peaks** **1** A mountain peak is the top of a mountain. **2** The peak on a cap is the part that sticks out in front.

peanut *noun* **peanuts** a small, round nut that grows in a pod in the ground

pear *noun* **pears** a sweet, juicy fruit that is narrow at the top and round at the bottom

pearl *noun* **pearls** (rhymes with *girl*) A pearl is a small, shiny, white ball that grows inside the shells of some oysters. People use pearls for making jewellery.

pebble *noun* **pebbles** a small, round stone

peculiar *adjective* strange

pedal *noun* **pedals** a part of a machine that you push with your foot to make it go

peel *noun* the skin of a fruit or vegetable
peel *verb* **peels, peeling, peeled** to take the skin off fruit or vegetables

peep *verb* **peeps, peeping, peeped** to look at something quickly

peg *noun* **pegs** **1** a small clip that you use for fixing washing onto a line **2** a piece of metal or wood that you can hang things on

pen *noun* **pens** something that you hold in your hand and use for writing with ink

pence *noun* **pennies**

pencil *noun* **pencils** something that you hold in your hand and use for writing or drawing

penguin *noun* penguins a large black and white bird that swims in the sea but cannot fly

penknife *noun* penknives a small knife that folds up so that you can carry it safely

penny *noun* pence a coin

pentagon *noun* pentagons a shape with five straight sides

people *noun* men, women, and children

pepper *noun* peppers **1** Pepper is a powder with a hot taste that you add to food. **2** A pepper is a green, yellow, orange, or red vegetable.

perch *noun* perches a place where a bird rests when it is not flying

percussion *noun* Percussion instruments are musical instruments that you play by banging, hitting, or shaking them. Drums, cymbals, and tambourines are percussion instruments.

perfect *adverb* Something that is perfect is so good that it cannot be any better.

perform *verb* performs, performing, performed to do something in front of people to entertain them

perfume *noun* perfumes a liquid with a nice smell that you put on your skin

perhaps *adverb* possibly

period *noun* periods a length of time

permanent *adjective* Something that is permanent will last for ever.

person *noun* people or persons a man, woman, or child

personal *adjective* Your personal things are the things that are to do with just you and no one else.

personality *noun* personalities Your personality is the type of person you are.

persuade *verb* persuades, persuading, persuaded If you persuade someone to do something, you make them agree to do it.

pester *verb* pesters, pestering, pestered to keep annoying someone until they do what you want them to do

pet *noun* pets an animal which you keep and look after

petal *noun* petals The petals on a flower are the coloured parts.

petrol *noun* a liquid that you put in cars to make them go

phone *noun* phones a telephone

phone *verb* phones, phoning, phoned to use a telephone to speak to someone

photo *noun* photos a photograph

photocopier *noun* photocopiers a machine which can make a copy of a piece of writing or a picture

photograph *noun* photographs a picture that you take with a camera

phrase *noun* phrases A phrase is a group of words which make sense, does not contain a verb and acts as one unit.

a
b
c
d
e
f
g
h
i
j
k
l
m
n
o
p
q
r
s
t
u
v
w
x
y
z

A B C D E F G H I J K L M N O **P** Q R S T U V W X Y Z

physical *adjective* Physical activities are activities that you do with your body, for example running and jumping.

piano *noun* pianos a large musical instrument which has white and black keys that you press with your fingers to make different musical notes

pick *verb* picks, picking, picked **1** to choose something **2** When you pick something up, you lift it up with your hand. **3** to take a flower or fruit off a plant

picnic *noun* picnics a meal of cold food that you eat outside

picture *noun* pictures **1** a painting, drawing, or photograph **2** When you go to the pictures, you go to a cinema to watch a film.

pie *noun* pies a type of food that has meat, vegetables, or fruit in the middle and pastry on the outside

piece *noun* pieces A piece of something is a bit of it.

pierce *verb* pierces, piercing, pierced to make a hole through something

pig *noun* pigs an animal with a large snout and a curly tail that is kept on farms for its meat

pigeon *noun* pigeons a grey bird that often lives in towns

pile *noun* piles a lot of things all on top of each other

pill *noun* pills a small tablet with medicine in, which you swallow when you are ill

pillar *noun* pillars a wooden or stone post that helps to hold up a building

pillow *noun* pillows a cushion that you rest your head on in bed

pilot *noun* pilots someone who flies an aeroplane

pin *noun* pins A pin is a thin piece of metal with a sharp point. You use pins to hold pieces of material together when you are sewing.

pinch *verb* pinches, pinching, pinched **1** to squeeze someone's skin between your thumb and finger so that it hurts **2** to steal something

pine *noun* pines a tree with leaves like needles that do not fall in winter

pineapple *noun* pineapples a large fruit with yellow flesh that grows in hot countries

pink *adjective* Something that is pink is very pale red.

pint *noun* pints We can measure liquids in pints. One pint is about half a litre.

pip *noun* pips a seed of a fruit such as an apple or orange

pipe *noun* pipes a hollow tube that gas or liquid can go along

pirate *noun* pirates someone who sails in a ship and attacks and robs other ships at sea

pitch *noun* pitches A sports pitch is a piece of ground that is marked out so that you can play a game on it.

pity *noun* **1** If you feel pity for someone, you feel sorry for them. **2** If something is a pity, it is a shame.

pizza *noun* **pizzas** a food made from a flat, bread-like mixture, with tomatoes, cheese, and other things on top

place *noun* **places** a building or area of land

place *verb* **places, placing, placed** to put something somewhere

plain *adjective* **plainer, plainest** ordinary, and not different or special

plain *noun* **plains** a large area of flat ground *You can see for miles over the plain.*

plait *verb* **plaits, plaiting, plaited** When you plait hair, you twist three pieces together by crossing them over and under each other.

plan *noun* **plans** 1 an idea about how to do something 2 a map of a building or a town

plan *verb* **plans, planning, planned** to decide what you are going to do and how you are going to do it

plane *noun* **planes** an aeroplane

planet *noun* **planets** A planet is a very large object in space that moves around a star or around our sun. The earth is a planet.

plant *noun* **plants** A plant is a living thing that grows in the soil. Trees, flowers, and vegetables are all plants.

plant *verb* **plants, planting, planted** to put something in the ground to grow

plaster *noun* **plasters** 1 a piece of sticky material that you put over a cut to keep it clean 2 Plaster is a soft mixture that goes hard when it dries. Plaster is put onto the walls of buildings. A different sort of plaster is put onto someone's arm or leg when they have broken a bone.

plastic *noun* a light, strong material that is made in factories and is used for making all kinds of things

plate *noun* **plates** a flat dish that you eat food from

platform *noun* **platforms** the place in a station where people wait beside the railway lines for a train to come

play *verb* **plays, playing, played** 1 to have fun 2 to use an instrument to make music *Can you play the piano?*

play *noun* **plays** a story which people act so that other people can watch

player *noun* **players** someone who takes part in a sport

playground *noun* **playgrounds** a place outside where children can play

pleasant *adjective* nice

please *verb* **pleases, pleasing, pleased** 1 to make someone happy 2 used when you want to ask for something politely *Please may I have another biscuit?*

pleasure *noun* the feeling that you have when you are happy and enjoying yourself

plenty *noun* If there is plenty of something, there is as much as you need.

plot *noun* **plots 1** a secret plan **2** the story of a novel, film, or play

plug *noun* **plugs 1** a round piece of plastic that you put into the hole in a bath or sink to stop the water from running out **2** the part of an electric machine or tool that you put into an electric socket to make it work

plum *noun* **plums** a juicy fruit with a stone in the middle

plumber *noun* **plumbers** a person whose job is to fit and mend water pipes and taps

plump *adjective* **plumper, plumpest** quite fat

plunge *verb* **plunges, plunging, plunged** If you plunge into water, you jump in.

plus *preposition* (in mathematics) add *Three plus three is six, 3 + 3 = 6.*

pocket *noun* **pockets** a part of a piece of clothing that is like a small bag that you can keep things in

poem *noun* **poems** a piece of writing that is written in lines and uses rhythms and rhymes in a clever way

poet *noun* **poets** someone who writes poems

poetry *noun* **poems** *Do you like reading poetry?*

point *noun* **points 1** a thin, sharp part on the end of something **2** a particular place or time **3** a mark that you score in a game

point *verb* **points, pointing, pointed 1** When you point at something, you show it to someone by holding your finger out towards it. **2** When you point a weapon at something, you aim the weapon towards it.

pointed *adjective* with a sharp point at one end

poison *noun* **poisons** something that will kill you or make you ill if you swallow it **poisonous** *adjective* If something is poisonous it will kill you or make you ill if you swallow it.

poke *verb* **pokes, poking, poked** to push something with your finger or with a stick

polar bear *noun* **polar bears** a very large, white bear that lives near the North Pole

pole *noun* **poles** a long stick

police *noun* The police are the people whose job is to catch criminals and make sure that people do not break the law.

polish *verb* **polishes, polishing, polished** to rub something to make it shine

polite *adjective* **politer, politest** Someone who is polite has good manners and is not rude to people. **politely** *adverb* If you do or say something politely you are not rude to people.

politician *noun* **politicians** a person who works in the government of a country

politics *noun* the work that the government of a country does

pollen *noun* Pollen is a yellow powder that you find inside flowers. Pollen is carried from one flower to another by the wind or by insects so that the flowers can produce seeds.

pollute *verb* polluting, polluting, polluted to make air or water dirty **pollution** *noun* when air or water is made dirty

polythene *noun* a type of plastic material that is used for making bags

pond *noun* ponds a small lake

pony *noun* ponies a small horse

ponytail *noun* ponytails If you wear your hair in a ponytail, you wear it tied in a long bunch at the back of your head.

pool *noun* pools a small area of water

poor *adjective* poorer, poorest
1 Someone who is poor does not have very much money. **2** A poor person is unlucky or unhappy. *You poor child!*

pop *verb* pops, popping, popped to burst with a loud bang

pop *noun* modern music that people dance to

popcorn *noun* a food that is made by heating grains of corn until they burst and become big and fluffy

popular *adjective* If something is popular, a lot of people like it.

population *noun* The population of a place is the number of people who live there.

porch *noun* porches a place in front of the door of a building where people can wait before they go in

pork *noun* meat from a pig

port *noun* ports a place on the coast where ships can come to the land to load or unload goods

portable *adjective* If something is portable, you can carry it or move it easily.

portion *noun* portions an amount of food that you give to one person

portrait *noun* portraits a painting or drawing of a person

position *noun* positions **1** the place where something is **2** the way that you are standing, sitting, or lying

possess *verb* possesses, possessing, possessed to own something

possible *adjective* If something is possible, it might happen, or it might be true. *It's possible that someone has stolen the money.* **possibly** *adverb* perhaps *Could we possibly leave for the park after lunch?* **possibility** *noun* something that might happen or might be true

post *noun* posts **1** a pole that is fixed in the ground **2** all the letters and parcels that are delivered to people's houses
post *verb* posts, posting, posted to send a letter or parcel to someone

a b c d e f g h i j k l m n o **p** q r s t u v w x y z

postcard *noun* **postcards** A postcard is a piece of card with a picture on one side. You write on the other side and send it to someone.

postcode *noun* **postcodes** letters and numbers that you put at the end of someone's address when you are sending them a letter

poster *noun* **posters** a large picture or notice that you put up on a wall

postman *noun* **postmen** A postman is a man who delivers letters and parcels to people's houses. A woman who does this is a **postwoman**.

post office *noun* **post offices** a place where you can go to buy stamps, and post letters and parcels

postpone *verb* **postpones, postponing, postponed** to decide to do something later

pot *noun* **pots** a round container that you can put or keep things in

potato *noun* **potatoes** a round white vegetable that you dig out of the ground

> Add **-es** for the plural.

pottery *noun* cups, plates, and other things that are made from clay

pounce *verb* **pounces, pouncing, pounced** to attack something by jumping on it suddenly

pound *noun* **pounds** **1** We can measure weight in pounds. One pound is about half a kilogram. **2** A pound is a unit of money. Pounds are used in Britain and some other countries.

pour *verb* **pours, pouring, poured** **1** to tip a liquid into a container **2** When a liquid is pouring out of something, it is coming out very quickly.

powder *noun* a substance like flour that is dry and made of lots of tiny bits

power *noun* **powers** **1** If you have power, you can do what you want, or make other people do what you want. **2** If you have special powers, you are able to do magic things. **3** Power is energy that makes machines work.

powerful *adjective* **1** Someone who is powerful has a lot of power over other people. **2** very strong

practical *adjective* A practical person is good at working with their hands and doing useful things.

practice *noun* when you do something again and again so that you will get better at it

practise *verb* **practises, practising, practised** to keep doing something over and over again so that you will get better at it

praise *verb* **praises, praising, praised** to tell someone that they have done well

pram *noun* **prams** a bed on wheels in which you can push a baby along

prawn *noun* **prawns** A prawn is a small sea creature with a shell. You can cook and eat prawns.

pray *verb* **prays, praying, prayed** to talk to a god

precious *adjective* worth a lot of money, or very special to someone

precise *adjective* exact and correct

predator *noun* **predators** an animal that hunts and kills other animals for food

predict *verb* **predicts, predicting, predicted** to say that something will happen in the future

prefer *verb* **prefers, preferring, preferred** to like one thing more than another *I don't like wearing skirts. I prefer to wear jeans.*

prehistoric *adjective* Prehistoric times were times long ago.

prepare *verb* **prepares, preparing, prepared** to get something ready

present *adjective* (prez-ent) **1** If you are present in a place, you are there. **2** The present time is the time that is happening now.

present *noun* (prez-ent) **presents** **1** something that you give to someone **2** The present is the time that is happening now.

present *verb* (pri-zent) **presents, presenting, presented 1** to give something to someone *The head presented the prizes to the winners.* **2** to introduce a show

president *noun* **presidents** someone who rules a country

press *verb* **presses, pressing, pressed** to push something with your finger

press *noun* The press is a general name for newspapers.

pressure *noun* **1** a force which pushes against something **2** If you put pressure on someone, you try to make them do something.

pretend *verb* **pretends, pretending, pretended** to say things or do things that are not really true

pretty *adjective* **prettier, prettiest 1** Something that is pretty is nice to look at **2** A pretty girl or woman has a beautiful face.

prevent *verb* **prevents, preventing, prevented** to stop something from happening

prey *noun* An animal's prey is the animal that it hunts and kills.

price *noun* **prices** the amount of money you have to pay for something

prick *verb* **pricks, pricking, pricked** When you prick something, you make a tiny hole in it with something sharp.

prickle *noun* **prickles** Prickles are sharp points on a plant. **prickly** *adjective* Something that is prickly has lots of sharp points. *He fell down the steep bank and landed in a prickly shrub.*

pride *noun* the feeling you have when you are proud

priest *noun* **priests** a Christian religious leader

prime minister *noun* **prime ministers** the leader of a country's government

prince *noun* **princes** the son of a king or queen

princess *noun* princesses **1** the daughter of a king or queen **2** the wife of a prince

print *verb* prints, printing, printed **1** to write words with letters that are not joined together **2** When a machine prints words or pictures, it puts them onto paper.

prison *noun* prisons a place where people are kept as a punishment

prisoner *noun* prisoners someone who is locked up in a place and not allowed to leave

private *adjective* only for some people, not for everyone

prize *noun* prizes something that you get if you win a game or competition

probably *adverb* You say that something will probably happen or is probably true when you think it is likely to happen or be true.

problem *noun* problems something that is difficult

process *noun* processes a series of actions that you do one after the other, and that take a long time

produce *verb* produces, producing, produced **1** to make something *Cows produce milk* **2** to bring something out of a box or bag

product *noun* products something that has been made so that it can be sold to people in shops

profit *noun* profits If you make a profit, you make money by selling something for more than you paid to buy it or make it.

program *noun* programs (*in ICT*) A computer program is a list of instructions that the computer follows.

programme *noun* programmes **1** a show on the radio or television **2** a small book that tells you what will happen at an event

progress *noun* When you make progress, you get better at doing something.

project *noun* projects a piece of work where you find out as much as you can about something interesting and write about it

promise *verb* promises, promising, promised to say that you will definitely do something

pronounce *verb* pronounces, pronouncing, pronounced The way you pronounce a word is the way you say it.

proof *noun* If there is proof that something happened, there is something that shows that it definitely happened.

prop *verb* props, propping, propped to lean something somewhere so that it does not fall over

propeller *noun* propellers a set of blades that spin round to make something move

A B C D E F G H I J K L M N O P Q R S T U V W X Y Z

proper *adjective* correct or right
properly *adverb* in the correct or right way

property *noun* **properties** If something is your property, it belongs to you.

prophet *noun* **prophets** a great religious teacher

protect *verb* **protects**, **protecting**, **protected** to keep someone safe and stop them being hurt

protein *noun* Protein is a substance that is found in some types of food, for example meat, eggs, and cheese. Your body needs protein to help you to grow.

protest *verb* **protests**, **protesting**, **protested** to say that you do not like something or do not agree with it

proud *adjective* **prouder**, **proudest** If you are proud of something, you are pleased with it and think that it is very good.

prove *verb* **proves**, **proving**, **proved** to show that something is definitely true

proverb *noun* **proverbs** a short, well-known saying which gives you advice about something

provide *verb* **provides**, **providing**, **provided** If you provide something for people, you give it to them.

pub *noun* **pubs** a place where people can go to have a drink and meet friends

public *adjective* Something that is public can be used by everyone.

publish *verb* **publishes**, **publishing**, **published** to prepare and sell a book

pudding *noun* **puddings** any sweet food which you eat after the main part of a meal

puddle *noun* **puddles** a small pool of water

pull *verb* **pulls**, **pulling**, **pulled** to get hold of something and move it towards you

pullover *noun* **pullovers** a jumper

pump *noun* **pumps** a machine that pushes air or water into something or out of something

pump *verb* **pumps**, **pumping**, **pumped** to force air or water into something or out of something

pumpkin *noun* **pumpkins** a very large, round orange vegetable

pun *noun* **puns** A pun is a joke that is funny because it uses words that sound the same, or words that have two different meanings. For example, *eggs are very eggs-pensive* is a pun.

punch *verb* **punches**, **punching**, **punched** to hit someone with your fist

punctuation *noun* Punctuation marks are used in sentences to make the meaning clear.

apostrophe	'
capital letter	A
colon	:
comma	,
dash	—
full stop	.
exclamation mark	!
ellipsis	…
bullet point	•
hyphen	-
inverted commas speech marks quotation marks	' ' or " "
semi-colon	;
question mark	?

puncture *noun* **punctures** a small hole in a tyre

punish *verb* **punishes**, **punishing**, **punished** to make someone suffer because they have done something wrong **punishment** *noun* when someone makes you suffer because you have done something wrong

pupil *noun* **pupils** **1** A pupil is a child who goes to school. **2** Your pupils are the black circles in the middle of your eyes.

puppet *noun* **puppets** a small doll that you can move by pulling on strings, or by putting it over your hand like a glove and then moving your hand

puppy *noun* **puppies** a young dog

pure *adjective* **purer**, **purest** one thing only, with nothing else mixed in

purple *adjective* Something that is purple is the colour that you make by mixing red and blue together.

purpose *noun* **on purpose** deliberately *I'm sorry, I didn't do it on purpose.*

purr *verb* **purrs**, **purring**, **purred** When a cat purrs, it makes a low, rumbling sound because it is happy.

purse *noun* **purses** a small bag that you carry money in

push *verb* **pushes**, **pushing**, **pushed** to use your hands to move something away from you

put *verb* **puts**, **putting**, **put** **1** to move something so that it is in a place **2** If you put something off, you decide to do it later instead of now.

puzzle *noun* **puzzles** a game in which you have to do something difficult or find the answer to a difficult question

puzzle *verb* **puzzles**, **puzzling**, **puzzled** If something puzzles you, it seems strange and you do not understand it.

pyjamas *noun* loose trousers and a top that you wear in bed

pyramid *noun* **pyramids** **1** a large, stone building that was made by the ancient Egyptians to bury a dead king or queen **2** a solid shape with a square base and four triangular sides that come together in a point at the top

Qq

quack *verb* quacks, quacking, quacked
When a duck quacks, it makes a loud sound.

quaint *adjective* quainter, quaintest
Something that is quaint is pretty and old-fashioned. *What a quaint little cottage!*

qualify *verb* qualifies, qualifying, qualified **1** to pass a test or exam so that you are allowed to do a job **2** to get enough points in a competition to go on to the next part of a competition

quality *noun* qualities how good or bad something is *You need good quality paper for model-making.*

quantity *noun* quantities an amount

quarrel *verb* quarrels, quarrelling, quarrelled When people quarrel, they argue with each other in an angry way.

quarter *noun* quarters One quarter of something is one of four equal parts that the thing is divided into. It can also be written as ¼.

quay *noun* quays (sounds like *key*) a place where ships can be loaded and unloaded

queen *noun* queens a woman who rules a country

query *noun* queries a question

question *noun* questions When you ask a question, you ask someone something because you want to know the answer.

questionnaire *noun* questionnaires a sheet of paper with a lot of questions on it to collect information from people

queue *verb* queues, queueing, queued to wait in a line

quick *adjective* quicker, quickest Something that is quick does not take very long. **quickly** *adverb* Something that is done quickly does not take very long.

quiet *adjective* quieter, quietest **1** If a place is quiet, there is no noise there. **2** not very loud **quietly** *adverb* Something that is done quietly is done with no or little noise.

quilt *noun* quilts a thick, warm cover for a bed

quit *verb* quits, quitting, quitted When you quit a file or program on a computer, you close it.

quite *adverb* **1** slightly, but not very *The film was quite good.* **2** completely *We haven't quite finished.*

quiz *noun* quizzes a game in which people try to answer a lot of questions

a b c d e f g h i j k l m n o p **q** r s t u v w x y z

Rr

rabbi *noun* a Jewish religious leader

rabbit *noun* **rabbits** A rabbit is a small furry animal with long ears. Rabbits live in holes in the ground and use their strong back legs to hop about.

race *verb* **races, racing, raced** When people race, they run or swim against each other to find out who is the fastest.

race *noun* **races** **1** a competition in which people run or swim against each other to find out who is the fastest **2** a group of people who come from the same part of the world and look the same because they have the same colour skin, the same type of hair, and so on

racist *noun* **racists** someone who treats other people unfairly because they have different colour skin or come from a different country

racket *noun* **rackets** **1** a bat that you use for hitting a ball in a game of tennis or badminton **2** If someone is making a racket, they are making a lot of loud noise.

radiator *noun* **radiators** a metal heater which hot water flows through to keep a room warm

radio *noun* **radios** a machine that picks up signals that are sent through the air and changes them into music or talking that you can listen to

radius *noun* **radii** how much a circle measures from the centre to the edge

raffle *noun* **raffles** A raffle is a competition in which people buy tickets with numbers on them. If their tickets are chosen, they win a prize.

raft *noun* **rafts** a flat boat made of logs joined together

rag *noun* **rags** a torn piece of cloth

rage *noun* **rages** a feeling of very strong anger

rail *noun* **rails** **1** a metal or wooden bar that is part of a fence **2** Rails are the long metal bars that trains travel on. **3** When you travel by rail, you travel in a train.

railings *noun* a fence made of a row of metal bars that stand upright next to each other

railway *noun* **railways** **1** A railway line is the long metal bars that trains travel on. **2** When you travel on the railway, you travel by train.

rain *noun* drops of water that fall from the sky

rain *verb* **rains, raining, rained** When it rains, drops of water fall from the sky.

rainbow *noun* **rainbows** a curved band of different colours you see in the sky when the sun shines through rain

rainforest *noun* **rainforests** a large forest in a tropical part of the world, where there is a lot of rain

raise *verb* **raises, raising, raised** **1** to lift something up so that it is higher **2** When you raise money, you collect it so that you can give it to a school or charity.

raisin *noun* raisins a dried grape that you use to make fruit cakes

Ramadan *noun* Ramadan is the ninth month of the Muslim year. During Ramadan, Muslims do not eat or drink anything from the time the sun comes up each morning until it sets in the evening.

ramp *noun* ramps a slope that you can walk or drive up to go from one level to another level

range *noun* ranges A range of things is a collection of different things.

rap *verb* raps, rapping, rapped to knock on a door

rap *noun* raps a type of poetry that you speak aloud with a strong rhythm

rapid *adjective* Something that is rapid happens very quickly.

rare *adjective* rarer, rarest If something is rare, you do not see it or find it very often.

rash *noun* rashes If you have a rash, you have red spots on your skin.

raspberry *noun* raspberries a soft, sweet, red berry

rat *noun* rats an animal that looks like a large mouse

rate *noun* rates The rate at which something happens is how quickly it happens.

rather *adverb* 1 quite *I was rather annoyed.* 2 If you would rather do something, you would prefer to do it.

rattle *noun* rattles a toy for a baby which makes a noise when you shake it

raw *adjective* not cooked

ray *noun* rays A ray of light or heat is a beam of it that shines onto something.

razor *noun* razors a very sharp blade that people use for shaving hair off their body

reach *verb* reaches, reaching, reached 1 to get to a place 2 When you reach for something, you put out your hand to touch it or pick it up.

react *verb* reacts, reacting, reacted The way that you react to something is the way that you behave when it happens.

read *verb* reads, reading, read to look at words that are written down and understand them

ready *adjective* 1 If you are ready, you are prepared so that you can do something straight away. 2 If something is ready, it is finished and you can have it or use it straight away.

real *adjective* 1 true, and not made-up or imaginary *There are no unicorns in real life.* 2 genuine, and not a copy *Is this a real diamond?*

realize *verb* realizes, realizing, realized to suddenly notice something or know that it is true

really *adverb* **1** very *The water's really cold!* **2** If something is really true, it is true in real life. *Are you really moving to Spain?*

reason *noun* reasons The reason for something is why it happens.

reasonable *adjective* fair and right

receive *verb* receives, receiving, received When you receive something, someone gives it to you or sends it to you.

recent *adjective* Something that is recent happened only a short time ago. recently *adverb* only a short time ago

recipe *noun* recipes a list of the things you need to cook something, and instructions that tell you how to cook it

recite *verb* recites, reciting, recited to say something out loud from memory

recognize *verb* recognizes, recognizing, recognized to know who someone is because you have seen them before

recommend *verb* recommends, recommending, recommended **1** to tell people that something is good *I would recommend this book to anyone who loves adventure stories.* **2** to tell someone that they should do something *I recommend that you see a doctor.*

record *noun* records **1** The record for something is the best that anyone has ever done. **2** If you keep a record of something, you write it down.

record *verb* records, recording, recorded **1** to store music or pictures on

a tape or CD *We can record the film and watch it later.* **2** to write information down

recorder *noun* recorders a musical instrument that you play by blowing into one end and covering holes with your fingers to make different notes

recover *verb* recovers, recovering, recovered to get better after you have been ill

rectangle *noun* rectangles A rectangle is a shape with four straight sides and four right angles. A rectangle looks like a long square and is also called an **oblong**.

recycle *verb* recycles, recycling, recycled to use things again instead of throwing them away

red *adjective* Something that is red is the colour of blood.

reduce *verb* reduces, reducing, reduced to make something smaller or less

refer *verb* refers, referring, referred When you refer to something, you talk about it. *She had never referred to her uncle before.*

referee *noun* referees someone who is in charge of a game and makes sure that all the players keep to the rules

reference book *noun* reference books A reference book is a book that gives you information. Dictionaries are reference books.

refresh *verb* refreshes, refreshing, refreshed to make you feel fresh and less tired

refreshments *noun* drinks and snacks

refrigerator *noun* refrigerators a fridge

refugee *noun* **refugees** someone who has had to leave their own country because of a war

refuse *verb* **refuses, refusing, refused** to say that you will not do something

region *noun* **regions** one part of a country

register *noun* **registers** a book in which people write down lists of names or other important information

regret *verb* **regrets, regretting, regretted** If you regret doing something, you are sorry that you did it.

regular *adjective* **1** Something that is regular happens at the same time every day or every week. **2** A regular pattern stays the same and does not change. **3** A regular shape has sides and angles that are all equal. **regularly** *adverb* often

rehearse *verb* **rehearses, rehearsing, rehearsed** to practise something before you do it in front of an audience

reign *verb* **reigns, reigning, reigned** When a king or queen reigns, they rule over a country.

reign *noun* **reigns** the time when a king or queen is ruling a country

reindeer *noun* **reindeer** a deer with large antlers that lives in very cold countries

related *adjective* belonging to the same family

relation *noun* **relations** Your relations are all the people who belong to your family.

relative *noun* **relatives** Your relatives are all the people who belong to your family.

relax *verb* **relaxes, relaxing, relaxed** to do things that make you calm and happy

reliable *adjective* If someone is reliable, you can trust them.

relief *noun* the feeling you have when you are no longer worried about something

relieved *adjective* happy because you are no longer worried about something

religion *noun* **religions** A religion is a set of ideas that people have about a god or gods. Different religions worship different gods, and have different festivals and traditions. **religious** *adjective* If someone is religious they have a set of ideas about a god or gods. If something is religious it is to do with religion.

rely *verb* **relies, relying, relied** If you rely on something, you need it. If you rely on someone, you need them to do something for you.

remain *verb* **remains, remaining, remained** to stay

remainder *noun* (*in mathematics*) an amount that is left over after you have worked out a sum

A
B
C
D
E
F
G
H
I
J
K
L
M
N
O
P
Q
R
S
T
U
V
W
X
Y
Z

remark *verb* remarks, remarking, remarked to say something

remark *noun* remarks something that you say

remember *verb* remembers, remembering, remembered If you can remember something, you can think of it and have not forgotten it.

remind *verb* reminds, reminding, reminded If you remind someone about something, you tell them about it again so that they do not forget it.

remove *verb* removes, removing, removed to take something off or take it away

rent *noun* rents an amount of money that you pay each week to live in a house that belongs to another person

repair *verb* repairs, repairing, repaired to mend something

repeat *verb* repeats, repeating, repeated to say or do something again

replace *verb* replaces, replacing, replaced to change something for something else *This computer is getting quite old now, so we will have to replace it soon.*

reply *noun* replies an answer

reply *verb* replies, replying, replied to answer someone

report *verb* reports, reporting, reported to tell someone about something that has happened *We reported the accident to the police.*

report *noun* reports **1** an account of something that has happened, for example in a newspaper **2** A school report is something that teachers write about each child, to say how well they have been working.

represent *verb* represents, representing, represented If a drawing or picture represents something, it is meant to be that thing.

reptile *noun* reptiles A reptile is an animal that has a dry, smooth skin, and lays eggs. Snakes and crocodiles are reptiles.

request *verb* requests, requesting, requested to ask for something politely

require *verb* requires, requiring, required If you require something, you need it.

rescue *verb* rescues, rescuing, rescued to save someone from danger

research *noun* When you do research, you find out about something so that you can learn about it.

reserve *verb* reserves, reserving, reserved to ask someone to keep something for you

reservoir *noun* reservoirs a big lake that has been built to store water in

resource *noun* **resources** something that is useful to people *Oil is an important natural resource.*

respect *noun* when you admire someone and think that their ideas and opinions are important

respect *verb* **respects, respecting, respected** to admire someone and think that their ideas and opinions are important

respond *verb* **responds, responding, responded** to answer someone

responsibility *noun* **responsibilities** something that you have to do because it is your job or duty to do it

responsible *adjective* **1** If you are responsible for doing something, it is your job to do it. *You are responsible for feeding the fish.* **2** If you are responsible for something, you did it or made it happen. *Who is responsible for all this mess?* **3** Someone who is responsible behaves in a sensible way.

rest *noun* **rests 1** When you have a rest, you sleep or sit still for a while. **2** The rest means all the others.

rest *verb* **rests, resting, rested** to sit or lie still for a while

restaurant *noun* **restaurants** a place where you can buy a meal and eat it

result *noun* **results 1** If something happens as a result of something else, it happens because of it. **2** the score at the end of a game

retire *verb* **retires, retiring, retired** When someone retires, they stop working because they are too old or ill.

retreat *verb* **retreats, retreating, retreated** to go back because it is too dangerous to go forwards

return *verb* **returns, returning, returned 1** If you return to a place, you go back there. **2** If you return something to someone, you give it back to them.

reveal *verb* **reveals, revealing, revealed** to uncover something so that people can see it

revenge *noun* If you take revenge on someone, you do something nasty to them because they have hurt you or one of your friends.

reverse *verb* **reverses, reversing, reversed** to go backwards in a car

revise *verb* **revises, revising, revised** to learn something again so that you are ready for a test

revolting *adjective* horrible and disgusting

reward *noun* **rewards** something that is given to someone because they have done something good, or done something to help someone

rhinoceros *noun* **rhinoceroses** A rhinoceros is a very big, wild animal that lives in Africa and Asia and has one or two large horns on its nose. It is also called a **rhino**.

A
B
C
D
E
F
G
H
I
J
K
L
M
N
O
P
Q
R
S
T
U
V
W
X
Y
Z

rhyme *noun* **rhymes** a word that has the same sound as another word

rhyme *verb* **rhymes, rhyming, rhymed** If two words rhyme, they sound the same. *Fish rhymes with dish.*

rhythm *noun* **rhythms** the regular beat of a piece of music

rib *noun* **ribs** Your ribs are the curved bones in your chest that protect your heart and lungs.

ribbon *noun* **ribbons** a strip of coloured material that you tie round a parcel or in your hair

rice *noun* white or brown grains that you cook and eat

rich *adjective* **richer, richest** Someone who is rich has a lot of money.

rid *verb* When you get rid of something, you throw it away or give it to someone else so that you no longer have it.

riddle *noun* **riddles** a clever question or puzzle that is difficult to answer because it is a trick or joke

ride *verb* **rides, riding, rode, ridden 1** to sit on a horse or bicycle while it moves along **2** to sit in a car, bus, or train while it moves along

ride *noun* **rides** When you go for a ride, you ride on a horse or bicycle, or in a bus, train, or car.

ridiculous *adjective* Something that is ridiculous is very silly and makes people laugh.

right *adjective* **1** The right side of something is the side that is opposite the left side. Most people write with their right hand, not their left hand. **2** correct *Yes, that's the right answer.* **3** fair and honest *It is not right to cheat.*

right angle *noun* **right angles** A right angle is an angle that measures 90 degrees. A square has four right angles.

rim *noun* **rims 1** the edge around the top of a cup or jug **2** the edge around the outside of a wheel

ring *noun* **rings 1** a circle **2** a circle of gold or silver that you wear on your finger

ring *verb* **rings, ringing, rang, rung 1** to make a sound like a bell **2** to phone someone

ringtone *noun* the special sound a mobile phone makes when it receives a call

rinse *verb* **rinses, rinsing, rinsed** to wash something in clean water after you have washed it using soap

rip *verb* **rips, ripping, ripped** to tear something

ripe *adjective* **riper, ripest** Fruit that is ripe is soft and ready to eat.

ripple *noun* **ripples** a tiny wave on the surface of water *The rain was making ripples on the surface of the pond.*

rise *verb* **rises, rising, rose, risen 1** to move upwards **2** to stand up **3** When the sun or moon rises, it moves up into the sky.

risk *noun* **risks** If there is a risk, there is a danger that something bad or dangerous might happen.

rival *noun* **rivals** someone who is trying to beat you in a competition or game

river *noun* **rivers** a large stream of water that flows into the sea

road *noun* **roads** a wide path that cars, buses, and lorries go along

roar *verb* **roars, roaring, roared** When an animal like a lion roars, it makes a loud, fierce sound.

roast *verb* **roasts, roasting, roasted** to cook meat or vegetables in the oven

rob *verb* **robs, robbing, robbed** to steal something from someone

robin *noun* **robins** a small, brown bird with a red patch on its chest

robot *noun* **robots** a machine that can do some of the jobs that a person can do

rock *noun* **rocks** 1 A rock is a very big stone. 2 Rock is the hard, stony substance that mountains, hills, and the ground are made of.

rock *verb* **rocks, rocking, rocked** to move gently backwards and forwards or from side to side

rocket *noun* **rockets** 1 a firework that shoots high into the air and then explodes with bright lights and a loud bang 2 A rocket is something that can travel very fast through the air or into space. Some

rockets are used as weapons, and some are used to take people up into space.

rod *noun* **rods** A fishing rod is a long, thin piece of wood or metal. You attach a piece of thin fishing line to it and use it for catching fish.

rodent *noun* **rodents** A rodent is an animal that has big front teeth, which it uses for biting and chewing things. Rats and mice are rodents.

roll *verb* **rolls, rolling, rolled** to move along on wheels or by turning over and over like a ball

roll *noun* **rolls** 1 a piece of cloth or paper that has been rolled up into the shape of a tube *a toilet roll* 2 a very small loaf of bread for one person

roller skate *noun* **roller skates** a special shoe or boot with wheels on the bottom

roof *noun* **roofs** the sloping part on the top of a building

room *noun* **rooms** 1 The rooms in a building are the different parts inside it. 2 If there is room for something, there is enough space for it.

root *noun* **roots** the part of a plant that grows under the ground

rope *noun* **ropes** a long piece of thick, strong material which you use for tying things together

rose *noun* **roses** a flower which has a sweet smell and sharp thorns on its stem

rot *verb* **rots, rotting, rotted** When something rots, it goes bad and soft and sometimes smells nasty.

rotate *verb* **rotates, rotating, rotated** to turn round in a circle, like a wheel

rotten *adjective* Something that is rotten is not fresh, but has gone bad and soft.

rough *adjective* **rougher, roughest** **1** not smooth or flat **2** not gentle **3** more or less right, but not exactly right

roughly *adverb* **1** in a way that is not gentle **2** about, but not exactly

round *adjective* shaped like a circle or ball

round *adverb & preposition* **1** turning in a circle *The wheels spun round and round.* **2** on all sides of something *There was a high wall round the garden.*

round *verb* **rounds, rounding, rounded** *(in mathematics)* When you round a number up or down, you raise it or lower it to the nearest 10, 100, or 1000.

rounders *noun* a game in which two teams try to hit a ball with a special bat and score points by running round a square

route *noun* **routes** the way you go to get to a place

routine *noun* **routines** the way in which you usually do things at the same time and in the same way

row *noun* **rows** (rhymes with *toe*) a long, straight line of people or things

row *verb* **rows, rowing, rowed** (rhymes with *toe*) to push oars through the water to make a boat move along

row *noun* **rows** (rhymes with *how*) **1** When you make a row, you make a lot of loud noise. **2** When people have a row, they have an angry, noisy argument.

royal *adjective* belonging to a king or queen

rub *verb* **rubs, rubbing, rubbed** **1** to move your hands backwards and forwards over something **2** When you rub out something that you have written, you make it disappear by rubbing it.

rubber *noun* **rubbers** **1** Rubber is a type of soft material that stretches, bends, and bounces. Rubber is used for making car tyres. **2** A rubber is a small piece of rubber that you use for rubbing out marks.

rubbish *noun* **1** things that you have thrown away because you do not want them any more **2** If something that you say is rubbish, it is silly and not true.

rucksack *noun* **rucksacks** a bag that you carry on your back

rude *adjective* **ruder, rudest** Someone who is rude says or does things that are not polite.

rug *noun* **rugs** **1** a small carpet **2** a thick blanket

rugby *noun* a game in which two teams throw, kick, and carry a ball, and try to score points by taking it over a line at one end of the pitch

ruin *noun* ruins a building that has fallen down

ruin *verb* ruins, ruining, ruined to spoil something completely

rule *noun* rules something that tells you what you must and must not do

rule *verb* rules, ruling, ruled to be in charge of a country

ruler *noun* rulers **1** someone who rules a country **2** a flat, straight piece of wood, metal, or plastic that you use for measuring things and drawing lines

rumour *noun* rumours something that a lot of people are saying, although it might not be true

run *verb* runs, running, ran, run **1** to move along quickly by taking very quick steps **2** to control something and be in charge of it

runway *noun* runways a strip of land where an aeroplane can take off and land

rush *verb* rushes, rushing, rushed to run or do something very quickly

rust *noun* a rough, red stuff that you see on metal that is old and has got wet

rustle *verb* rustles, rustling, rustled to make a soft sound like the sound of dry leaves or paper being squashed

Ss

sack *noun* sacks a large, strong bag

sad *adjective* sadder, saddest unhappy

saddle *noun* saddles the seat that you sit on when you are riding a bicycle or a horse

safari *noun* safaris a trip to see lions and other large animals in the wild

safe *adjective* safer, safest **1** If you are safe, you are not in any danger. **2** If something is safe, you will not get hurt if you go on it or use it. *The bridge wasn't safe.*

safe *noun* safes a strong metal box with a lock where you can keep money and jewellery **safety** *noun* being safe and not in danger **safely** *adverb* without the chance of harm or danger

sail *noun* sails A sail is a large piece of strong cloth which is attached to a boat. The wind blows into the sail and makes the boat move along.

sail *verb* sails, sailing, sailed to go somewhere in a boat

sailor *noun* sailors someone who works on a ship

salad *noun* salads a mixture of vegetables that you eat raw or cold

sale *noun* sales **1** If something is for sale, people can buy it. **2** When a shop has a sale, it sells things at lower prices than usual.

saliva *noun* the liquid in your mouth

salmon *noun* salmon a large fish that you can eat

salt *noun* a white powder that people often add to food for its flavour

salute *verb* salutes, saluting, saluted to touch your forehead with your fingers to show that you respect someone

same *adjective* **1** Things that are the same are like each other. *Your jeans are the same as mine.* **2** If two people share the same thing, they share one thing and do not have two different ones. *We both go to the same school.*

sample *noun* samples a small amount of something that you can try to see what it is like

sand *noun* sands Sand is a powder made from tiny bits of crushed rock. You find sand in a desert or on a beach.

sandal *noun* sandals Sandals are shoes with straps that you wear in warm weather.

sandwich *noun* sandwiches two slices of bread and butter with a layer of a different food in between them

sap *noun* the sticky liquid inside a plant

sardine *noun* sardines a small sea fish you can eat

sari *noun* saris A sari is a type of dress that women and girls from India and other countries in Asia wear. It is a long piece of cloth that you wrap round your body.

satellite *noun* satellites A satellite is a machine that is sent into space to collect information and send signals back to earth. Satellites travel in orbit round the earth.

satellite dish *noun* satellite dishes an aerial shaped like a large dish which can receive television signals sent by satellite

satisfy *verb* satisfies, satisfying, satisfied to be good enough to make you feel pleased or happy

Saturday *noun* Saturdays the day after Friday

sauce *noun* sauces a thick liquid that you put over food

saucepan *noun* saucepans a metal pan that you use for cooking

saucer *noun* saucers a small plate that you put a cup on

sausage *noun* sausages minced meat that has been made into a long, thin shape and cooked

savage *adjective* A savage animal is wild and fierce.

save *verb* saves, saving, saved **1** to take someone away from danger and make them safe **2** to keep money so that you can use it later **3** *(in ICT)* When you save a computer file, you instruct the computer to keep a copy of it on its hard disk.

savings *noun* money that you have saved to use later

saw *noun* saws A saw is a tool that you use to cut wood. It has a row of sharp teeth which you push backwards and forwards over the wood to cut it.

saw *verb* saws, sawing, sawed, sawn to cut wood with a saw

say *verb* **says, saying, said** When you say something, you speak.

scale *noun* **scales** 1 The scale of a map is how big things on the map are compared to how big they are in real life. 2 The scales on a fish are the small, round pieces of hard skin all over its body.

scales *noun* something that you use for weighing things

scar *noun* **scars** a mark that is left on your skin after a cut or burn has healed

scare *verb* **scares, scaring, scared** to make someone feel frightened

scarecrow *noun* **scarecrows** something that looks like a person and is put in a field to frighten away birds

scarf *noun* **scarves** a piece of material that you wear round your neck to keep you warm

scarlet *adjective* Something that is scarlet is bright red.

scatter *verb* **scatters, scattering, scattered** to throw things all around you

scene *noun* **scenes** 1 The scene of something is the place where it happens. 2 one part of a play

scenery *noun* 1 things that you can see around you when you are out in the country 2 things that you put on the stage of a theatre to make it look like a real place

scent *noun* **scents** 1 perfume that you put on your skin so that you will smell nice

2 a pleasant smell 3 An animal's scent is its smell.

school *noun* **schools** a place where children go to learn things

science *noun* **sciences** the subject in which you study the things in the world around you, for example plants and animals, wood and metal, light, and electricity

scissors *noun* a tool that you use for cutting paper or cloth

> The first /s/ sound is spelled **sc-**.

scoop *noun* **scoops** 1 a deep spoon that you use for serving ice cream 2 an amount of something served by a scoop *two scoops of strawberry ice cream*

score *noun* **scores** The score in a game is the number of points that each player or team has.

score *verb* **scores, scoring, scored** to get a point or a goal in a game

scowl *verb* **scowls, scowling, scowled** (rhymes with *owl*) to look cross

scrap *noun* **scraps** 1 A scrap of paper or cloth is a small piece. 2 Scrap is anything that you do not want any more.

scrape *verb* **scrapes, scraping, scraped** 1 If you scrape something off, you get it

135

off by pushing it with something sharp. *Scrape the mud off your shoes.* **2** If you scrape a part of your body, you cut it by rubbing it against something.

scratch *verb* scratches, scratching, scratched **1** to cut something or make a mark on it with something sharp **2** to rub your skin because it is itching

scream *verb* screams, screaming, screamed to shout or cry loudly because you are frightened or hurt

screech *verb* screeches, screeching, screeched to shout or cry in a loud, high voice

screen *noun* screens **1** the part of a television or computer where the words and pictures appear **2** the large, flat surface at a cinema, on which films are shown

screw *noun* screws a pointed piece of metal that you use for fixing pieces of wood together

screw *verb* screws, screwing, screwed **1** When you screw things together, you fix them together using screws. **2** When you screw a lid on or off, you put it on or take it off by turning it round and round.

screwdriver *noun* screwdrivers a tool that you use for fixing screws into wood

scribble *verb* scribbles, scribbling, scribbled to write or draw something quickly, in an untidy way

script *noun* scripts all the words that the characters say in a play

scroll *verb* scrolls, scrolling, scrolled *(in ICT)* When you scroll up or down on a computer screen, you move up or down on the screen to see what comes before or after.

scrub *verb* scrubs, scrubbing, scrubbed to rub something hard to clean it

sculpture *noun* sculptures a statue made out of stone or wood

sea *noun* seas the salty water that covers large parts of the earth

seal *noun* seals A seal is an animal that has flippers and lives in the sea. Seals have thick fur to keep them warm in cold water.

seam *noun* seams a line of sewing that joins two pieces of material together

search *verb* searches, searching, searched to look for something very carefully

search engine *noun* search engines a computer program that helps you find information on the Internet

seaside *noun* a place by the sea where people go on holiday to enjoy themselves

season *noun* seasons **1** The four seasons are the four parts of the year, which are spring, summer, autumn, and winter. **2** The season for a sport is the time of year when it is played. *When does the cricket season start?*

seat *noun* **seats** anything that you can sit on

seat belt *noun* **seat belts** a strap that you wear round your body to keep you safe in a car

seaweed *noun* a plant that grows in the sea

second *adjective* The second thing is the one that comes after the first.
second *noun* **seconds** We measure time in seconds. There are sixty seconds in one minute.

secret *adjective* A secret thing is one that not very many people know about.
secret *noun* **secrets** If something is a secret, not many people know about it and you must not tell anyone. **secretly** *adverb* Something done secretly is done so that not many people know about it.

secretary *noun* **secretaries** someone whose job is to assist with office jobs and answer the telephone at work

section *noun* **sections** one part of something

secure *adjective* **securer, securest** **1** Something that is secure is safe and firm. **2** If you feel secure, you feel safe.

see *verb* **sees, seeing, saw, seen** **1** to notice something with your eyes **2** to understand something *Do you see what I mean?*

seed *noun* **seeds** a small thing that a new plant grows from

seem *verb* **seems, seeming, seemed** to look, sound, or appear

see-saw *noun* **see-saws** A see-saw is a toy that children can play on. It is made of a long piece of wood that is balanced on something in the middle so that someone can sit on each end and make it go up and down.

seize *verb* **seizes, seizing, seized** (rhymes with *sneeze*) to grab something roughly

select *verb* **selects, selecting, selected** to choose something

selfish *adjective* only thinking about yourself and not caring what other people want

sell *verb* **sells, selling, sold** When you sell something, you give it to someone and they give you money for it.

Sellotape *noun* (trademark) a type of sticky tape that you use for sticking pieces of paper together

send *verb* **sends, sending, sent** **1** When you send something somewhere, you arrange for someone to take it there. *My grandma sent me a birthday card.* **2** When you send someone somewhere, you tell them to go there. *He was sent to the headteacher for behaving badly.*

senior *adjective* older or more important than other people

sense *noun* **senses** **1** Your senses are your ability to see, hear, smell, feel, and taste. *Dogs have a good sense of smell.* **2** If you have good sense, you know what the right thing to do is. *She had the sense to call an ambulance.*

sensible *adjective* If you are sensible, you think carefully and you do the right thing.

sensitive *adjective* **1** Someone who is sensitive is easily upset by other people. **2** Something that is sensitive reacts to things around it. *Some people have very sensitive skin.*

sentence *noun* sentences **1** A sentence tells you something, asks you something, asks you to do something or exclaims about something. **2** a punishment that is given to someone by a judge

separate *adjective* Things that are separate are not joined together or not next to each other.

separate *verb* separates, separating, separated to take people or things away from each other so that they are no longer together

> Remember there is **a rat** in the middle of this word.

September *noun* the ninth month of the year

sequence *noun* sequences A sequence is a series of numbers that come after each other in a regular order. For example, *2, 4, 6, 8* is a sequence.

series *noun* series **1** a number of things that come one after another **2** a television show that is on regularly and is about the same thing each week

serious *adjective* **1** very important *This is a very serious matter.* **2** Someone who is serious does not smile or joke, but thinks carefully about things. **3** very bad *There has been a serious accident on the motorway.* **seriously** *adverb* If someone is seriously ill, injured, or hurt it means that they are very badly ill, injured, or hurt.

servant *noun* servants someone who works at another person's home, doing jobs such as cleaning and cooking

serve *verb* serves, serving, served **1** to help someone in a shop find and buy the things that they want **2** to put food on people's plates **3** to start a game of tennis by hitting the ball to the other player

service *noun* services something that is done to help people or give them something that they need *Letters are delivered by the postal service.*

set *verb* sets, setting, set **1** to change the controls on a machine to a particular position *We set the alarm clock for six o'clock.* **2** to go hard *Has the glue set yet?* **3** When the sun sets, it goes down at the end of the day. **4** To set off means to leave.

set *noun* sets a group of people or things that belong together

settle *verb* settles, settling, settled **1** When you settle an argument, you agree on what to do about it. **2** When you settle down somewhere, you sit or lie down comfortably.

seven *noun* sevens the number 7

seventeen *noun* the number 17

seventy *noun* the number 70

several *determiner* Several things means more than two but not many.

severe *adjective* severer, severest very bad

sew *verb* sews, sewing, sewed, sewn to use a needle and thread to join pieces of cloth together

sex *noun* sexes The sex of a person or an animal is whether they are male or female.

shade *noun* shades **1** If a place is in the shade, it is quite dark because the light of the sun cannot get to it. **2** The shade of a colour is how light or dark it is.

shadow *noun* shadows the dark shape that forms on the ground when something is blocking out the light

shake *verb* shakes, shaking, shook, shaken **1** to move something about quickly **2** to move about **3** When you shake, you cannot keep your body still because you are very cold or frightened.

shall *verb* I shall do something means that I will do it.

shallow *adjective* not very deep

shame *noun* the feeling you have when you are unhappy because you have done wrong

shampoo *noun* shampoos liquid soap that you use to wash your hair

shape *noun* shapes what the outline of something looks like, for example whether it is square, round, or oval *What shape is this room?*

share *verb* shares, sharing, shared **1** When you share something, you give some of it to other people. **2** When people share something, they both use it. *I share a bedroom with my sister.*

shark *noun* sharks a big, fierce sea fish that has sharp teeth and hunts and kills other fish to eat

sharp *adjective* sharper, sharpest **1** Something that is sharp can cut things because it is thin or pointed. **2** If someone speaks in a sharp voice, they say something angrily. **sharply** *adverb* If you say something sharply, you say it angrily.

shatter *verb* shatters, shattering, shattered to break into tiny pieces

shave *verb* shaves, shaving, shaved to cut all the hair off a part of your body to make it smooth

she *pronoun* You use **she** to talk about a girl, woman, or female animal.

shed *noun* sheds a small wooden building

sheep *noun* sheep an animal that is kept on farms for its wool and meat

sheet *noun* sheets **1** a large piece of cloth that you put on a bed **2** a thin, flat piece of something *I need another sheet of paper.*

shelf *noun* shelves a piece of wood that is fastened to a wall so that you can put things on it

shell *noun* shells A shell is a hard part on the outside of something. Eggs and nuts have shells, and some animals such as snails and tortoises have a shell on their back.

shelter *noun* shelters a place that protects people from bad weather or from danger

shelter *verb* shelters, sheltering, sheltered **1** to keep someone safe from bad weather or danger **2** to stay in a place that is safe from bad weather or danger

shepherd *noun* shepherds someone whose job is to look after sheep

139

A B C D E F G H I J K L M N O P Q R (S) T U V W X Y Z

sheriff *noun* **sheriffs** In America, a sheriff is a person who makes sure that people do not break the law.

shield *noun* **shields** something that soldiers or the police hold in front of their bodies to protect themselves during a battle

shift *verb* **shifts, shifting, shifted** to move something *I can't shift this rock.*

shin *noun* **shins** Your shins are the front parts of your legs below your knees.

shine *verb* **shines, shining, shone** to give out light or look very bright *The sun shone all day.* **shiny** *adjective* Something that is shiny looks very bright and gives out light.

ship *noun* **ships** a very large boat

shirt *noun* **shirts** A shirt is a piece of clothing that you wear on the top half of your body. It has buttons down the front, sleeves, and a collar.

shiver *verb* **shivers, shivering, shivered** to shake because you are cold or frightened

shock *noun* **shocks** 1 If something is a shock, you were not expecting it and it upsets you when it happens. 2 If you get an electric shock, electricity gets into your body and hurts you.
shock *verb* **shocks, shocking, shocked** to give someone a nasty surprise and upset them

shoe *noun* **shoes** something that you wear on your feet to keep them warm and dry when you go outside

shoot *verb* **shoots, shooting, shot** 1 to fire a gun or other weapon 2 to try to score a goal in a game such as football

shop *noun* **shops** a place where you can go to buy things
shop *verb* **shops, shopping, shopped** to go into a shop to buy something

shore *noun* **shores** the land by the edge of the sea

short *adjective* **shorter, shortest** 1 not very tall 2 not very long 3 not lasting very long

shorts *noun* short trousers that only cover the top part of your legs

shot *noun* **shots** 1 the sound of someone firing a gun 2 a photograph 3 one kick or hit of the ball in a game such as football or tennis

should *verb* If you should do something, you ought to do it. *I should go home now.*

shoulder *noun* **shoulders** Your shoulders are the parts of the body between your neck and your arms.

shout *verb* **shouts, shouting, shouted** to speak in a very loud voice

show *noun* **shows** something that people perform for other people to watch at the theatre or on television
show *verb* **shows, showing, showed, shown** 1 When you show something to someone, you let them see it. 2 If you show someone how to do something, you do it so that they can watch you and learn how to do it. 3 If something shows, people can see it.

shower *noun* **showers 1** When there is a shower, it rains or snows for a short time. **2** When you have a shower, you stand under a stream of water to wash yourself.

shriek *verb* **shrieks, shrieking, shrieked** to shout or scream in a high voice

shrill *adjective* **shriller, shrillest** A shrill sound is high and loud.

shrimp *noun* **shrimps** a small sea animal that you can eat

shrink *verb* **shrinks, shrinking, shrank, shrunk** to get smaller

shrug *verb* **shrugs, shrugging, shrugged** to lift your shoulders up to show that you do not know something or do not care about it

shuffle *verb* **shuffles, shuffling, shuffled 1** to walk slowly, without lifting your feet off the ground **2** to mix cards up so that they are ready for a game

shut *verb* **shuts, shutting, shut 1** to close something **2** When a shop shuts, it closes and people cannot use it. **3** When you shut down a computer, you close all the programs and switch it off.

shy *adjective* **shyer, shyest** frightened and nervous when you meet people you do not know

sick *adjective* **sicker, sickest 1** ill **2** If you are sick, food comes back up out of your mouth after you have eaten it.

side *noun* **sides 1** The sides of something are the parts on the left and right of it, not at the back or the front. *There were some people standing at one side of the field.* **2** Your sides are the parts of your body on your left and right. *He had a big bruise on his right side.* **3** The sides of something are its edges. *A triangle has three sides.* **4** The two sides of a piece of paper or cloth are its front and back. **5** One side in a game or fight is one group that is playing or fighting against another group. *Whose side are you on?*

sideways *adverb* towards the side rather than forwards or backwards

sigh *verb* **sighs, sighing, sighed** (rhymes with *by*) to breathe out heavily because you are sad or tired

sight *noun* **1** how well you can see things **2** something that you see

sign *noun* **signs** (rhymes with *mine*) **1** a picture or mark that means something *The sign for a dollar is $* **2** a notice that tells you something **3** If you give someone a sign, you move your body to tell them something.

sign *verb* **signs, signing, signed** to write your name on something

signal *noun* **signals** a light, sound, or movement that tells people what they should do, or tells them that something is going to happen

signature *noun* **signatures** your own special way of writing your name

sign language *noun* a way of communicating by using your hands to make words

Sikh *noun* **Sikhs** a person who follows the Indian religion of Sikhism

silent *adjective* **1** Something that is silent does not make any noise. Someone who is silent does not speak or make a noise. **2** If a place is silent, there is no noise in it.

141

A
B
C
D
E
F
G
H
I
J
K
L
M
N
O
P
Q
R
S
T
U
V
W
X
Y
Z

silk *noun* a type of smooth cloth that is made from threads spun by insects called **silkworms** **silky** *adjective* feeling smooth and soft

silly *adjective* **sillier**, **silliest** stupid, not clever or sensible

silver *noun* a shiny, white metal that is very valuable

similar *adjective* Things that are similar are the same in some ways, but not exactly the same.

simple *adjective* **simpler**, **simplest** **1** very easy **2** plain and clear

since *preposition & conjunction* **1** from that time *We have been friends since last summer.* **2** because *We couldn't play outside since it was raining.*

sing *verb* **sings**, **singing**, **sang**, **sung** to use your voice to make music

single *adjective* **1** only one *The tree had a single apple on it.* **2** not married

sink *noun* **sinks** a large bowl with taps where you can wash things
sink *verb* **sinks**, **sinking**, **sank**, **sunk** **1** to go under water **2** to go downwards

sip *verb* **sips**, **sipping**, **sipped** to drink a drink slowly, a little bit at a time

sir *noun* a word you use when you are speaking politely to a man

sister *noun* **sisters** a girl who has the same parents as you

sit *verb* **sits**, **sitting**, **sat** **1** to rest on your bottom **2** If something is sitting somewhere, it is there. *My school bag was sitting by the back door.*

site *noun* **sites** A site is a piece of ground that is used for something. For example, a campsite is a place where people can camp.

situation *noun* **situations** all the things that are happening to you and to the people around you

six *noun* **sixes** the number 6

sixteen *noun* the number 16

sixty *noun* the number 60

size *noun* **sizes** The size of something is how big or small it is. *These trousers are the wrong size for me.*

skate *noun* **skates** **1** a boot with a special blade on the bottom, which you use for skating on ice **2** a special shoe or boot with wheels on the bottom
skate *verb* **skates**, **skating**, **skated** to move smoothly over ice or over the ground wearing ice skates or roller skates

skateboard *noun* **skateboards** a small board on wheels that you can stand on and ride

skeleton *noun* **skeletons** Your skeleton is all the bones that are in your body.

sketch *verb* **sketches**, **sketching**, **sketched** to draw something quickly and roughly

ski *noun* **skis** Skis are long, flat sticks that you strap to your feet and use for moving over snow.

ski *verb* skis, skiing, skied to move over snow on skis

skill *noun* skills If you have skill, you can do something well.

skin *noun* skins **1** the part of you that covers all of your body **2** the tough part on the outside of a fruit or vegetable

skip *verb* skips, skipping, skipped **1** to run along lightly taking a little jump with each step **2** to turn a rope over your head and under your feet and jump over it each time it goes under your feet

skirt *noun* skirts A skirt is a piece of clothing that a woman or girl wears. It fastens around her waist and hangs down over her legs.

sky *noun* skies the space above the earth where you can see the sun, moon, and stars

slam *verb* slams, slamming, slammed to push a door shut so that it makes a loud bang

slang *noun* words that you use when you are talking to your friends, but not when you are writing or talking politely to people

slap *verb* slaps, slapping, slapped to hit someone with the front of your hand

slate *noun* slates Slate is a type of smooth, grey rock. Pieces of slate are sometimes used to cover the roofs of houses.

sledge *noun* sledges a piece of wood or plastic, which you sit on to slide along on snow or ice

sleep *verb* sleeps, sleeping, slept to close your eyes and rest your body and your mind

sleet *noun* a mixture of rain and snow

sleeve *noun* sleeves The sleeves on a shirt, jumper, or coat are the parts that cover your arms.

sleigh *noun* sleighs a large sledge that is pulled along by animals

slice *noun* slices a thin piece of something that has been cut off

slide *verb* slides, sliding, slid to move along smoothly

slide *noun* slides **1** A slide is a toy that children can play on. It is made of steps that you climb up, and a long sloping part that you can slide down. **2** a clip that girls sometimes wear in their hair to keep it tidy

slight *adjective* slighter, slightest small and not very important or not very bad **slightly** *adverb* by a small amount

slim *adjective* slimmer, slimmest thin

slime *noun* nasty wet, slippery stuff

sling *noun* slings A sling is a piece of cloth that goes round your arm and is

a
b
c
d
e
f
g
h
i
j
k
l
m
n
o
p
q
r
s
t
u
v
w
x
y
z

tied round your neck. You wear a sling to support your arm if you have hurt it.

slip *verb* slips, slipping, slipped **1** If you slip, your foot accidentally slides on the ground. *I slipped and fell over.* **2** to go somewhere quickly and quietly

slipper *noun* slippers Slippers are soft shoes that you wear indoors.

slippery *adjective* smooth or wet and difficult to get hold of or walk on

slit *noun* slits a long, narrow cut in something

slope *verb* slopes, sloping, sloped Something that slopes is not flat but goes up or down at one end.

slope *noun* slopes a piece of ground that goes up or down like the side of a hill

slot *noun* slots a narrow opening that you can put a coin into

slow *adjective* slower, slowest **1** Something that is slow does not move very quickly. Someone who is slow does not do things quickly. **2** If a clock or watch is slow, it shows a time that is earlier than the right time. **slowly** *adverb* not quickly

slug *noun* slugs a small, soft animal that looks like a snail but has no shell

sly *adjective* slyer, slyest clever at tricking people secretly to get what you want

smack *verb* smacks, smacking, smacked to hit someone with the front of your hand

small *adjective* smaller, smallest not very big

smart *adjective* smarter, smartest
1 clean and neat with nice clothes on
2 clever

smash *verb* smashes, smashing, smashed to break into a lot of pieces with a loud noise

smell *verb* smells, smelling, smelled, smelt **1** When you smell something, you notice it through your nose. **2** If something smells, you can notice it through your nose.

smell *noun* smells **1** something that you can notice with your nose **2** Your sense of smell is how well you can smell things. *Dogs have a very good sense of smell.*

smile *verb* smiles, smiling, smiled to move your mouth to show that you are happy

smoke *noun* grey or black gas from a fire
smoke *verb* smokes, smoking, smoked
1 When something smokes, smoke comes off it. **2** If someone smokes they breathe in the smoke from rolled up leaves from a plant.

smooth *adjective* smoother, smoothest flat and level, with no bumps or rough parts

smoothie *noun* a thick, smooth drink with fresh fruit and milk, yogurt, or ice cream *I had a banana smoothie for breakfast.*

smudge *noun* smudges a dirty mark on something

smudge *verb* smudges, smudging, smudged to touch paint or ink while it is still wet and make it messy

smuggle *verb* smuggles, smuggling, smuggled to take something into a place or out of a place secretly

snack *noun* snacks something you can eat quickly instead of a meal

snail *noun* snails a small animal with a soft body, no legs, and a hard shell on its back

snake *noun* snakes an animal with a long, thin body and no legs

snap *verb* snaps, snapping, snapped **1** to break suddenly **2** If an animal snaps at you, it tries to bite you. **3** To snap at someone means to shout at them angrily.

snarl *verb* snarls, snarling, snarled When an animal snarls, it makes a fierce sound and shows its teeth.

snatch *verb* snatches, snatching, snatched to grab something quickly

sneak *verb* sneaks, sneaking, sneaked to go somewhere quietly so that people do not see you or hear you

sneeze *verb* sneezes, sneezing, sneezed When you sneeze, air suddenly comes out of your nose with a loud noise.

sniff *verb* sniffs, sniffing, sniffed to breathe in noisily through your nose

snooze *verb* snoozes, snoozing, snoozed to have a short sleep

snore *verb* snores, snoring, snored to breathe very noisily while you are asleep

snow *noun* small, light flakes of frozen water that fall from the sky when it is very cold

snowball *noun* snowballs a ball of snow that you throw at someone

snowboard *noun* snowboards a narrow board that you stand on to slide down a slope over snow

snowflake *noun* snowflakes Snowflakes are small light pieces of snow that fall from the sky.

snug *adjective* snugger, snuggest warm, cosy, and comfortable

snuggle *verb* snuggles, snuggling, snuggled to curl up somewhere so that you are warm and comfortable

so *conjunction* for that reason *I have no money left so can't buy any more sweets.*

soak *verb* soaks, soaking, soaked **1** to make something very wet **2** If something soaks up water, the water goes into it.

soap *noun* soaps **1** Soap is something that you use with water for washing yourself. **2** A soap or a **soap opera** is a regular television series about the lives of ordinary people.

sob *verb* sobs, sobbing, sobbed to cry in a noisy way

soccer *noun* the game of football

a
b
c
d
e
f
g
h
i
j
k
l
m
n
o
p
q
r
s
t
u
v
w
x
y
z

A B C D E F G H I J K L M N O P Q R **S** T U V W X Y Z

society *noun* **societies** **1** all the people who live together in the same country **2** a club

sock *noun* **socks** a piece of clothing that you wear over your feet

socket *noun* **sockets** a place on a wall that an electric plug fits into

sofa *noun* **sofas** a long, comfortable seat for more than one person

soft *adjective* **softer, softest** **1** not hard or stiff **2** not very loud **softly** *adverb* quietly

software *noun* *(in ICT)* the programs that you put into a computer to make it work

soggy *adjective* **soggier, soggiest** wet and soft

soil *noun* the brown earth that plants grow in

solar *adjective* to do with the sun *Some houses now use solar energy.*

soldier *noun* **soldiers** someone who is a member of an army

sole *noun* **soles** the part underneath your foot or shoe

solid *adjective* **1** not hollow in the middle **2** hard and firm *Water becomes solid when it freezes.*

solid *noun* **solids** A solid is any substance that is hard and is not a liquid or a gas. Wood, rock, and plastic are all solids.

solo *noun* **solos** a piece of music or a dance that one person performs on their own

solution *noun* **solutions** **1** the answer to a puzzle or problem **2** *(in science)* a liquid in which something has been dissolved

solve *verb* **solves, solving, solved** to find the answer to a puzzle or problem

some *determiner & pronoun* **1** a few *Some of us can swim, but the others can't.* **2** an amount of something *Would you like some cake?*

somebody, someone *pronoun* a person *Somebody's taken my pencil!*

somehow *adverb* in some way *We must get away somehow.*

somersault *noun* **somersaults** When you do a somersault, you roll over forwards or backwards.

something *pronoun* a thing *I'm sure I've forgotten something.*

sometimes *adverb* at some times *Sometimes I cycle to school, sometimes I walk.*

somewhere *adverb* in some place *I put the book somewhere but I've forgotten where.*

son *noun* **sons** someone's male child

song *noun* **songs** a piece of music with words that you sing

soon *adverb* in a very short time *We must go home soon.*

sore *adjective* **sorer**, **sorest** If a part of your body is sore, it hurts.

sorry *adjective* **sorrier**, **sorriest** **1** If you are sorry that you did something, you are sad about it and wish that you had not done it. **2** If you feel sorry for someone, you feel sad because something nasty has happened to them.

sort *noun* **sorts** a kind *Which sort of ice cream do you like?*

sort *verb* **sorts**, **sorting**, **sorted** to put things into different groups

sound *noun* **sounds** anything that you can hear

soup *noun* **soups** a hot liquid made from meat or vegetables

sour *adjective* **sourer**, **sourest** Something that is sour has a nasty bitter taste, like a lemon.

source *noun* **sources** the place where something comes from, or the place where it starts

south *noun* South is one of the directions in which you can face or travel. On a map, south is the direction towards the bottom of the page.

souvenir *noun* **souvenirs** something that you keep because it reminds you of a person or place

sow *verb* **sows**, **sowing**, **sowed**, **sown** (rhymes with *low*) to put seeds into the ground so that they will grow

space *noun* **spaces** **1** Space is the place around the Earth and far beyond the Earth, where the stars and planets are. **2** A space is a place with nothing in it.

spade *noun* **spades** a tool with a long handle and a wide blade that you use for digging

spaghetti *noun* a type of pasta that is made in long, thin pieces

spanner *noun* **spanners** a tool that you use for tightening and undoing nuts

spare *verb* **spares**, **sparing**, **spared** If you can spare something, you have some extra that you can give to someone else.

spare *adjective* If something is spare, you are not using it at the moment but you can use it if you need it.

spark *noun* **sparks** **1** a tiny flash of electricity **2** a tiny piece of something burning that shoots out from a fire

sparkle *verb* **sparkles**, **sparkling**, **sparkled** to shine brightly

sparrow *noun* **sparrows** a small, brown bird that you often see in gardens

speak *verb* **speaks**, **speaking**, **spoke**, **spoken** to say something

speaker *noun* **speakers** the part of a radio, television, or music player that the sound comes out of

a b c d e f g h i j k l m n o p q r **s** t u v w x y z

147

spear *noun* **spears** a long stick with a sharp point that is used as a weapon

special *adjective* **1** different and more important than other things **2** for one particular person or job *You use a special tool to get the strings on a piano in tune.*

spectator *noun* **spectators** a person watching a sporting event or game

speech *noun* **speeches** **1** Speech is the ability to speak. **2** A speech is a talk that someone gives to a group of people.

speed *noun* how fast something moves or how quickly it happens

spell *verb* **spells, spelling, spelled, spelt** The way in which you spell a word is the letters that you use when you write it.

spell *noun* **spells** a set of words that people say in stories when they want something magic to happen

spellcheck *noun* **spellchecks** *(in ICT)* When you do a spellcheck on a computer, you tell the computer to check the spellings of all the words you have typed.

spend *verb* **spends, spending, spent** **1** to use money to pay for things **2** to use time to do something *We spent all day trying to mend the boat.*

sphere *noun* **spheres** the shape of a ball

spice *noun* **spices** a powder or seed which is added to food to give it a strong flavour **spicy** *adjective* **spicier, spiciest** having a strong flavour and a hot taste

spider *noun* **spiders** a small animal with eight legs that spins sticky webs to catch insects for food

spill *verb* **spills, spilling, spilled, spilt** If you spill something, you let some of it fall out onto the floor.

spin *verb* **spins, spinning, spun** **1** to turn round and round **2** to make thread from wool or cotton **3** to make a web

spine *noun* **spines** **1** the long line of bones down the middle of your back **2** The spines on a plant or animal are sharp points on it.

spiral *noun* **spirals** a line that keeps going round and round in circles, with each circle getting slightly bigger

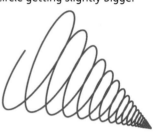

spire *noun* **spires** a tall, pointed part on the top of a tower on a building

spite *noun* If you do something out of spite, you do it to hurt or upset someone.

spiteful *adjective* Someone who is spiteful does nasty things to hurt or upset other people.

splash *verb* **splashes, splashing, splashed** to hit water so that it makes a noise and flies up into the air

splinter *noun* **splinters** a small, sharp bit of wood or glass

split *verb* **splits, splitting, split** **1** to break or tear **2** to break something into pieces

spoil *verb* **spoils, spoiling, spoiled, spoilt** **1** to damage something so that it is not as good or as nice as it was before **2** to give a child everything that they want so that they always expect to get their own way and behave badly if they do not

spoke *noun* **spokes** The spokes on a wheel are the pieces of metal that go from the centre of the wheel to the edge.

sponge *noun* sponges **1** A sponge is a thick, soft thing with a lot of small holes in. A sponge soaks up water easily, and you use it for washing things. **2** a type of cake

sponsor *verb* sponsors, sponsoring, sponsored to promise to give someone money if they do something difficult

spoon *noun* spoons a thing that you use for eating soft or liquid foods such as soup and ice cream

sport *noun* sports a game that you play or something difficult that you do to exercise your body

spot *noun* spots **1** a small round mark on something **2** a small, sore, red lump on your skin

spot *verb* spots, spotting, spotted to see something

spotless *adjective* perfectly clean

spout *noun* spouts the part of a jug or teapot that you pour liquid out of

spray *verb* sprays, spraying, sprayed to cover something with tiny drops of water

spread *verb* spreads, spreading, spread **1** to open something out to its full size **2** When you spread butter or jam, you put a thin layer of it onto bread.

spring *verb* springs, springing, sprang, sprung to jump

spring *noun* springs **1** a piece of metal that is wound into rings so that it jumps back into shape after it has been pressed down **2** the time of the year when plants start to grow and the days get lighter and warmer

sprinkle *verb* sprinkles, sprinkling, sprinkled to shake a few drops or small pieces of something over something else

sprint *verb* sprints, sprinting, sprinted to run as fast as you can over a short distance

sprout *verb* sprouts, sprouting, sprouted When a plant sprouts, it starts to grow new parts.

spy *noun* spies someone who works secretly to find out information about another person or country

spy *verb* spies, spying, spied **1** When you spy on someone, you watch them secretly. **2** When you spy something, you see it.

square *noun* squares **1** A square is a shape with four straight sides and four right angles. The sides of a square are all the same length. **2** *(in mathematics)* The square of a number is the number you get when you multiply it by itself. *The square of 4 is 16.* **3** an open space in a town with buildings all round it

squash *verb* squashes, squashing, squashed to press something hard so that it becomes flat

squash *noun* a sweet drink made from fruit juice and sugar

squat *verb* squats, squatting, squatted to bend your knees under you so that your bottom is almost touching the ground

squawk *verb* squawks, squawking, squawked When a bird squawks, it makes a loud, rough sound in its throat.

squeak *verb* squeaks, squeaking, squeaked to make a very high sound

squeal *verb* squeals, squealing, squealed to shout or cry in a high voice

squeeze *verb* squeezes, squeezing, squeezed **1** to press something hard with your hands **2** If you squeeze something into a place, you push it in even though

a
b
c
d
e
f
g
h
i
j
k
l
m
n
o
p
q
r
s
t
u
v
w
x
y
z

there is not very much room. *Can we squeeze six people in the car?*

squirrel *noun* **squirrels** A squirrel is a small animal with a thick tail. Squirrels live in trees and eat nuts and seeds.

squirt *verb* **squirts, squirting, squirted** When water squirts out of something, it shoots out quickly.

stable *noun* **stables** a building in which horses are kept

stack *noun* **stacks** a neat pile of things

stadium *noun* **stadiums** a large building where people can watch sports and games

staff *noun* all the people who work in a school, shop, or office

stage *noun* **stages** the raised part in a theatre or hall on which people act, sing, or dance to entertain other people

stagger *verb* **staggers, staggering, staggered** to walk with unsteady legs, almost falling over with each step

stain *noun* **stains** a dirty mark on something that does not come out when you wash it or rub it

stair *noun* **stairs** Stairs are steps inside a building.

staircase *noun* **staircases** a set of stairs inside a building

stale *adjective* **staler, stalest** not fresh *We had nothing to eat except stale bread.*

stalk *noun* **stalks** the part of a flower, leaf, or fruit that joins it to the plant

stall *noun* **stalls** **1** a table that things are arranged on so that they can be sold, for example in a market **2** a place for one animal in a stable

stammer *verb* **stammers, stammering, stammered** to keep repeating the sounds at the beginning of words when you speak

stamp *noun* **stamps** A stamp is a small piece of sticky paper with a picture on it. You stick a stamp on a letter or parcel to show that you have paid to post it.

stamp *verb* **stamps, stamping, stamped** to bang your foot heavily on the ground

stand *verb* **stands, standing, stood** **1** to be on your feet, not sitting or lying down **2** If you cannot stand something, you do not like it at all.

stand *noun* **stands** something that you can put things on *Put your music on the music stand.*

standard *noun* **standards** The standard of something is how good or bad it is.

standard *adjective* ordinary and not special

star *noun* stars **1** one of the tiny, bright lights you see in the sky at night **2** a shape that has five or more points sticking out all round it **3** a famous person

star *verb* stars, starring, starred to have an important part in in a film or show

starch *noun* starches Starch is a substance in food that gives you energy. There is starch in bread and potatoes.

stare *verb* stares, staring, stared to keep looking at something for a long time, without moving your eyes

start *verb* starts, starting, started **1** When you start to do something, you begin to do it. *Georgina started to cry.* **2** When something starts, it begins.

start *noun* starts The start of something is when it begins.

startle *verb* startles, startling, startled to give someone a sudden shock *The sudden noise startled me.*

starve *verb* starves, starving, starved to be ill or to die because you have not got enough food

state *noun* states **1** the condition that something is in, for example whether it is clean, tidy, or broken **2** a country or one part of a country that has its own laws and government

statement *noun* statements a sentence that is not a question or an exclamation

station *noun* stations **1** a place where trains and buses stop so that people can get on and off **2** a building where the police or firefighters work

stationery *noun* paper, pens, and other things that you use for writing and drawing

statue *noun* statues a model of a person made from stone, wood, or metal

stay *verb* stays, staying, stayed **1** to remain somewhere and not go away *Please stay in your seats.* **2** to live in a place for a while *I'm going to stay with my grandma for the summer holidays.* **3** to remain *I hope it stays dry for sports day.*

steady *adjective* steadier, steadiest **1** Something that is steady is firm and does not shake or move about. **2** If something moves in a steady way, it moves along at the same speed all the time.

steak *noun* steaks a thick slice of meat or fish

steal *verb* steals, stealing, stole, stolen to take something that belongs to someone else

steam *noun* the hot gas that comes off water when it boils

steel *noun* a type of strong, shiny metal

steep *adjective* steeper, steepest sloping sharply up or down

steer *verb* steers, steering, steered to make a car or bicycle go in the direction you want

a
b
c
d
e
f
g
h
i
j
k
l
m
n
o
p
q
r
s
t
u
v
w
x
y
z

stem *noun* stems the long, thin part of a plant that grows up out of the ground

step *noun* steps **1** When you take a step, you move one foot forwards or backwards. **2** Steps are stairs.

stepbrother *noun* stepbrothers a boy whose father or mother has married your father or mother

stepfather *noun* stepfathers a man who has got married to your mother but is not your real father

stepmother *noun* stepmothers a woman who has got married to your father but is not your real mother

stepsister *noun* stepsisters a girl whose father or mother has married your father or mother

stereo *noun* stereos a machine that plays music from tapes or CDs through two speakers

stern *adjective* sterner, sternest serious and strict

stew *noun* stews a mixture of meat or vegetables cooked in a sauce

stick *noun* sticks a long, thin piece of wood

stick *verb* sticks, sticking, stuck **1** If you stick a pin or nail into something, you push it in. **2** When you stick things together, you fix them together using glue. *I stuck the pictures into my book.* **3** If something sticks, it gets jammed and you cannot move it.

sticker *noun* stickers a small piece of paper with a picture or writing on one side and glue on the other side

sticky *adjective* stickier, stickiest Something that is sticky will stick to things when it touches them.

stiff *adjective* stiffer, stiffest Something that is stiff is hard and does not bend easily.

still *adjective* stiller, stillest **1** not moving **2** not fizzy

still *adverb* **1** When you stand, sit, or lie still, you do not move. **2** even now *He's still asleep.*

sting *verb* stings, stinging, stung If an insect stings you, it jabs you with a sharp part of its body and hurts you.

stink *verb* stinks, stinking, stank, stunk to smell nasty

stir *verb* stirs, stirring, stirred to move something about with a spoon

stitch *noun* stitches **1** a loop of thread that you make when you are sewing or knitting **2** a sudden pain in your side that you sometimes get when you have been running

stomach *noun* stomachs the part inside your body where your food goes after you have eaten it

A B C D E F G H I J K L M N O P Q R S T U V W X Y Z

stone *noun* stones **1** rock *The castle is built of solid stone.* **2** a small piece of rock **3** the hard seed in the middle of some fruits such as a cherry or peach **4** We can measure weight in stones. One stone is just under 6½ kilograms.

stool *noun* stools a small seat without a back

stop *verb* stops, stopping, stopped **1** to make something stand still **2** to stand still **3** When you stop doing something, you no longer do it. *The baby finally stopped crying.*

store *verb* stores, storing, stored to keep things until you need them

store *noun* stores a large shop

storey *noun* storeys One storey of a tall building is one floor.

storm *noun* storms When there is a storm, there is a strong wind and a lot of rain or snow. **stormy** *adjective* If the weather is stormy, there is a strong wind and a lot of rain or snow.

story *noun* stories something in a book that tells you about things that have happened

straight *adjective* straighter, straightest Something that is straight does not bend or curl.

strain *verb* strains, straining, strained **1** If you strain a muscle, you hurt it by stretching it too much. **2** When you strain a liquid, you take out any lumps.

strange *adjective* stranger, strangest **1** unusual and surprising **2** A strange place is one that you have not seen before.

stranger *noun* strangers someone you do not know

strap *noun* straps a strip of leather or cloth that you hold when you are carrying something or use for fastening things

straw *noun* straws **1** Straw is dry stalks of corn or wheat that you put on the ground for animals to lie on. **2** A straw is a thin tube that you sometimes put into a drink and use to drink through.

strawberry *noun* strawberries a small, red, juicy fruit

stray *adjective* A stray dog or cat does not have a home but lives outside.

stream *noun* streams a small river

street *noun* streets a road in a town or city with houses along each side

strength *noun* how strong something is

stretch *verb* stretches, stretching, stretched **1** to pull something so that it becomes longer or bigger **2** to move your arms or legs as far as you can

strict *adjective* stricter, strictest Someone who is strict does not allow people to behave badly.

strike *verb* strikes, striking, struck **1** When you strike a match, you rub it so that it makes a flame. **2** When a clock strikes, it makes a sound.

string *noun* strings **1** String is thin rope. **2** The strings on a guitar or violin are the parts that you touch to make music.

strip *verb* strips, stripping, stripped to take off all your clothes

a
b
c
d
e
f
g
h
i
j
k
l
m
n
o
p
q
r
s
t
u
v
w
x
y
z

153

strip *noun* **strips** a long, narrow piece of something

stripe *noun* **stripes** a band of colour on something

stroke *verb* **strokes, stroking, stroked** to move your hand over something gently

stroll *verb* **strolls, strolling, strolled** to walk along slowly

strong *adjective* **stronger, strongest** **1** If you are strong, you can lift and move heavy things. **2** Something that is strong will not break easily. **3** A strong taste or smell is not mild or weak. **strongly** *adverb* If something is built strongly, it will not break easily. If something smells strongly, it doesn't smell mild or weak.

structure *noun* **structures** anything that has been built

struggle *verb* **struggles, struggling, struggled** **1** to fight with your arms and legs to try to get free **2** If you struggle to do something, you work hard to do it because it is difficult.

stubborn *adjective* Someone who is stubborn will not change their mind even though they might be wrong.

student *noun* **students** someone who is studying at college or university

studio *noun* **studios** **1** a place where people make films or radio or television programmes **2** a room where an artist or photographer works

study *verb* **studies, studying, studied** **1** to learn about a subject **2** to look at something very carefully

study *noun* **studies** a room in a house where someone works or studies

stuff *noun* anything that you can see and touch

stuff *verb* **stuffs, stuffing, stuffed** **1** When you stuff something, you fill it with things. **2** When you stuff something somewhere, you push it there roughly.

stumble *verb* **stumbles, stumbling, stumbled** to trip and fall over

stupid *adjective* **1** very silly *That was a really stupid thing to do.* **2** not very clever

stutter *verb* **stutters, stuttering, stuttered** to keep repeating the sounds at the beginning of words when you speak

style *noun* **styles** the shape and design of something

subject *noun* **subjects** **1** A subject is something that you learn about at school. Maths, English, history, and art are all subjects. **2** The subjects of a king or queen are the people they rule over.

submarine *noun* **submarines** a ship that can go under the water

substance *noun* **substances** anything that is a liquid, solid, or gas

A B C D E F G H I J K L M N O P Q R S T U V W X Y Z

subtract *verb* subtracts, subtracting, subtracted *(in mathematics)* When you subtract one number from another, you take it away to make a smaller number. *If you subtract six from nine, you get three, 9 - 6 = 3.*

subway *noun* subways a path or tunnel under a busy road or railway

succeed *verb* succeeds, succeeding, succeeded to manage to do something

success *noun* successes If something is a success, it works well and people like it.

successful *adjective* **1** If you are successful, you manage to do something. **2** If something is successful, it works well and people like it. **successfully** *adverb* Something done successfully works well. If someone does something successfully they manage to do it.

such *determiner* so much *That was such fun!*

suck *verb* sucks, sucking, sucked **1** When you suck something into your mouth, you pull it in. *Sarah sucked some milk up through the straw.* **2** When you suck on something, you keep moving it about in your mouth without chewing it or swallowing it. *Ben was sucking on a sweet.*

sudden *adjective* happening quickly without any warning **suddenly** *adverb* quickly and without warning

There is a double **d** in this word.

suffer *verb* suffers, suffering, suffered When you suffer, something hurts you or upsets you.

sugar *noun* a sweet powder that you add to drinks and other foods to make them taste sweet

suggest *verb* suggests, suggesting, suggested to say that something would be a good idea

suggestion *noun* suggestions an idea or possibility that you can think about

suit *noun* suits a jacket and a pair of trousers or a skirt that are made of the same material and meant to be worn together

suit *verb* suits, suiting, suited If something suits you, it looks nice on you.

suitable *adjective* Something that is suitable is the right type of thing.

suitcase *noun* suitcases a bag with stiff sides that you use for carrying clothes and other things on journeys

sulk *verb* sulks, sulking, sulked When you sulk, you are bad-tempered and do not speak to people because you are cross about something.

sum *noun* sums **1** The sum of two numbers is the number that you get when you add them together. *The sum of seven and three is ten, 7 + 3 = 10.* **2** When you do a sum, you find an answer to a question by working with numbers. **3** A sum of money is an amount of money.

summarize *verb* summarizes, summarizing, summarized to give a summary of something

summary *noun* summaries When you give a summary of something, you describe the important parts of it and leave out the parts that are not so important.

summer *noun* summers the time of the year when the weather is hot and it stays light for longer in the evenings

sun *noun* **1** The sun is the star that we see shining in the sky during the day. The sun gives the earth heat and light. **2** If you are in the sun, the sun is shining on you.

sunburn *noun* If you have sunburn, your skin becomes red and painful because you have spent a long time in the sun.

Sunday *noun* Sundays the day of the week after Saturday

sunflower *noun* sunflowers a big yellow flower that grows very tall and always turns to face the sun

sunglasses *noun* dark glasses that you wear to protect your eyes from the bright sun

sunlight *noun* light from the sun

sunny *adjective* sunnier, sunniest When the weather is sunny, the sun is shining.

sunrise *noun* the time in the morning when the sun comes up and it becomes light

sunset *noun* the time in the evening when the sun goes down and it becomes dark

sunshine *noun* the light and heat that come from the sun

super *adjective* very good

supermarket *noun* supermarkets a large shop where you can buy food and other things

supper *noun* suppers a meal or snack that you eat in the evening

supply *verb* supplies, supplying, supplied to give or sell something to someone

supply *noun* supplies If you have a supply of things, you are keeping them ready to be used later.

support *verb* supports, supporting, supported **1** to hold something up and stop it from falling down **2** to help someone and encourage them to do well *Which football team do you support?*

suppose *verb* supposes, supposing, supposed to think that something is true although you do not know for sure

sure *adjective* **1** If you are sure about something, you know that it is definitely true. **2** If something is sure to happen, it will definitely happen.

surf *verb* surfs, surfing, surfed **1** to stand on a special board called a **surfboard** and ride in towards the shore on big waves **2** *(in ICT)* When you surf the Internet, you look at different websites to find information.

surface *noun* surfaces The surface of something is the top or outside part, not the middle.

surgery *noun* surgeries the room where you go to see a doctor or dentist

surname *noun* surnames your last name, which is the name you share with other members of your family

surprise *noun* surprises **1** If something is a surprise, you were not expecting it to happen. **2** Surprise is the feeling you have when something happens that you were not expecting.

surprise *verb* surprises, surprising, surprised If something surprises you, you were not expecting it to happen.

surrender *verb* surrenders, surrendering, surrendered to stop fighting or hiding and give yourself up

surround *verb* surrounds, surrounding, surrounded to form a circle all around a place

survey *noun* surveys a set of questions that you ask people to find out information about something

survive *verb* survives, surviving, survived **1** If you survive, you do not die but carry on living. *A few people survived the plane crash.* **2** If something survives, it is not destroyed.

suspect *verb* suspects, suspecting, suspected to have a feeling that something might be true

suspense *noun* excitement that you feel because you do not know what is going to happen next

suspicious *adjective* **1** If someone behaves in a suspicious way, they behave in a strange, secret way which makes you think they are doing something wrong. **2** If you are suspicious of someone, you have a feeling that they have done something wrong and you do not trust them.

swallow *verb* swallows, swallowing, swallowed to make something go down your throat

swan *noun* swans a big white bird with a long neck that lives near water and often swims on the water

swap *verb* swaps, swapping, swapped to give something to someone and get something else in return

sway *verb* sways, swaying, swayed to move gently from side to side

sweat *verb* sweats, sweating, sweated When you sweat, salty liquid comes out from your skin when you are very hot.

sweater *noun* sweaters a warm jumper

sweatshirt *noun* sweatshirts a jumper made of thick cotton cloth

sweep *verb* sweeps, sweeping, swept to clean a floor by pushing a brush over it

sweet *adjective* sweeter, sweetest **1** tasting of sugar **2** very nice *What a sweet little girl!*

sweet *noun* sweets **1** something small and sweet which you eat as a snack **2** a pudding

sweetcorn *noun* the yellow seeds of a corn plant, which you cook and eat as a vegetable

swell *verb* swells, swelling, swelled, swollen When something swells, it gets bigger.

a
b
c
d
e
f
g
h
i
j
k
l
m
n
o
p
q
r
s
t
u
v
w
x
y
z

A
B
C
D
E
F
G
H
I
J
K
L
M
N
O
P
Q
R
S
T
U
V
W
X
Y
Z

swerve *verb* swerves, swerving, swerved If a car swerves, it suddenly moves to the side so that it does not hit something. *The bus swerved to avoid a dog in the road.*

swim *verb* swims, swimming, swam, swum to move through water by floating and moving your arms and legs

swimming costume *noun* swimming costumes a piece of clothing that a woman or girl wears when she goes swimming

swimming pool *noun* swimming pools a large pool that has been built for people to swim in

swimming trunks *noun* a piece of clothing that a man or boy wears when he goes swimming

swing *verb* swings, swinging, swung to move backwards and forwards in the air

swing *noun* swings A swing is a seat that hangs down from a frame. You can sit on it and move backwards and forwards.

switch *noun* switches something that you turn or press to make a machine work or a light come on

switch *verb* switches, switching, switched When you switch something on, you turn or press a control so that it starts working. When you switch something off, you turn or press a control so that it stops working.

swop *verb* swops, swopping, swopped Swop is another spelling of **swap**.

sword *noun* swords a weapon that has a handle and a long, thin, sharp blade

syllable *noun* syllables A syllable is one of the sounds or beats in a word. The word *chim-pan-zee* has three syllables. The word *sweet-corn* has two syllables.

symbol *noun* symbols A symbol is a sign which stands for something or means something. The + symbol means that you add numbers together.

symmetrical *adjective* having two halves that are exactly alike

symmetry *noun* If a shape or object has symmetry, its two halves are exactly alike. The line of symmetry in a shape is the line through the middle, which divides the two symmetrical halves.

sympathy *noun* If you have sympathy for someone, you feel sorry for them.

synagogue *noun* synagogues a building where Jewish people pray and worship

synonym *noun* synonyms a word that means the same as another word, such as *courageous* and *brave*

syrup *noun* syrups a very sweet, sticky, liquid

system *noun* systems **1** If you have a system for doing something, you do it in a particular order or way every time. **2** a set of machines that work together *The school has a new heating system.*

Tt

table *noun* **tables 1** a piece of furniture with a flat top that you can put things on **2** a list of numbers or words arranged in rows or columns

tablet *noun* **tablets** a small pill with medicine in, which you swallow when you are ill

tackle *verb* **tackles, tackling, tackled 1** to start doing a difficult job **2** to try to get the ball from someone in a game such as football or rugby

tadpole *noun* **tadpoles** a tiny animal that lives in water and will turn into a frog or toad

tail *noun* **tails** the long part at the end of an animal's body

take *verb* **takes, taking, took, taken 1** to get hold of something *I offered him a sweet, and he took one.* **2** If you take something to a place, you have it with you when you go there. **3** to steal something **4** If someone takes you to a place, you go there with them. *Dad promised to take us to the cinema.* **5** (in mathematics) If you take one number away from another, you subtract it. **6** When a rocket takes off, it goes up into space.

talc, talcum powder *noun* a fine powder you put on your skin to make it feel smooth and smell nice

tale *noun* **tales** a story

talent *noun* **talents** If you have a talent for something, you can do it very well.

talk *verb* **talks, talking, talked** to speak to someone

tall *adjective* **taller, tallest 1** Someone who is tall measures a lot from their head to their feet. **2** A tall tree or building is very high.

Talmud *noun* a book of writings about the Jewish religion

tame *adjective* **tamer, tamest** An animal or bird that is tame is not wild or fierce, and is not afraid of people.

tan *noun* When you have a tan, your skin is darker than usual because you have been in the hot sun.

tangle *noun* **tangles** If things are in a tangle, they are all twisted or knotted together and it is difficult to separate them.

tank *noun* **tanks 1** a very large container that you keep liquid in **2** a very strong, heavy truck that is used in war and moves on metal tracks, not wheels

tap *noun* **taps** a handle which you turn to start or stop water flowing through a pipe

tap *verb* **taps, tapping, tapped** to hit something gently

tape *noun* **tapes 1** Sticky tape is a strip of sticky paper that you use for sticking things together. **2** a special magnetic strip that you can record sound and picture on

tape *verb* **tapes, taping, taped** to record sound or pictures

tape measure *noun* **tape measures** a long strip of cloth or plastic with measurements marked on it, which you use for measuring things

a
b
c
d
e
f
g
h
i
j
k
l
m
n
o
p
q
r
s
t
u
v
w
x
y
z

target *noun* **targets** something that you aim at and try to hit when you are shooting or throwing something

tart *noun* **tarts** a type of food that has pastry on the bottom and fruit, meat, or vegetables on top

task *noun* **tasks** a job that you have to do

taste *verb* **tastes, tasting, tasted**
1 When you taste food, you eat a small amount to see what it is like. **2** The way something tastes is the flavour that it has. *The food tasted horrible.*

taste *noun* **1** what something is like when you eat it **2** Your sense of taste is how well you can recognize things when you eat them.

tax *noun* **taxes** money that people have to pay to the government

taxi *noun* **taxis** a car that you can travel in if you pay the driver

tea *noun* **1** a hot drink that you make by pouring boiling water over the dried leaves of the tea plant **2** a meal that you eat in the afternoon or early evening

teach *verb* **teaches, teaching, taught** to tell someone about something or show them how to do it

teacher *noun* **teachers** a person who teaches someone

team *noun* **teams** a group of people who work together or play together on the same side in a game

teapot *noun* **teapots** a container with a spout that you use for making and pouring tea

tear *verb* **tears, tearing, tore, torn** (rhymes with *fair*) to pull something apart so that it splits or makes a hole

tear *noun* **tears** (rhymes with *fear*) Tears are drops of salty water that come from your eyes when you cry.

tease *verb* **teases, teasing, teased** to make fun of someone

technology *noun* Technology is using science and machines to help people in their lives.

teddy bear *noun* **teddy bears** a stuffed toy bear

teenager *noun* **teenagers** someone who is between 13 and 19 years old

telephone *noun* **telephones** A telephone is a machine that you use to speak to someone who is far away from you. It is also called a **phone**.

telephone *verb* **telephones, telephoning, telephoned** to use a telephone to speak to someone

telescope *noun* **telescopes** A telescope is a tube with special lenses in. When you look through a telescope, things that are far away look bigger and closer.

television *noun* **televisions** a machine that picks up signals that are sent through the air and changes them into pictures and sound so that people can watch them

tell *verb* **tells, telling, told** **1** to speak to someone about something **2** If you can tell the time, you can look at a clock and say what time it is. **3** To tell someone off means to speak to them angrily because they have done something wrong.

temper *noun* **1** Your temper is how you are feeling. If you are in a good temper, you are happy and cheerful. If you are in a bad temper, you are cross and grumpy. **2** If you are in a temper, you are very angry. If you lose your temper, you suddenly become very angry.

temperature *noun* **1** how hot or cold something is **2** If you have a temperature, your body is hotter than usual because you are ill.

temple *noun* **temples** a place where people go to pray and worship a god

temporary *adjective* only lasting for a short time

tempt *verb* **tempts, tempting, tempted** If something tempts you, it seems nice and you want it, but you think it would be wrong or dangerous.

ten *noun* **tens** the number 10

tender *adjective* **tenderer, tenderest** **1** kind and loving **2** soft and easy to eat *The meat was lovely and tender.*

tennis *noun* a game in which players use a special racket to hit a ball backwards and forwards over a net

tense *noun* **tenses** The different tenses of a verb are the different forms that you use to show whether you are talking about the past or present. The past tense of *come* is *came.*

tent *noun* **tents** A tent is a shelter made of cloth that is stretched over poles. You sleep in a tent when you go camping.

tentacle *noun* **tentacles** The tentacles of a sea animal such as an octopus are the long parts that it can move about.

term *noun* **terms** A school term is a time when you go to school and are not on holiday.

terrace *noun* **terraces** a row of houses that are all joined together

terrible *adjective* very bad

terrify *verb* **terrifies, terrifying, terrified** to make someone feel very frightened

terror *noun* a feeling of very great fear

test *noun* **tests** a set of questions that you have to answer to show what you have learned
test *verb* **tests, testing, tested** **1** to give someone questions to answer to show what they have learned **2** to use something so that you can find out whether it works

tetrahedron *noun* **tetrahedrons** a solid shape that has four triangular sides

text *noun* **texts** a piece of writing
text *verb* **texts, texting, texted** to send someone a text message

textbook *noun* **textbooks** a book which gives you information about a subject

text message *noun* **text messages** a written message that you send to someone on a mobile phone

a b c d e f g h i j k l m n o p q r s **t** u v w x y z

texture *noun* **textures** what something feels like when you touch it

than *conjunction* compared with another person or thing *My brother is smaller than me.*

thank *verb* **thanks, thanking, thanked** to tell someone that you are grateful for something they have given you or done for you

that *determiner & pronoun* **those** the one there *That hat is red. That is yours.*

thatched *adjective* A thatched house has a roof made of reeds or straw.

thaw *verb* **thaws, thawing, thawed** When something thaws, it melts and is no longer frozen.

the *determiner* You use **the** in front of a noun when you are talking about that thing in particular, for example *the tree, the bus, the dog.*

theatre *noun* **theatres** a place where plays and shows are performed and people can go to watch them

their *determiner* You use **their** when you are talking about something that belongs to one person that isn't, or more people that aren't, you. *Their coats are hanging up in the cloakroom.*

theirs *pronoun* You use **theirs** when you want to say something belongs to one person, or more people, that aren't you. *These coats are theirs.*

them *pronoun* You use **them** when you are talking about two or more people. *I asked them to my party.*

theme *noun* **themes** the main idea that a book or film is about

then *adverb* **1** after that *I got up and then went to school.* **2** at that time *I was only five 5 old then.*

there *adverb* in that place *You can sit there.*

therefore *adverb* so *We haven't got very much money and therefore we can't go on holiday.*

thermometer *noun* **thermometers** something that you use for measuring temperature

thesaurus *noun* **thesauruses** a book which gives you lists of words that have similar meanings

they *pronoun* You use **they** when you are talking about the people or things already mentioned. *Your mum and dad don't have a dog, do they?*

thick *adjective* **thicker, thickest** **1** wide and not thin **2** made of heavy material **3** A thick liquid is not very runny.

thief *noun* **thieves** someone who steals things

thigh *noun* **thighs** Your thighs are the top parts of your legs.

thin *adjective* **thinner, thinnest** **1** not very thick or wide **2** not very fat **3** A thin liquid is runny.

thing *noun* **things** an object, or anything that is not a person, animal, or plant

think *verb* **thinks, thinking, thought** **1** to have thoughts and ideas in your mind *Think carefully before you answer the question.* **2** to believe that something is true when you do not know for sure *I think we break up next Friday.*

third *adjective* The third thing is the one that comes after the second.

third *noun* One third of something is one of three equal parts that the thing is divided into. It can also be written as ⅓.

thirsty *adjective* thirstier, thirstiest feeling that you want to drink something

thirteen *noun* the number 13

thirty *noun* the number 30

this *determiner* & *pronoun* these the one here *This pencil is mine. This is the one that I want.*

thorn *noun* thorns a sharp, prickly point that grows on some plants

though *adverb* (rhymes with *go*) although

thought *noun* thoughts an idea you think of

thoughtful *adjective* **1** If you look thoughtful, you look quiet, as if you are thinking about something. **2** If you are thoughtful, you are kind and think about what other people want.

thousand *noun* thousands the number 1000

thread *noun* threads a long, thin piece of cotton that you use for sewing

thread *verb* threads, threading, threaded When you thread a needle, you put a thread through it so that you can use it for sewing.

threaten *verb* threatens, threatening, threatened to say that you will do something nasty to someone

three *noun* threes the number 3

three-dimensional *adjective* A three-dimensional object is solid rather than flat. A cube is a three-dimensional shape.

throat *noun* throats the part at the back of your mouth where you swallow food and drink

throb *verb* throbs, throbbing, throbbed If a part of your body throbs, it hurts a lot.

throne *noun* thrones a special chair that a king or queen sits on

through *preposition* (rhymes with *threw*) from one side of something to the other

throw *verb* throws, throwing, threw, thrown **1** to hold something in your hand and then push it away so that it flies through the air **2** When you throw something away, you get rid of it because you do not want it any more.

thud *noun* thuds a dull banging sound

thumb *noun* thumbs the short, thick finger at the side of your hand

thump *verb* thumps, thumping, thumped to hit someone hard

thunder *noun* the loud, rumbling noise that you hear after a flash of lightning in a storm

Thursday *noun* Thursdays the day after Wednesday

tick *noun* ticks a small mark like this ✓ that shows that something is right

tick *verb* ticks, ticking, ticked **1** to put a tick next to something **2** When a clock ticks, it makes a regular clicking sound.

a
b
c
d
e
f
g
h
i
j
k
l
m
n
o
p
q
r
s
t
u
v
w
x
y
z

163

ticket *noun* **tickets** a piece of paper that you buy so that you can travel on a bus or train or get into a place such as a cinema or theatre

tickle *verb* **tickles, tickling, tickled** to touch someone lightly with your fingers to make them laugh

tide *noun* **tides** the regular movement of the sea towards the land and then away from the land

tidy *adjective* **tidier, tidiest** If a place is tidy, everything is in the right place and there is no mess.

tie *verb* **ties, tying, tied** to fasten something with a knot or a bow

tie *noun* **ties** 1 a strip of material that you wear round your neck, under the collar of a shirt 2 If there is a tie in a game, two people or teams have the same number of points.

tiger *noun* **tigers** A tiger is a large wild cat that lives in Asia. It has orange fur with black stripes. A female tiger is called a **tigress**.

tight *adjective* **tighter, tightest** Tight clothes fit your body closely and are not loose.

tights *noun* a piece of clothing that women and girls wear over their feet, legs, and bottom

tile *noun* **tiles** Tiles are thin pieces of baked clay that people use to cover walls or floors.

till *conjunction & preposition* until *Wait till I'm ready!*

till *noun* **tills** a machine that people use in a shop to keep money in and add up how much customers have to pay

time *noun* **times** 1 the thing that we measure in seconds, minutes, hours, days, weeks, months, and years *What time is it?* 2 If it is time to do something, it should be done now. 3 If you do something one or two times, you do it once or twice.

times *verb* (*in mathematics*) One number times another number is one number multiplied by another number. *Two times four equals eight.*

timetable *noun* **timetables** a list of times when things will happen or buses or trains will leave

timid *adjective* shy and not very brave

tin *noun* **tins** 1 a round metal container that food is sold in 2 a metal container for putting things in

tiny *adjective* **tinier, tiniest** very small

tip *noun* **tips** 1 the part right at the end of something long and thin 2 a small amount of money that you give someone to thank them for serving you in a restaurant or helping you 3 a rubbish dump

tiptoe *verb* **tiptoes, tiptoeing, tiptoed** to walk quietly on your toes

tired *adjective* 1 feeling as if you need to sleep 2 If you are tired of something, you are bored or fed up with it.

tissue *noun* **tissues** 1 Tissue paper is very thin, soft paper that you use for wrapping up fragile things to stop them breaking. 2 a paper handkerchief

title *noun* **titles** 1 The title of a book, film, picture, or piece of music is its name. 2 Someone's title is the word like *Dr, Mr,* and *Mrs* that is put in front of their name.

to *preposition* When you go to a place, you go there.

> This sounds the same as **too** or **two**.

toad *noun* toads A toad is an animal that looks like a big frog. It has rough, dry skin and lives on land.

toadstool *noun* toadstools a plant that looks like a mushroom but is poisonous to eat

toast *noun* a slice of bread that has been cooked until it is crisp and brown

toboggan *noun* toboggans a sledge that you use for sliding down slopes covered in snow

today *noun* & *adverb* this day I'm not very well today.

toddler *noun* toddlers a young child who is just beginning to walk

toe *noun* toes Your toes are the parts of your body on the ends of your feet.

together *adverb* **1** with each other I stuck two pieces of paper together. **2** at the same time as each other They all sang together.

toilet *noun* toilets a large bowl with a seat that you use when you need to empty waste from your body

tomato *noun* tomatoes a soft, round, red fruit that you can eat raw in a salad or cook as a vegetable

tomorrow *noun* & *adverb* the day after today I'll see you tomorrow.

> There is only one **m** in this word.

ton *noun* tons We can measure weight in tons. One ton is about 1,016 kilograms.

tongue *noun* tongues (rhymes with sung) the part inside your mouth that you can move about and use for speaking

tonight *noun* & *adverb* this evening or night I'll phone you tonight.

tonne *noun* tonnes We can measure weight in tonnes. One tonne is 1,000 kilograms.

too *adverb* **1** also Can I come too? **2** more than you need Don't use too much salt.

> This sounds the same as **to** or **two**.

tool *noun* tools A tool is something that you use to help you to do a job. Hammers and saws are tools.

tooth *noun* teeth Your teeth are the hard, white parts inside your mouth which you use for biting and chewing.

toothbrush *noun* a long-handled brush that you use to clean your teeth

top *noun* tops **1** the highest part of something **2** the lid of a bottle or jar **3** a piece of clothing that you wear on the top part of your body, over your chest and arms

topic *noun* **topics** a subject that you are writing or talking about

Torah *noun* the law of God as given to Moses and recorded in the first five books of the Bible in the Jewish religion

torch *noun* **torches** an electric light that you can carry about with you

tortoise *noun* **tortoises** A tortoise is an animal that has four legs and a hard shell over its body. Tortoises move slowly and hide their head and legs inside their shell when they are in danger.

toss *verb* **tosses, tossing, tossed** **1** to throw something through the air **2** When you toss a coin, you throw it into the air to see which way it lands.

total *noun* the amount that you get when you have added everything up

total *adjective* complete *There was total silence in the hall.*

touch *verb* **touches, touching, touched** **1** to feel something with your hand **2** to be very close together, with no space between

tough *adjective* **tougher, toughest** **1** very strong **2** brave and strong

tour *noun* **tours** when you visit a lot of different places

tourist *noun* **tourists** someone who is visiting a place on holiday

tournament *noun* **tournaments** a competition in which a lot of different people or teams play matches against each other until a winner is found

tow *verb* **tows, towing, towed** to pull something along *The car was towing a caravan.*

towards *preposition* in the direction of

towel *noun* **towels** a piece of cloth that you use for drying things that are wet

tower *noun* **towers** a tall, narrow part of a building

town *noun* **towns** A town is a place where a lot of people live close to each other. A town is smaller than a city.

toy *noun* **toys** something that children can play with

trace *verb* **traces, tracing, traced** **1** to copy a picture using thin paper that you can see through **2** to find something by getting information and following clues

track *noun* **tracks** **1** The tracks that a person or animal leaves are the marks that they leave on the ground as they walk. **2** a path **3** A railway track is a railway line. **4** A racing track is a piece of ground with lines marked on it so that people can use it for racing.

tractor *noun* **tractors** a strong, heavy truck with large wheels that people drive on a farm and use for pulling farm machines

trademark *noun* **trademarks** a picture or name that a company always puts on the things that it makes

tradition *noun* **traditions** something that people have done it in the same way for a very long time

traffic *noun* cars, buses, bicycles, lorries, and other things that travel on roads

tragedy *noun* **tragedies** something very sad that happens, especially something in which people are hurt or killed

trail *noun* **trails** **1** a rough path across fields or through woods **2** the smells or marks that an animal leaves behind as it goes along *We were able to follow the animal's trail.*

trailer *noun* **trailers** a short part of a film that is shown to people to encourage them to watch it

train *noun* **trains** something that carries passengers or goods on a railway

train *verb* **trains, training, trained** **1** to teach a person or animal how to do something **2** to practise the skills you need to do a sport

trainer *noun* **trainers** **1** someone who trains people or animals **2** Trainers are shoes that you wear for running or doing sport.

tram *noun* **trams** a type of bus which runs along rails in the road

trampoline *noun* **trampolines** a large piece of thick cloth that is joined to a metal frame and is used for jumping up and down on

translate *verb* **translates, translating, translated** to change something from one language into another

transparent *adjective* If something is transparent, you can see through it.

transport *noun* anything that is used to take people, animals, or things from one place to another, for example buses, trains, and lorries

trap *noun* **traps** something that is used to catch a person or an animal

trapdoor *noun* **trapdoors** a door in the floor or ceiling which you can open to make people fall through

travel *verb* **travels, travelling, travelled** to go from one place to another

tray *noun* **trays** a flat piece of wood, metal, or plastic that you use for carrying cups, plates, and other things

tread *verb* **treads, treading, trod, trodden** If you tread on something, you walk on it.

treasure *noun* gold, silver, jewels, and other valuable things

treat *verb* **treats, treating, treated** **1** The way in which you treat someone is the way you behave towards them. **2** When doctors treat someone, they give them medicine or do things to them to make them better when they are ill.

treat *noun* **treats** something special that you enjoy

tree *noun* **trees** a tall plant that has a thick trunk, branches, and leaves

tremble *verb* **trembles, trembling, trembled** to shake because you are cold or frightened

trial *noun* **trials** **1** when you try something to see how well it works **2** when a prisoner and witnesses are questioned in a court to decide whether the prisoner has done something wrong

triangle *noun* **triangles** a shape with three straight edges and three angles

tribe *noun* **tribes** a group of people who live together and are ruled by a chief

trick *noun* **tricks** **1** something that you do to cheat someone or make them look silly **2** something clever that you have learned to do

trick *verb* **tricks, tricking, tricked** to make someone believe something that is not true

trickle *verb* **trickles, trickling, trickled** When water trickles, it moves very slowly.

trigger *noun* **triggers** the part of a gun that you pull with your finger to fire it

trim *verb* **trims, trimming, trimmed** to cut something so that it looks neat and tidy

trip *verb* **trips, tripping, tripped** to catch your foot on something and nearly fall over

trip *noun* **trips** a short journey

triumph *noun* **triumphs** a great success

trolley *noun* **trolleys** a large container on wheels that you can put things in and push along

troops *noun* soldiers

trophy *noun* **trophies** a cup that you can win

tropical *adjective* A tropical place has a very hot, wet climate.

trouble *noun* **troubles** **1** If something causes trouble for you, it causes problems for you or upsets you. **2** If you are in

trouble, you have a problem or someone is cross with you.

trousers *noun* a piece of clothing that you wear over your legs and bottom

trout *noun* **trout** a fish that lives in rivers and lakes and can be cooked and eaten

truck *noun* **trucks** a small lorry

trudge *verb* **trudges, trudging, trudged** When you trudge along, you walk along slowly, with heavy steps.

true *adjective* **truer, truest** real and not made-up or pretended

trumpet *noun* **trumpets** A trumpet is a musical instrument made of brass. You blow into it and press down buttons to make different notes.

trunk *noun* **trunks** **1** the thick stem on a tree that grows up out of the ground **2** an elephant's long nose **3** a large box that you use for carrying things on a journey

trust *verb* **trusts, trusting, trusted** to believe that someone is good and honest and will not hurt you or tell you lies

truth *noun* something that is true *Is he telling the truth?*

truthful *adjective* Someone who is truthful tells the truth.

try *verb* **tries, trying, tried** **1** If you try to do something, you make an effort to do it. **2** to do or use something to see what it is like

T-shirt *noun* T-shirts A T-shirt is a piece of clothing that you wear on the top half of your body. It has a round neck and short sleeves.

tub *noun* tubs a container *We bought a tub of ice cream.*

tube *noun* tubes **1** a long, thin container that you can squeeze a thick liquid out of **2** a long, round, hollow thing

tuck *verb* tucks, tucking, tucked If you tuck a piece of clothing in, you push the ends of it into another piece of clothing.

Tuesday *noun* Tuesdays the day after Monday

tug *verb* tugs, tugging, tugged to pull something hard

tuna *noun* tuna a large sea fish that you can eat

tune *noun* tunes a group of musical notes which make a nice sound when they are played in order

tunnel *noun* tunnels a long hole under the ground that you can walk or drive through

turban *noun* turbans a long piece of material that you wear wrapped round your head

turkey *noun* turkeys a large bird that is kept on farms for its meat

turn *verb* turns, turning, turned **1** When you turn round, you move round. **2** to move something round *He turned the key in the lock.* **3** to become *A lot of leaves turn red and orange in the autumn.* **4** To turn into something means to change and become that thing.

turn *noun* turns If it is your turn to do something, you are the person who should do it next.

turtle *noun* turtles a sea animal that looks like a tortoise

tusk *noun* tusks An elephant's tusks are its two very long, pointed teeth.

TV *noun* TVs a television

twelve *noun* the number 12

twenty *noun* the number 20

twice *adverb* two times

twig *noun* twigs a very small, thin branch on a tree

twin *noun* twins Twins are two children who are born to the same mother at the same time.

twinkle *verb* twinkles, twinkling, twinkled to shine with little flashes of light

twirl *verb* twirls, twirling, twirled to spin round and round

twist *verb* twists, twisting, twisted to turn something round

two *noun* twos the number 2

This sounds the same as **to** or **too**.

two-dimensional *adjective* A two-dimensional shape is flat rather than solid. A square is a two-dimensional shape.

a
b
c
d
e
f
g
h
i
j
k
l
m
n
o
p
q
r
s
t
u
v
w
x
y
z

type *noun* **types** a kind or sort *What type of car have your parents got?*

type *verb* **types, typing, typed** to write with a computer keyboard

typical *adjective* normal and usual

tyre *noun* **tyres** a circle of rubber that goes round the outside of a wheel

Uu

ugly *adjective* **uglier, ugliest** horrible to look at

umbrella *noun* **umbrellas** a round cover that you hold over your head to keep the rain off you

unable *adjective* If you are unable to do something, you cannot do it.

unbelievable *adjective* If something is unbelievable, it is so strange that you cannot believe it.

uncertain *adjective* not sure about something

uncle *noun* **uncles** the brother of your mother or father, or your aunt's husband

uncomfortable *adjective* **1** If you are uncomfortable, part of your body hurts or is not relaxed. **2** If a chair or bed is uncomfortable, it does not feel nice when you sit on it or lie on it.

unconscious *adjective* When you are unconscious, you are in a very deep sleep

and cannot understand what is happening around you.

under *preposition* **1** below *The cat is under the table.* **2** less than *You can't drive if you are under 17.*

underground *adjective* under the ground

underground *noun* a railway that runs through tunnels under the ground

underline *verb* **underlines, underlining, underlined** to draw a straight line underneath a word

underneath *preposition* under

understand *verb* **understands, understanding, understood** If you can understand something, you know what it means or how it works.

undo *verb* **undoes, undoing, undid, undone** to open something so that it is no longer tied or fastened

undress *verb* **undresses, undressing, undressed** to take your clothes off

unemployed *adjective* Someone who is unemployed does not have a job.

uneven *adjective* not smooth or flat

unexpected *adjective* If something is unexpected, it is surprising because you did not expect it to happen.

unfair *adjective* If something is unfair, it is not fair or right because it treats some people badly. **unfairly** *adverb* in a way that is not fair or right

unfortunate *adjective* happening because of bad luck

ungrateful *adjective* If you are ungrateful, you do not thank someone when they have helped you or given you something.

unhappy *adjective* unhappier, unhappiest sad and not happy

unhealthy *adjective* **1** not strong and healthy **2** Things that are unhealthy are not good for you and can make you ill.

unicorn *noun* unicorns an animal in stories that has one long, straight horn growing from the front of its head

uniform *noun* uniforms a special set of clothes that everyone in the same school, job, or club wears

unique *adjective* If something is unique, there is nothing else like it.

unit *noun* units *(in mathematics)* Units are ones. When you add or subtract big numbers, you work with hundreds, tens, and units.

unite *verb* unites, uniting, united to join together and work together

universe *noun* everything in space, including the earth, the sun, and all the stars and planets

university *noun* universities a place where you can go to study after you have left school

unkind *adjective* unkinder, unkindest nasty or cruel to another person

unless *conjunction* if something does not happen

unlock *verb* unlocks, unlocking, unlocked to open a lock with a key

unlucky *adjective* unluckier, unluckiest If you are unlucky, you have bad luck.

unnecessary *adjective* If something is unnecessary, you do not need it.

unpack *verb* unpacks, unpacking, unpacked to take things out of a bag, box, or suitcase

unpleasant *adjective* nasty or horrible

unpopular *adjective* If something is unpopular, not many people like it. If someone is unpopular, not many people like them.

unsafe *adjective* dangerous and not safe

untidy *adjective* untidier, untidiest messy and not tidy

untie *verb* unties, untying, untied to undo a knot in a piece of rope or string

until *conjunction* & *preposition* up to a certain time

untrue *adjective* not true or correct

unusual *adjective* strange and not normal or usual

up *adverb* & *preposition* towards a higher place *Time to get up! She ran up the hill.*

upright *adjective* standing up straight

uproar *noun* If there is an uproar, a lot of people shout and make a noise.

upset *adjective* sad or crying
upset *verb* upsets, upsetting, upset to make someone feel sad and disappointed

upside-down *adjective* turned over so that the bottom is at the top

urgent *adjective* If something is urgent, you have to do it immediately.

us *pronoun* You use **us** when you are talking about yourself and at least one more other person.

A
B
C
D
E
F
G
H
I
J
K
L
M
N
O
P
Q
R
S
T
U
V
W
X
Y
Z

use *verb* **uses, using, used** **1** When you use something, you do a job with it. **2** If you used to do something, you did it in the past but you do not do it now.

use *noun* **uses** If something has a use, you can use it to make something or do a job.

useful *adjective* good and helpful

useless *adjective* If something is useless, you cannot use it.

user-friendly *adjective* A machine that is user-friendly is easy to understand and use.

usual *adjective* normal and happening quite often **usually** *adverb* normally and quite often

Vv

vaccination *noun* **vaccinations** an injection that stops you getting an illness

vague *adjective* **vaguer, vaguest** not clear or certain

vain *adjective* **vainer, vainest** **1** If you are vain, you think too much about how nice you look and how clever you are. **2** If you try in vain to do something, you try to do it but do not manage it.

valley *noun* **valleys** low land between two hills

valuable *adjective* worth a lot of money, or very useful

value *noun* how much money something is worth, or how important or useful it is

van *noun* **vans** a type of car with a large, covered part at the back for carrying things in

vandal *noun* **vandals** someone who deliberately breaks things that belong to other people

vanilla *noun* something that is added to ice cream and other sweet food to make it taste nice

vanish *verb* **vanishes, vanishing, vanished** to disappear

variety *noun* **varieties** **1** A variety of things is a lot of different things. *We have a variety of colours to choose from.* **2** One variety of something is one type. *They sell over twenty varieties of ice cream.*

various *adjective* Various things means a lot of different things. *There were various things to eat.*

vase *noun* **vases** a pot that you put flowers in

vast *adjective* very big

vegetable *noun* **vegetables** A vegetable is a part of a plant that we can eat. Potatoes, carrots, and beans are vegetables.

vegetarian *noun* vegetarians a person who does not eat meat

vehicle *noun* vehicles A vehicle is anything that can travel on land and take people or things from one place to another. Cars, vans, buses, trains, and lorries are vehicles.

veil *noun* veils a piece of thin material that some women or girls wear over their face or head

vein *noun* veins Your veins are the narrow tubes inside your body that carry blood to your heart.

velvet *noun* a type of thick, soft cloth

verse *noun* verses **1** One verse of a song or poem is one part of it that is not the chorus. **2** Verse is poetry.

version *noun* versions one form of something, which is slightly different from all the other forms

vertical *adjective* standing or pointing straight up

very *adverb* extremely *That was a very silly thing to do!*

> There is only one **r** in this word.

vest *noun* vests a piece of clothing that you wear on the top half of the body under your other clothes

vet *noun* vets a doctor for animals

via *preposition* When you go via a place, you go through that place to get somewhere else.

vibrate *verb* vibrates, vibrating, vibrated to shake

vicar *noun* vicars a Christian religious leader who is in charge of a church and the area around it

vicious *adjective* violent and cruel

victim *noun* victims someone who has been hurt, robbed, or killed *We must help the victims of this terrible earthquake.*

victory *noun* victories when you win a game or battle

video *verb* videos, videoing, videoed to record a television programme on a video so that you can watch it later

view *noun* views everything that you can see from a place

village *noun* villages A village is a small group of houses and other buildings in the country. A village is smaller than a town.

vinegar *noun* a sour liquid which you use in cooking to give a sharp, sour taste to food

violin *noun* violins A violin is a musical instrument made of wood with strings across it. You hold a violin under your chin and play it by pulling a bow across the strings.

virus *noun* viruses a tiny living thing that can make you ill if it gets into your body

vision *noun* how well you can see things

visit *verb* visits, visiting, visited When you visit a person, you go to see them. When you visit a place, you go there to see what it is like.

vital *adjective* very important

a
b
c
d
e
f
g
h
i
j
k
l
m
n
o
p
q
r
s
t
u
v
w
x
y
z

vitamin *noun* vitamins A vitamin is something that is found in your food. Your body needs vitamins to stay strong and healthy. *Oranges are full of vitamin C.*

vivid *adjective* **1** Vivid colours are very bright. **2** A vivid dream or memory is so clear that it seems real.

vocabulary *noun* all the words that someone knows and uses

voice *noun* voices the sound you make with your mouth when you are speaking or singing

volcano *noun* volcanoes a mountain or other place on the earth's surface from which hot, liquid rock sometimes bursts from inside the earth

volume *noun* volumes **1** how much space something takes up **2** how loud a sound is **3** one book that is part of a set of books

voluntary *adjective* If something is voluntary, you can choose to do it if you want, but you do not have to do it.

volunteer *verb* volunteers, volunteering, volunteered to offer to do a job

volunteer *noun* volunteers someone who offers to do a job

vote *verb* votes, voting, voted to say which person or thing you choose

voucher *noun* vouchers a piece of printed paper you can use instead of money to pay for something

vowel *noun* vowels Vowels are the letters, *a, e, i, o, u,* and sometimes *y*. All the other letters of the alphabet are consonants.

voyage *noun* voyages a long journey in a boat or spacecraft

vulture *noun* vultures a large bird that eats dead animals

Ww

wade *verb* wades, wading, waded to walk through water

wag *verb* wags, wagging, wagged When a dog wags its tail, it moves it quickly from side to side because it is happy or excited.

wagon *noun* wagons a cart with four wheels that is pulled by horses

wail *verb* wails, wailing, wailed to give a long, sad cry

waist *noun* waists the narrow part in the middle of your body

wait *verb* waits, waiting, waited to stay in a place until someone comes or until something happens

wake *verb* wakes, waking, woke, woken When you wake up, you stop sleeping.

walk *verb* walks, walking, walked to move along on your feet

walk *noun* walks When you go for a walk, you walk somewhere.

wall *noun* **walls** **1** The walls of a building are the parts that hold up the roof and separate the building into different rooms. **2** something built from bricks or stone around a garden or field

wallet *noun* **wallets** a small, flat case that you carry money in

wallpaper *noun* **1** colourful paper that you stick onto the walls of a room to make it look nice **2** *(in ICT)* the background pattern or picture that you choose to have on the screen of your computer or mobile phone

wand *noun* **wands** a stick that you use for casting magic spells or doing magic tricks

wander *verb* **wanders, wandering, wandered** to walk about in no particular direction

want *verb* **wants, wanting, wanted** If you want something, you would like to have it or do it. *Do you want a drink?*

war *noun* **wars** When there is a war, two countries fight against each other.

wardrobe *noun* **wardrobes** a cupboard where you hang clothes

warm *adjective* **warmer, warmest** quite hot

warn *verb* **warns, warning, warned** to tell someone about a danger

wash *verb* **washes, washing, washed** **1** to clean something with water **2** When you wash up, you wash the plates, knives, and forks at the end of a meal.

washing *noun* clothes that need to be washed or are being washed

washing machine *noun* **washing machines** a machine for washing clothes

wasp *noun* **wasps** A wasp is an insect with black and yellow stripes on its body. Wasps can sting you.

waste *noun* something that is left over and cannot be used

waste *verb* **wastes, wasting, wasted** to use more of something than you really need to

watch *verb* **watches, watching, watched** to look at something

watch *noun* **watches** a small clock that you wear on your wrist

water *noun* Water is the clear liquid that is in rivers and seas. All living things need water to live.

water *verb* **waters, watering, watered** **1** to pour water onto a plant to help it to grow **2** When your eyes water, tears come into them.

waterfall *noun* **waterfalls** part of a river where the water falls down over rocks

waterproof *adjective* made of material that does not let water through

wave *verb* **waves, waving, waved** **1** to lift up your hand and move it from side to side **2** to move backwards and forwards or from side to side *The flags were waving in the wind.*

wave *noun* **waves** Waves in the sea are the parts that move up and down across the top of it.

wax *noun* the substance that candles are made from

way *noun* **ways** **1** the roads or paths you follow to get to a place **2** how you do something *What's the best way to cook potatoes?*

we *pronoun* You use **we** when you're talking about yourself and one or more people.

weak *adjective* **weaker, weakest** **1** not very strong **2** likely to break easily **3** A weak drink has a lot of water in it and so does not have a very strong taste.

wealthy *adjective* **wealthier, wealthiest** rich

weapon *noun* **weapons** A weapon is something that a person can use to hurt or kill someone. Knives and guns are weapons.

wear *verb* **wears, wearing, wore, worn** (rhymes with *air*) **1** When you wear clothes, you have them on your body. **2** When something wears out, it becomes so old that you cannot use it any more.

weary *adjective* **wearier, weariest** very tired

weather *noun* what it is like outside, for example whether the sun is shining, or it is rainy, or windy

weave *verb* **weaves, weaving, wove, woven** to make cloth from threads

web *noun* **webs** **1** a thin net that a spider spins to trap insects **2** *(in ICT)* The Web is the World Wide Web, where information is kept on computers all over the world and people can use it by using the Internet.

webbed *adjective* Animals with webbed feet have skin between the toes of their feet.

webcam *noun* **webcams** *(in ICT)* a camera that films things that are happening and broadcasts them live over the Internet

website *noun* **websites** *(in ICT)* a place on the Internet where you can find information about something

wedding *noun* **weddings** the time when a man and woman get married

Wednesday *noun* **Wednesdays** the day after Tuesday

weed *noun* **weeds** Weeds are wild plants that grow in a garden or field when you do not want them to.

week *noun* **weeks** a period of seven days

weekend *noun* **weekends** Saturday and Sunday

weep *verb* **weeps, weeping, wept** to cry

A B C D E F G H I J K L M N O P Q R S T U V **W** X Y Z

weigh *verb* weighs, weighing, weighed **1** When you weigh something, you use a machine to find out how heavy it is. **2** The amount that something weighs is how heavy it is *How much do you weigh?*

weight *noun* weights **1** how heavy something is **2** Weights are pieces of metal that you use for weighing things. **3** Weights are heavy pieces of metal that people lift to make their bodies stronger.

weird *adjective* weirder, weirdest very strange

welcome *verb* welcomes, welcoming, welcomed If you welcome someone, you show that you are pleased when they arrive.

well *noun* wells a deep hole in the ground from which you can get water or oil

well *adverb* better, best **1** in a good or successful way *I can play the piano quite well now.* **2** a lot *Shake the bottle well before you open it.* as well also *Can I come as well?*

well *adjective* healthy and not ill

west *noun* West is the direction where the sun sets in the evening.

wet *adjective* wetter, wettest **1** covered or soaked in water **2** When the weather is wet, it rains.

whale *noun* whales A whale is a very large sea animal. Whales are mammals and breathe air, but they live in the sea like fish.

what *adjective & pronoun* Use this word when you are asking about something.

wheat *noun* Wheat is a plant that farmers grow. It is used to make flour.

wheel *noun* wheels Wheels are the round objects that cars, buses, bicycles, and trains go along on.

wheelbarrow *noun* wheelbarrows a small cart that you push along and use for carrying things

wheelchair *noun* wheelchairs a chair on wheels for a person who cannot walk very well

when *adverb & conjunction* Use this word when you are talking about the time that something happens.

where *adverb & conjunction* Use this word when you are talking about the place that something happens.

whether *conjunction* if *The teacher asked whether I had finished my work.*

which *determiner & pronoun* Use this word when you are choosing one thing or talking about one particular thing.

while *conjunction* during the time that something else is happening

whimper *verb* whimpers, whimpering, whimpered to cry softly because you are frightened or hurt *The puppy whimpered in his basket because he wanted to be in the room with the children.*

whine *verb* whines, whining, whined **1** to make a long, high, sad sound **2** to complain about something

whip *noun* whips a long piece of rope or leather that is used for hitting people or animals

whip *verb* whips, whipping, whipped **1** to hit a person or animal with a whip **2** to stir cream quickly until it goes thick

a b c d e f g h i j k l m n o p q r s t u v **w** x y z

whirl *verb* whirls, whirling, whirled to turn round and round very fast

whirr *verb* whirrs, whirring, whirred When a machine whirrs, it makes a gentle humming sound.

whisk *verb* whisks, whisking, whisked to stir eggs or cream round and round very fast

whisker *noun* whiskers An animal's whiskers are the long, stiff hairs near its mouth.

whisper *verb* whispers, whispering, whispered to speak very quietly

whistle *verb* whistles, whistling, whistled to make a high sound by blowing air through your lips

whistle *noun* whistles something that you can blow into to make a loud, high sound

white *adjective* whiter, whitest **1** Something that is white is the colour of snow. **2** Someone who is white has a skin that is naturally pale in colour. **3** White bread is made with just the white part of the wheat grain, not the whole grain.

whiteboard *noun* whiteboards a large board with a smooth white surface that you can write on with special pens

who *pronoun* which person

whole *adjective* **1** all of something, with nothing left out **2** in one piece *The bird swallowed the fish whole.*

wholemeal *adjective* Wholemeal bread is brown bread.

whose *adjective & pronoun* belonging to which person *Whose coat is this?*

why *adverb* Use this word when you are talking about the reason that something happens.

wicked *adjective* very bad or cruel

wide *adjective* wider, widest Something that is wide measures a lot from one side to the other.

width *noun* widths how wide something is

wife *noun* wives the woman a man is married to

wig *noun* wigs false hair that some people wear on their head

wild *adjective* wilder, wildest **1** Wild animals and plants live or grow in a natural way and are not looked after by people. **2** Wild behaviour is rough and not calm.

wildlife *noun* wild animals

will *verb* would If you will do something, you are going to do it in the future. *I will be there at ten o'clock.*

will *noun* wills something that a person writes down to tell other people what they want to happen to their things after they have died

willing *adjective* happy to do something *We are willing to help.*

win *verb* wins, winning, won to beat the other people or teams in a game, competition, or battle

wind *noun* winds (rhymes with *tinned*) air that moves over the earth

wind *verb* winds, winding, wound (rhymes with *find*) **1** to twist or turn something round *She wound her scarf round her neck.* **2** When you wind up a clock or clockwork toy, you turn a key so that it will work.

windmill *noun* windmills a building with large sails that move in the wind and use the power of the wind to make a machine work

window *noun* windows **1** an opening in a wall that is filled with glass to let the light in **2** *(in ICT)* one area of a computer screen where you can see information or a document

windscreen *noun* windscreens the big window at the front of a car

wind turbine *noun* wind turbines a tall, thin building that has large sails which move in the wind to produce electricity

windy *adjective* windier, windiest When the weather is windy, there is a strong wind.

wine *noun* wines an alcoholic drink that is made from grapes

wing *noun* wings **1** A bird's wings are the parts that it moves up and down when it is flying. **2** The wings on an aeroplane are the parts that stick out on each side and help the aeroplane to fly smoothly.

wink *verb* winks, winking, winked to close one eye

winner *noun* winners the person or team that wins a game or competition

winter *noun* winters the time of the year when the weather is cold and it gets dark early in the evenings

wipe *verb* wipes, wiping, wiped to rub something gently to clean it

wire *noun* wires A wire is a long, thin strip of metal. Electricity goes along wires, and wires are also used to hold things in place.

wireless *adjective* able to send and receive signals without using wires *You can get a wireless Internet connection for your computer.*

wise *adjective* wiser, wisest Someone who is wise understands a lot of things and knows the most sensible thing to do.

wish *verb* wishes, wishing, wished to say that you would really like something to happen *I wish I had lots of money.*

wish *noun* wishes When you make a wish, you say what you would like to happen.

witch *noun* witches a woman in stories who uses magic

with *preposition* **1** If one thing is with another thing, the two things are together. *We had apple pie with cream.* **2** using *You can cut paper with scissors.*

There is only one **h** in this word.

within *preposition* inside *You must stay within the school grounds.*

without *preposition* not having *The family was left without any money.*

witness *noun* witnesses someone who sees a crime or an accident happen

a
b
c
d
e
f
g
h
i
j
k
l
m
n
o
p
q
r
s
t
u
v
w
x
y
z

A B C D E F G H I J K L M N O P Q R S T U V **W** X Y Z

wizard *noun* **wizards** a man in stories who uses magic

wobble *verb* **wobbles, wobbling, wobbled** to move and shake about

wolf *noun* **wolves** a wild animal that is like a large, grey dog

woman *noun* **women** a grown-up female person

wonder *noun* when you feel amazed and very glad

wonder *verb* **wonders, wondering, wondered** to ask yourself about something

wonderful *adjective* amazing and fantastic

won't *verb* will not *I won't put up with this bad behaviour!*

wood *noun* **woods** **1** Wood is the hard material that trees are made of. You can burn wood as fuel or use it for making things. **2** A wood is an area of land where a lot of trees grow. *Don't go into the woods on your own.*

wool *noun* the thick, soft hair that sheep have on their bodies

word *noun* **words** **1** a group of sounds or letters that mean something **2** If you give your word, you promise.

word processor *noun* **word processors** *(in ICT)* a computer program that you use when you want to write something

work *noun* a job that you have to do

work *verb* **works, working, worked** **1** to do a job or do something useful **2** If a machine works, it does what it is meant to do. **3** When you work out the answer to a question, you find the answer.

world *noun* all the countries and people on the earth

World Wide Web *noun (in ICT)* The World Wide Web is the system for keeping information on computers all over the world so that people can use it by using the Internet.

worm *noun* **worms** a long, thin animal with no legs that lives in the soil

worry *verb* **worries, worrying, worried** to feel upset and nervous because you think something bad might happen

worse *adjective* **1** less good than another thing **2** more ill than before

worship *verb* **worships, worshipping, worshipped** To worship a god means to show your love and respect.

worst *adjective* The worst person or thing is the one that is worse than any other.

worth *adjective* **1** If something is worth an amount of money, you could sell it for that amount of money. *How much are these old coins worth?* **2** If something is worth doing or having, it is good or useful. *This film is well worth seeing.*

wound *noun* **wounds** (rhymes with *spooned*) a cut on your body

wound *verb* **wounds, wounding, wounded** (rhymes with *spooned*) to hurt someone

wrap *verb* wraps, wrapping, wrapped to put cloth or paper around something

wreath *noun* wreaths a circle of flowers or leaves twisted together

wreck *verb* wrecks, wrecking, wrecked to break something or destroy it completely

wreck *noun* wrecks a car, ship, or aeroplane that has been damaged in an accident

wrestle *verb* wrestles, wrestling, wrestled When people wrestle, they fight with each other by holding each other and trying to force each other to the ground.

wriggle *verb* wriggles, wriggling, wriggled to twist and turn with your body

wrinkle *noun* wrinkles Wrinkles are small lines in your skin that often appear as you get older.

wrist *noun* wrists the thin part of your arm where it is joined to your hand

write *verb* writes, writing, wrote, written to put letters and words onto paper so that people can read them

writing *noun* **1** A piece of writing is something that you have written. **2** Your writing is the way you write.

wrong *adjective* **1** not right or correct *He gave the wrong answer.* **2** bad *Stealing is wrong.*

Xx

X-ray *noun* X-rays a photograph that shows the bones and other things inside your body so that doctors can see if there is anything wrong

xylophone *noun* xylophones a musical instrument with a row of wooden or metal bars that you hit with small hammers

Yy

yacht *noun* yachts a boat with sails that people use for racing or for pleasure

yard *noun* yards **1** We can measure length in yards. One yard is just under one metre. **2** a piece of ground that is next to a building and has a wall round it

yawn *verb* yawns, yawning, yawned to open your mouth and breathe in deeply because you are tired

year *noun* years a period of twelve months, or 365 days

yell *verb* yells, yelling, yelled to shout very loudly

a b c d e f g h i j k l m n o p q r s t u v **w** **x** **y** z

A
B
C
D
E
F
G
H
I
J
K
L
M
N
O
P
Q
R
S
T
U
V
W
X
Y
Z

yellow *adjective* Something that is yellow is the colour of a lemon.

yes *interjection* You use **yes** to agree or accept something or as an answer meaning, *I am here.*

yesterday *noun* the day before today

yet *adverb & preposition* **1** until now *He hasn't arrived yet.* **2** If you do not want to do something yet, you do not want to do it until later. **3** but *It was the middle of winter, yet it was quite warm.*

yogurt *noun* a thick liquid that is made from milk and has a slightly sour taste

yolk *noun* yolks (rhymes with *joke*) the yellow part inside an egg

you *pronoun* the person or people that you are talking to and nobody else

young *adjective* younger, youngest not very old

your *adjective* belonging to you

yourself *pronoun* yourselves the person that you are talking to and nobody else

youth *noun* youths **1** a boy or young man **2** the time in your life when you are young

yo-yo *noun* yo-yos a toy that spins round on a piece of string

Zz

zebra *noun* zebras an animal that looks like a horse and has black and white stripes on its body

zebra crossing *noun* zebra crossings a place where there are black and white stripes across a road to show that cars must stop to let people cross the road

zero *noun* zeros the number **0**

zigzag *noun* zigzags a line with a lot of sudden, sharp turns in it like this ∿∿∿

zip, zipper *noun* zips, zippers A zip joins two pieces of cloth. It has two lines of teeth that come together and grip each other when you close it.

zone *noun* zones an area of land that has a special use

zoo *noun* zoos a place where different kinds of wild animals are kept so that people can go and see them

zoom *verb* zooms, zooming, zoomed to move along very quickly

Top Ten
Writing Tips

Charlie Higson

Who, what, where, when, why? Ask yourself these questions . . .

Andy Stanton

Give your characters memorable names . . .

Jeremy Strong

Surprises keep the reader interested . . .

Jacqueline Wilson

Use lots of conversation . . .

Make Your Writing
More Exciting

Read on to find out more!

Charlie Higson

Charlie is a novelist who has written for both adults and younger readers, as well as writing and performing comedy on television.

ideas

readi

practice

2
Who, what, where, when?
Ask yourself these questions before you start writing. Who is the story about – a boy a girl, a monster, a cat? What type of story is it – a love story, a horror story, a crime story? Where does it take place – at school, on the moon, in a fantasy world? When does it take place – today, yesterday, 100 years ago, in the future?

1
Where do you get your ideas?
Every time I watch television, every time I read a book, every time I talk to a friend, or listen to people chatting on a bus, I get ideas for stories. Ideas are all around us, you just have to let them in.

3
And *why*?
Why do the peop in your story do the things they do?

7
Don't be afraid to copy.
You're young, you haven't seen that much of the world, you'll mostly know about life from books, TV and films, so, there's nothing wrong with borrowing from grown-up writers who will know more than you. Find an author you like and write a story in their style, or using some of their ideas, it's very good practice.

6
Use all the writer's tools.
As well as getting inside your characters' heads and hearts you need to use: DESCRIPTION – where you tell us what things look like. ACTION – where things happen. DIALOGUE – where you show what characters are saying to each other.

... television work includes *The ...st Show*, *Randall and Hopkirk ...eceased* and the sitcom *Swiss ...oni*. His books for younger readers include the best-selling Young James Bond series and the Enemy series of zombie books for teenagers.

4

A story is not just one thing happening after another.

That would get boring. "The man walked into the room and the other ...n hit him with a frying pan, and then ...ldier came in and blew the house up ...d then a monster flew down and ate ...everyone…" That's not a story. The events need to be connected so the reader thinks "I wonder what happens next."

5

Make the reader care about your characters.

Let the reader know what they're thinking and feeling. Don't be afraid to put emotions into your story. Show us what's in your characters' hearts. Make them real.

feeling

9

Starting a story is easy, finishing one is difficult.

It really helps if you know how your story ends. If you know where you're heading it makes it all much easier. It doesn't matter how you get there but it's good to have a destination.

ialogue

8

Don't be afraid _not_ to copy.

Despite what you may have been told at school ...here is no right or wrong way to write a story. Have the confidence to write it the way you want to write it.

confidence

10

Write, write, write, write, write and read, read, read, read, read.

Writing is like any other skill. The more you do it, the better you'll get at it. And read as many books as possible to see how the experts do it.

Andy Stanton

Andy Stanton is best known for his award-winn
Mr Gum books, which have sold more than a
million copies in the UK and been published in

1

Read as many books as possible.
The more you read, the more you'll understand the tricks and techniques that other writers use.

character

2

Don't worry about pleasing anyone else,
write what interests you. If you like it, chances are that other people will like it too.

3

Some writers plan out everything that's going to happen in a story before they begin writing – and some just start with one or two ideas and dive right in. **There's no right or wrong way.**

edit

tricks

8

Give your characters memorable names that stand out.
Also, you can use a name to hint at what a character is like. For instance, I called my villain Mr Gum because it sounds a bit grubby and nasty, like chewing gum stuck on the sole of your shoe.

7

The first version of your story doesn't have to be perfect, so **don't give up.**
The important thing is to get it all down from start to finish – you can make it better later, when you edit it.

style

ver thirty countries worldwide. hey have won multiple awards, ncluding the Red House Children's ook Award and the first ever oald Dahl Funny Prize.

When he's not writing, Andy enjoys reading, watching cartoons and playing the electric guitar really, really badly (he thinks).

5

technique

Try to write every day.
Find the time of day that works best for you. Some writers like to write in the morning and others get their best work done late at night.

4

If you really don't know where to begin, **open this dictionary at a random page,** take the first word you see and start a story based on that word!

6

ALWAYS carry a notebook so that you can write down ideas before you forget them.

names

10

9

Look for interesting ways of saying things.
Instead of saying 'Frank had a terrible headache,' you might say, 'Frank felt like there was a tiny angry pixie inside his head, whacking his brains with a sledgehammer.' Avoid overused phrases and come up with a style of your own.

Play around until you find the best possible ending for your story.
A good ending should feel like it has naturally 'grown out of' what has come before it – but at the same time it shouldn't be predictable. It has to be satisfying AND surprising.

Good luck, everyone! Keep writing!

Jeremy Strong

Jeremy Strong has published over one hundred children's books, mostly for the 7-11 age group. His books have been short-listed for numerous awards and he has won The Children's Book Awar

memorable

1

Get off to a great start.
Don't hang around or your reader will die of boredom. Capture their interest with the first few sentences.

2

Memorable main characters
that come alive in your imagination will help you write the story.

3

Create tension.
Who or what is going to try and stop your heroes from achieving their goal? How will they do that?

tension

7

Edit your work.
You must be ruthless in cutting out words and sentences, even whole paragraphs and pages if they are not necessary for the story or they are simply not good enough. One page of good writing is far more effective than five pages of poor quailty wordage.

8

Stories are always improved by removing material. (See Tip 7!)
The biggest problem with writing is trying to make the story on paper as good as that wonderful story in your head.

alive

e Hundred Mile-An-Hour Dog),
e Nottingham Big Three Award
y Mum's Going to Explode), and
s novel *Beware – Killer Tomatoes*
n four awards including the
effield Book Award. *There's a*

Viking in My Bed! was dramatised for CBBC and further TV projects are in the pipeline. Jeremy visits schools and festivals world-wide to encourage children's reading and writing.

5

wonderful

Make sure you use dialogue
to show what your characters are thinking. and also to give variety to your writing.

6

Adjectives and adverbs are useful words but **don't overdo it!** Readers get tired of too many.

4

As you go long read your story out loud to yourself.
t's a great way to get a feel for how the story is going. You can change things as you go along to improve them.

variety

9

10

Put in surprises for the reader
that will make them think – 'Oh! I wasn't expecting that!' Surprises keep the reader interested and involved.

Read as many books as you can
and try to work out why you like your favourites and why you don't like others. Reading top writing by great authors will help you become a good author too.

surprises

Jacqueline Wilson

Jacqueline Wilson is one of the best-selling children's writers in the UK where her books have sold over 35 million copies. She has won the Smarties Prize, the Children's Book Award

unusual

1
Read as many books as you can, to enrich your imagination.

2
Keep a daily diary so you get into a regular writing habit.

3
Make writing fun use colourful notebooks or a different font on your computer.

fun

7
Use lots of conversation in your stories.

8
Try to choose unusual interesting words and describe things with care.

interesting

the Guardian Children's Fiction
ard. She trained as a journalist
leaving school and then started
iting after she married and had
r daughter, Emma. Her interests
e reading books, visiting the
smaller and shabbier stately
homes, going to the theatre
and art galleries and, most
of all, browsing around
bookshops. She became Dame
Jacqueline Wilson in 2008.

colourful

5
Other times
just start writing and
see where your
stories take
you.

6
Think
hard about
your characters
so that they become
real to you.

4
Sometimes
plan out a story
carefully,
working out the
beginning, the middle
and the end.

imagination

10
Write the
sort of stories
you'd like
to read
– that's what I do.

9
Don't worry
if you can't
always finish
your story.
Simply start a
new one.

conversation

Fun Words
to use in your writing

shrill
tender
unique
scarlet
marvellous
magic
nocturnal
vertical
wild
lunar
ferocious
gigantic
fizzy
remote
dangerous
wonderful
kind
chilly
brilliant
haunted
opaque
quaint
ancient
dramatic
indignant
young
prehistoric
jagged
enchanted
precious